Commerce and Coalitions

Commerce and Coalitions

HOW TRADE AFFECTS DOMESTIC POLITICAL ALIGNMENTS

Ronald Rogowski

PRINCETON UNIVERSITY PRESS

PRINCETON, NEW JERSEY

Published by Princeton University Press, 41 William Street,
Princeton, New Jersey 08540
In the United Kingdom: Princeton University Press, Chichester, West Sussex

Library of Congress Cataloging-in-Publication Data

Rogowski, Ronald.
Commerce and coalitions : how trade affects domestic political alignments
/ Ronald Rogowski.
p. cm.   Bibliography: p.   Includes index.
ISBN 0-691-07812-2 (alk.paper)
ISBN 0-691-02330-1
1. International trade—Political aspects—History. 2. Coalition
(Social sciences)—History. 3. Political stability—History. 4. World politics. I. Title.
HF1379.R64 1989   382'.3—dc19   89-3630

First Princeton Paperback printing, 1990

9   8   7   6   5

This book has been composed in Linotron Galliard

Princeton University Press books are printed on acid-free paper and meet the
guidelines for permanence and durability of the Committee on Production
Guidelines for Book Longevity of the Council on Library Resources

Printed in the United States of America

FOR MY PARENTS,

Lindall and Iola Rogowski

Generalizations that are sound resemble a large-scale map of an extended terrain, such as an airplane pilot might use in crossing a continent. Such maps are essential for certain purposes just as more detailed maps are necessary for others. No one seeking a preliminary orientation to the terrain wants to know the location of every house and footpath. Still, if one explores on foot . . . there can be long periods when the investigator feels lost in an underbrush of facts inhabited by specialists engaged in savage disputes about whether the underbrush is a pine forest or a tropical jungle. He is unlikely to emerge from such encounters without scratches and bruises. And if he draws a map of the area he has visited, one of the natives may well accuse him of omitting his own house and clearing, a sad event if the researcher has actually found much sustenance and refreshment there. The outcry is likely to be all the sharper if at the end of the journey the explorer tries to set down in very brief form for those who may come later the most striking things he has seen.

—Barrington Moore, Jr.,
Social Origins of Dictatorship and Democracy

Contents

List of Illustrations

List of Tables

Preface and Acknowledgments

THE STORIES are familiar from the great studies of comparative politics, sociology, and history.[1] In the 1860s, Americans divided over slavery and the tariff: western farmers joined northern workers and industrialists to oppose southern plantation owners. A decade later, German politics was riven by issues of protection and parliamentarism; but in that case industrialists, *Junker* estate owners, and smallholding peasants united against workers. In the Populist revolt of the 1890s, American politics was "realigned": radical farmers of the West and South aroused the united opposition of urban workers and industrialists, insuring a Republican hegemony that endured until the depression of the 1930s. In that depression, Swedish and Norwegian farmers and workers forged "Red-Green" coalitions against urban elites; those same years of crisis engendered in Latin America populist alliances of urban workers, industrialists, and middle classes that undermined the traditional rule of landed elites. After World War II, peasant revolutions swept much of Asia and some of Caribbean and Central America: tenant farmers and rural laborers, usually led by urban intellectuals, combated both rural and urban elites.

If the actors in these various dramas bear at least a similarity of nomenclature, their couplings and conflicts do not. Every possible permutation seems actually to have arisen at some historical juncture; certainly none can be excluded a priori. Moreover, as I shall try to show, cleavages and coalitions of these kinds do not belong only to our own age; they can be discerned with equal clarity in sixteenth-century Europe or ancient Greece.

Naturally enough, students of comparative politics have persistently endeavored to explain this bewildering array: to say why countries have the political cleavages that they do, and why those cleavages change. Among the many factors that have been adduced as partial explanations are preexisting cultural and religious divisions, the strength of the feudal tradition, the rapidity and timing of industrialization or of the grant of the mass suffrage, the sequence of "crises" of modernization, the institutional setting, the impact of foreign threat or invasion, and—most recently—the product cycle.[2]

I do not propose to deny the importance of any of these variables. In-

---

[1] See, among many others: Moore 1967, esp. chaps. 3 and 7–9; Burnham 1970; Dahl 1966, esp. chaps. 3 and 4; Huntington 1968.

[2] See, inter alia: Rokkan 1970 and 1981; Lipset 1970 and 1983; Moore 1967; Lipset and Rokkan 1967; Binder et al. 1971; Duverger 1959; Dahl 1966, chap. 12; Johnson 1962; Skocpol 1979; and Kurth 1979a and 1979b.

deed, as will become clear in the several substantive chapters of this volume, no sensible explanation can dispense with them. I shall however argue that a much fuller account can be had if one admits the relevance of a factor that, until now, has been almost universally neglected: externally induced changes, in countries and regions with different factor endowments, in exposure to international trade.

To be sure, some studies of individual countries, and even a few comparative inquiries, have argued that domestic politics is affected by changing international trade in particular circumstances: Rosenberg (1943), Gerschenkron (1943), and more recently Gourevitch (1977; and 1986, chap. 3) have analyzed the ways in which cheaper imports, particularly of foodstuffs, affected domestic European cleavages and coalitions after 1873; Sunkel with Paz (1973), Cardoso and Faletto (1979), and others of the "dependency" school have pointed to shifting flows and patterns of trade as sources of Latin America's volatile divisions and alliances. Cameron (1978) has argued that both leftist strength and the public sector's rate of growth may be affected by countries' degrees of exposure to international trade. Abraham (1981) has attempted, in part, to link Weimar Germany's conflicts to its fluctuating export markets; and, perhaps most provocatively, Wallerstein (1974 and 1980) has contended that regional variations in political institutions and cleavages in the early modern period can be explained by the rise of a world market, and of an international division of labor within that market.

The argument that I undertake in this volume is more general. Briefly, I try to show that basic results of the theory of international trade—including, above all, the well-known theorem of Stolper and Samuelson (1941)—imply that increases or decreases in the costs and difficulty of international trade should powerfully affect domestic political cleavages and should do so differently, but predictably, in countries with different factor endowments; and I suggest that these implications conform surprisingly well with what has been actually observed about patterns of cleavage, and about changes in those patterns, in a great variety of countries during five periods of global change in exposure to trade.

Chapter 1 outlines and defends the theoretical connection between trade and political cleavage. Chapters 2, 3, and 4 apply it to three recent periods of change: the great expansion of world trade in the nineteenth century, its major contraction in the depression of the 1930s, and its revival and extension after 1945. In chapter 5 I attempt to demonstrate the theory's generality by using it to illuminate three eras of changing trade that may be less familiar to present-day students of politics: the expansions of the classical period in ancient Greece and of early modern Europe's "long" sixteenth century, and the collapse of long-range trade that was central to the collapse of the Roman Empire. Chapter 6 indicates both avenues of future research and ways in which the approach adopted here may be able to shed light on some other mysteries of comparative politics.

Despite the evidence that I shall be able to adduce in support of the theory, it remains conjectural and preliminary, and its application to specific cases is suggestive rather than conclusive. Much work remains to be done.

·　·　·

I have incurred many debts in the long gestation of this short book, and it is pleasant to redeem them, however partially, here. The greatest is surely to the Tuesday Luncheon Group in Political Economy at the University of California, Los Angeles,[3] among whom I first read the original Stolper-Samuelson article, and who encouraged and repeatedly sharpened my halting efforts to see in it a broader political significance. Within that group, I owe a special debt to my colleague Michael Wallerstein; he above all pressed me to develop these ideas into publishable form.

Second only to that group, I want to thank the Center for Advanced Study in the Behavioral Sciences (CASBS) in Palo Alto, California, where as a Fellow in 1983–1984 I first grappled—at that time, with limited success—with the issues that this book addresses. Among that year's other Fellows, Roger Noll was especially helpful in discussing (and, often enough, demolishing) early drafts; so were such Stanford University colleagues as John Ferejohn, Judith Goldstein, and Stephen Krasner.

My third principal debt is to my wife, Katherine Rogowski. Not only has she put up with much turmoil and disruption in the research and writing of this book; it was she who first urged me, at Christmas of 1986, to abandon an earlier, more diffuse project and to devote my energies single-mindedly to this effort. My good friend Joel Aberbach, when I consulted him, supported Kay in that endeavor to impose sanity, and I shall always be grateful.

Stephen McMillan, my superb and painstaking research assistant from 1986 to the present, not only searched down references but offered trenchant criticisms of early drafts. Without his unfailing and prompt perfor-

---

[3] Few institutions have done more than this simple and fluid interdisciplinary reading group to make UCLA, in my modest and disinterested judgment, one of the world's most intellectually exciting and fertile locations. In 1985–1986, when I first began to formulate these notions, the group consisted of (in alphabetical order) Joel Aberbach, Richard Baum, Peter Bernholz, Leonard Binder, Jeff Frieden, Barbara Geddes, Jack Hirshleifer, David Lake, Karen Orren, Arthur Stein, and Michael Wallerstein. Aberbach, Bernholz, and Orren no longer attend regularly; but James DeNardo, David Dollar, Daniel Garst, Louis Goldberg, Miriam Golden, Mary Hampton, Douglas Rivers, Richard Rosecrance, Richard Sklar, Thomas Schwartz, George Tsebelis, John Wiley, and David Wilson have joined the circle.

mance of duty, this book could simply not have been written. If he would only permit me to win occasionally at handball, he would be perfect. David D'Lugo and Michael Van Dyck provided additional research assistance; and Celia Carrera has served, in the later stages of this project, as the kind of supercompetent secretary of whom most academics can only dream.

Many colleagues, at UCLA and elsewhere, have been kind enough to read substantial parts of the manuscript and, at critical junctures, to offer the invaluable combination of correction and support. I owe particular thanks to Peter Katzenstein, who has read every draft (including some discarded ones) and has more than once revived my flagging spirits. I heartily second Gøsta Esping-Andersen's nomination of Peter as "America's most generous academic."[4] I would place Robert Bates, Jeff Frieden, and Richard Rosecrance in almost the same category. My colleague Rick Baum suggested the title, which easily displaced my blander alternative. Others who deserve special mention are James Alt, Harry Eckstein, Jack Hirshleifer, Miles Kahler, James Kurth, David Lake, David Laitin, Edward Leamer, Afaf Marsot, James Rosenau, Samuel Popkin, Richard Sklar, Amanda Tillotson, and an anonymous referee.

Sandy Thatcher, Editor-in-Chief at Princeton University Press, has managed the difficult feat of continually encouraging me while treating me with absolute professional detachment. He resembles, and for all I know may have modelled himself on, Max Perkins; may he find his future A. Scott Berg. Brian R. MacDonald performed the copyediting with superb expertise and dispatch. Trained as a classicist, he saved me from more errors in ancient history than either of us will care to count; still, he will doubtless be relieved when I reemphasize here the traditional formula that the remaining blunders, especially in that section, are my very own.

In addition to my year at CASBS, which was supported in part by National Science Foundation grant BNS 76-22943 to that institution, this project has been sustained financially by grants from the Committee on Research of the Los Angeles Division of the Academic Senate of the University of California. I am also grateful to Provost Raymond Orbach, Dean David Sears, and then Department Chair J. Richard Sisson for freeing up most of academic year 1986–1987 to permit me to finish this project. The editors of the *American Political Science Review* have kindly granted permission to reprint those parts of this preface and of chapter 1 that originally appeared as an article in that journal; and I appreciate also the recognition of the American Political Science Association, which awarded that paper its Franklin L. Burdette–Pi Sigma Alpha Prize as the best presented at the 1987 Annual Meeting.

Finally, I owe a special but almost undefinable debt to my colleagues,

[4] Esping-Andersen 1985, xvii.

between 1984 and 1986, on that grand and peculiar institution, UCLA's Council on Academic Personnel (CAP). From that interdisciplinary group, whose recommendation must be sought on all promotions and tenured appointments on the campus, I learned the unity and glory of excellent research. I discovered that, with close attention and a little tutoring, one can tell good from bad work almost as readily in physics or microbiology as in history or political science; that standards are much the same in Moscow or New Delhi as in New Haven or Los Angeles; and that this larger perspective can, and should, help to assess and prioritize one's own work.

To my astonishment, an onerous "administrative" task that was widely supposed to interdict all one's own research and writing turned out to redirect and invigorate my own. That is a profound debt, and I am proud to acknowledge it.

List of Abbreviations

APRA   Alianza Popular Revolucionaria Americana
CDU   Christlich-Demokratische Union
CGIL   Confederazione Generale Italiana del Lavoro
CNIP   Centre National des Indépendents et Paysans
CNPF   Conseil National du Patronat Français
DGB   Deutscher Gewerkschaftsbund
DNVP   Deutsch-Nationale Volkspartei
FNSEA   Fédération Nationale des Syndicats d'Exploitants Agricoles
KMT   Kuomintang
MRP   Mouvement Républicain Populaire
NEP   New Economic Program
PCF   Parti Communiste Français
PCI   Partito Comunista Italiano
PRI   Partido Revolucionario Institucional
SFIO   Section Française de l'Internationale Ouvrière
SPD   Sozialdemokratische Partei Deutschlands

Commerce and Coalitions

CHAPTER ONE

Why Changing Exposure to Trade
Should Affect Political Cleavages

THE STOLPER-SAMUELSON THEOREM

IN 1941, Wolfgang Stolper and Paul Samuelson solved conclusively the old riddle of gains and losses from protection (or, for that matter, from free trade).[1] In almost[2] any society, they showed, protection benefits (and liberalization of trade harms) owners of factors in which, relative to the rest of the world, that society is *poorly* endowed, as well as producers who use that scarce factor intensively.[3] Conversely, protection harms (and liberalization benefits) those factors that—again, relative to the rest of the world—the given society holds *abundantly*, and the producers who use those locally abundant factors intensively.[4] Thus, in a society rich in labor but poor in capital, protection benefits capital and harms labor; and liberalization of trade benefits labor and harms capital.[5]

So far, the theorem is what it is usually perceived to be, merely a statement, albeit an important and sweeping one,[6] about the effects of tariff

---

[1] I briefly discuss two partially dissenting perspectives, conventionally labeled the "specific-factors model" and the "Leontieff paradox," later in this chapter.

[2] The principal exceptions are economies that specialize to the extent of abandoning, instead of merely reducing, production of goods in which they lack comparative advantage (Stolper and Samuelson 1941, 70–71). An example would be a society that ceased all agricultural production.

[3] In fact, the effect flows backward from products and is an extension of the Heckscher-Ohlin theorem: under free trade, countries export those products whose manufacture uses intensively their abundant factors, and import ones that employ intensively factors in which they are poorly endowed. Stolper and Samuelson 1941, 65–66; cf. Leamer 1984, esp. 8–10.

[4] Admittedly, these results depend on simplifying assumptions that are never achieved in the real world, among them perfect mobility of factors within national boundaries and a world of only two factors (Stolper and Samuelson 1941, 72). Still, as an approximation to reality, they remain highly serviceable. On the specific issue of extension of the theorem to cases of more than two factors—where, in essence, it continues to hold as a correlation rather than a certainty—see Ethier 1984, esp. 63–64 and 181.

[5] To dispel a misunderstanding that occasionally arises: these effects befall both the country that imposes protection *and* its trading partners—i.e., they flow simply from the constriction of trade. Hence any retaliatory tariffs from other countries will only magnify the benefit to scarce, and the harm to abundant, factors. Cf. Magee 1978, 149.

[6] Especially for those of us who may have received from our textbooks a more restrictive impression of the theorem's import, it is essential to emphasize how sweeping the original statement was—and, indeed, to reread the original essay. It does not describe only the effect

policy. The picture is altered, however, when one realizes that *exogenous* changes can have exactly the same effects as increases or decreases in protection. A cheapening of transport costs, for example, is indistinguishable in its impact from an across-the-board decrease in every affected state's tariffs;[7] so is any change in the international regime that decreases the risks or the transaction costs of trade. The converse is of course equally true: when a nation's external transport becomes dearer or its trade less secure, it is affected exactly as if it had imposed a higher tariff.

The point is of more than academic interest because we know, historically, that major changes in the risks and costs of international trade have occurred: notoriously, the railroads and steamships of the nineteenth century brought drastically cheaper transportation; so, in their day, did the improvements in shipbuilding and navigation of the fifteenth and sixteenth centuries; and so, in our own generation, have supertankers, cheap oil, and containerization.[8] According to the familiar argument of Kindleberger (1973) and others, international hegemony decreases both the risks and the transaction costs of international trade; and the decline of hegemonic power makes trade more expensive, perhaps—as, some have argued, in the 1930s—prohibitively so. Analyzing a much earlier period, the Belgian historian Henri Pirenne (1939) attributed much of the final decline of the Roman Empire to the growing insecurity of interregional, and especially of Mediterranean, trade after A.D. 600.[9]

Global changes of these kinds, it follows, should have had global consequences. The "transportation revolutions" of the sixteenth, the nineteenth, and scarcely less of the mid-twentieth century must have benefited in each affected country owners and intensive employers of locally abundant factors and must have harmed owners and intensive employers of locally scarce factors. The events of the 1930s should have had exactly the opposite effect. What, however, will have been the *political* consequences of those shifts of wealth and income? To answer that question, we require a rudimentary model of the political process and a somewhat more definite one of the economy.

Simple Models of the Polity and the Economy

Concerning domestic political processes, I shall make only three assumptions: that the beneficiaries of a change will try to continue and accelerate

---

of particular kinds of protection (e.g., of industrial goods), but of blanket protection of precisely the kind that is analogous to a shift in the costs or risks of trade.

[7] See, e.g., Mundell 1957, 330.

[8] Landes 1969, 153–54, 196, and 201–2; Hobsbawm 1975, chap. 3; Cipolla 1965; Rosecrance 1986, 142.

[9] Later historians have of course largely rejected Pirenne's attribution of this insecurity to

it, while the victims of the same change will endeavor to retard or halt it; that those who enjoy a sudden increase in wealth and income will thereby be enabled to expand their political influence as well (cf. Becker 1983); and that, as the desire and the means for a particular political preference increase, the likelihood grows that political entrepreneurs will devise mechanisms that can surmount the obstacles to collective action.[10]

For our present concerns, the first assumption implies that the beneficiaries of safer or cheaper trade will support yet greater openness, while gainers from dearer or riskier trade will pursue even greater self-sufficiency. Conversely, those who are harmed by easier trade will demand protection or imperialism;[11] and the victims of exogenously induced constrictions of trade will seek offsetting reductions in barriers. More important, the second assumption implies that the beneficiaries, potential or actual, of any such exogenous change will be strengthened politically (although they may still lose); the economic losers will be weakened politically as well. The third assumption gives us reason to think that the resultant pressures will not remain invisible but will actually be brought to bear in the political arena.

The issue of potential benefits is an important one, and a familiar example may help to illuminate it. In both great wars of this century, belligerent governments have faced an intensified demand for industrial labor and, because of the military's need for manpower, a reduced supply. That situation has positioned workers—and, in the U.S. case, such traditionally disadvantaged workers as blacks and women—to demand greatly increased compensation: these groups, in short, have had large *potential* gains. Naturally, governments and employers have endeavored to deny them those gains; but in many cases—Germany in World War I, the United States in World War II, Britain in both world wars—the lure of sharing in the potential gains has induced trade union leaders, and workers themselves, to organize and demand more.[12] Similarly, when transportation costs fall, governments may at first partially offset the effect by imposing protection.

---

the rise of Islam and its alleged blockade of Mediterranean commerce (Havighurst 1958). It can hardly be doubted, however, that the decline of Roman power by itself rendered interregional trade far less secure. See chapter 5.

[10] Olson 1968; Frohlich, Oppenheimer, and Young 1971.

[11] Countries that lack essential resources can only beggar themselves by protection. Ultimately, those threatened by trade in such a society must advocate conquest of the missing resources, as indeed occurred in Japan and Germany in the 1930s. It should be self-evident, however, that not all imperialisms originate in this way: those of ancient Rome, and of nineteenth-century Britain, aimed to expand trade. Doyle 1986, chaps. 4 and 11.

[12] In the United States and Britain, union membership as a share of total work force increased dramatically in wartime; in Germany, unions simply asserted and won a larger share in the formulation of policy. In general, strike rates rose after an initial decline. Bain and Price 1980, 37–88; Stein 1980, 47–51; Feldman 1966, esp. 116–35.

FIGURE 1.1
Four Main Types of Factor Endowments

Land-Labor Ratio

	High	Low
Economy Advanced	ABUNDANT: Capital Land SCARCE: Labor	ABUNDANT: Capital Labor SCARCE: Land
Economy Backward	ABUNDANT: Land SCARCE: Capital Labor	ABUNDANT: Labor SCARCE: Capital Land

Owners of abundant factors nonetheless still have substantial *potential* gains from trade, which they may mortgage, or on which others may speculate, to pressure policy toward lower levels of protection.

So much for politics. As regards the economic aspect, I propose to adopt with minor refinements the traditional three-factor model—land, labor, and capital—and to assume, for now, that the land-labor ratio informs us fully about any country's endowment of those two factors. (I shall presently relax this assumption, but it is useful at this stage of the exposition.) No country, in other words, can be rich in both land and labor: a high land-labor ratio implies abundance of land and scarcity of labor; a low ratio signifies the opposite. Finally, I shall simply define an *advanced* economy as one in which capital[13] is abundant.

This model of factor endowments inevitably oversimplifies reality and will require amendment. Its present starkness, however, permits us in theory to place any country's economy into one of four cells (see Figure 1.1), according to whether it is advanced or backward and whether its land-labor ratio is high or low. We recognize, in other words, only economies that are: (1) capital rich, land rich, and labor poor; (2) capital rich, land

---

[13] The capital may be either human or physical, but—as political scientists must sometimes be reminded—it must be distinguished from mere wealth. Capital is productive investment, not cash. For example, Kuwait has the per capita income and wealth but not the endowments of physical or human capital of European or North American economies.

poor, and labor rich; (3) capital poor, land rich, and labor poor; or (4) capital poor, land poor, and labor rich.

POLITICAL EFFECTS OF EXPANDING TRADE

The Stolper-Samuelson theorem, applied to our simple model, implies that increasing exposure to trade must result in *urban-rural conflict* in two kinds of economies, and in *class conflict* in the two others. Consider first the upper right-hand cell of Figure 1.1: the advanced (therefore capital-rich) economy endowed abundantly in labor but poorly in land. Expanding trade must benefit both capitalists and workers; it harms only landowners and the pastoral and agricultural enterprises that use land intensively. Both capitalists and workers—which is to say, almost the entire urban sector—should favor free trade; agriculture should on the whole be protectionist.[14] Moreover, we expect the capitalists and the workers to try, very likely in concert, to expand their political influence. Depending on preexisting circumstances, they may seek concretely an extension of the franchise, a reapportionment of seats, a diminution in the powers of an upper house or of a gentry-based political elite, or a violent "bourgeois" revolution.

Urban-rural conflict should also arise in backward, land-rich economies (the lower left-hand cell of Figure 1.1) when trade expands, albeit with a complete reversal of fronts. In such "frontier" societies, both capital and labor are scarce; hence both are harmed by expanding trade and, normally, will seek protection. Only land is abundant, and therefore only agriculture will gain from free trade. Farmers and pastoralists will try to expand their influence in some movement of a "populist" and antiurban stripe.

Conversely, in backward economies with low land-labor ratios (the lower right-hand cell of Figure 1.1), land and capital are scarce and labor is abundant. The model therefore predicts *class conflict*: labor will pursue free trade and expanded political power (including, in some circumstances, a workers' revolution);[15] landowners, capitalists, and capital-intensive industrialists will unite to support protection, imperialism, and a politics of continued exclusion.[16]

[14] Trade may, however, not emerge as the dominant issue, or even as an explicit one. To take only two examples: in small states, protection may seem so suicidal, and imperialism so ludicrous, that neither gains serious advocates (Katzenstein, 1985); or the parasitism of traditional elites may appear as the immediate obstacle, even while expanding trade has made rebellion desirable and possible.

[15] In such an economy, much of the labor may well be rural; and its aims will often include a land reform—i.e., a change of ownership structure—that can institute a more efficient (more labor-intensive) mix of factors and a more export-oriented production. The case of land reform and olive cultivation in ancient Greece (chapter 5) is startlingly instructive. The larger issues of ownership and property rights are discussed later in the present chapter.

[16] Lest the picture of a popular rising in support of freer markets seem too improbable a

FIGURE 1.2

Predicted Effects of Expanding Exposure to Trade

Land-Labor Ratio

	High	Low
Economy Advanced	CLASS CLEAVAGE: Land and Capital free-trading, assertive; Labor defensive, protectionist	URBAN-RURAL CLEAVAGE: Capital and Labor free-trading, assertive; Land defensive, protectionist Radicalism
Economy Backward	URBAN-RURAL CLEAVAGE: Land free-trading, assertive; Labor and Capital defensive, protectionist U.S. Populism	CLASS CLEAVAGE: Labor free-trading, assertive; Labor and Capital defensive, protectionist Socialism

The reverse form of class conflict is expected to arise in the final case, that of the advanced but land-rich economy (the upper left-hand cell of Figure 1.1) under increasing exposure to trade. Because both capital and land are abundant, capitalists, capital-intensive industries, and agriculture will all benefit from, and will endorse, free trade; labor being scarce, workers and labor-intensive industries will resist, normally embracing protection and (if need be) imperialism. The benefited sectors will seek to expand their political power, if not by disfranchisement then by curtailment of workers' economic prerogatives and suppression of their organizations.

These implications of the theory of international trade (summarized in Figure 1.2) seem clear, but do they in any way describe reality? Obviously I shall try to address that question more fully in subsequent chapters, but for now it is worth observing how closely the experience of three major countries—Germany, Britain, and the United States[17]—conforms to this analysis in the period of rapidly expanding trade in the last third of the

priori, I observe at once its general conformity with Popkin's (1979) astute interpretation of the Vietnamese revolution.

[17] A fuller treatment of these cases is presented in chapter two.

nineteenth century; and how far it can go to explain otherwise puzzling disparities in those states' patterns of political evolution.

Germany and the United States were both relatively backward (i.e., capital-poor) societies: both imported considerable amounts of capital in this period, and neither had until late in the century anything like the per capita industrial capacity of the United Kingdom or Belgium.[18] Germany, however, was rich in labor and poor in land; the United States, of course, was in exactly the opposite position. (Again, we observe that the United States imported, and Germany exported—not least to the United States—workers, which is not surprising since, at midcentury, Prussia's labor-land ratio was fifteen times that of the United States.)[19]

The theory predicts class conflict in Germany, with labor the "revolutionary" and free-trading element, and with land and capital united in support of protection and imperialism. Surely this description will not ring false to any student of German socialism or of Germany's infamous "marriage of iron and rye."[20] For the United States, conversely, the theory predicts—quite accurately, I submit—urban-rural conflict, with the agrarians now assuming the "revolutionary" and free-trading role; capital and labor unite in a protectionist and imperialist coalition. Neither E. E. Schattschneider nor Walter Dean Burnham could have described more succinctly the history of the Populist movement or of the election of 1896.[21]

Britain, on the other hand, was already an advanced economy in the nineteenth century. Its per capita industrial output far exceeded that of any

[18] Feis 1965, 24–25 and chap. 3. Nowadays, of course, governments' fiscal and monetary policies can drastically affect flows of capital: the United States' massive imports of capital under Reagan do not imply—not yet, at least—that capital has become scarce in America. In the nineteenth century, when almost all governments adhered to the gold standard, these flows tended much more to reflect real disparities of endowment. For evidence on per capita levels of industrialization, see chapter 2.

[19] Between 1871 and 1890, just under two million Germans emigrated to points outside Europe; over the same period, some seven million immigrants entered the United States. For labor-land ratios at midcentury, see Table 2.4. Migration may of course occur for reasons quite other than local scarcity or abundance, notably to escape political persecution; yet in these years the economic motive seems to have predominated. See for example Hobsbawm 1979, chap. 11.

[20] The Stolper-Samuelson analysis also helps to clear up what had seemed even to the perspicacious Gerschenkron (1943, 26–27) an insoluble riddle: why the *smallholding* German peasants had quickly become as protectionist as the *Junker*. Not only landowners, we now see, but all enterprises that *used land intensively*, will have been harmed by free trade. On the other hand—and later the distinction will become crucial—agricultural *wage-labor* should have been free-trading. See further discussion in chapter 2.

[21] Schattschneider 1960, 78–85; Burnham 1970, esp. 53–54. That the farmers of the Great Plains were hardly prospering is no refutation of the analysis advanced here. Their *potential* gains were great (as noted previously), and their suffering could plausibly be attributed not to expanded trade but to the obstacles or exploitation laid upon that trade by other sectors. As in Marxist analysis, the older relations of production and of rule could be seen as "fetters."

other nation, and it exported capital in vast quantities.[22] That it was also rich in labor is suggested by its extensive exports of that factor to the United States, Canada, Australia, New Zealand, and Africa; in fact, Britain's labor-land ratio then exceeded Japan's by 50 percent and was over thirty times that of the United States.[23] Britain therefore falls into the upper right-hand quadrant of Figure 1.1 and is predicted to exhibit a rural-urban cleavage whose fronts are opposite those found in the United States: capitalists and labor unite in support of free trade and in demands for expanded political power, while landowners and agriculture support protection and imperialism.

Although this picture surely obscures important nuances, it illuminates crucial differences—between, for example, British and German political development in this period. In Britain, capitalists and labor united in the Liberal party and forced an expanded suffrage and curtailment of (still principally land-owning) aristocratic power. In Germany, liberalism shattered,[24] the suffrage at the crucial level of the individual states was actually contracted, and—far from eroding aristocratic power—the bourgeoisie grew more and more *verjunkert* in style and aspirations.

POLITICAL EFFECTS OF DECLINING TRADE

When rising costs or declining security substantially increases the risks or costs of external trade, the gainers and losers in each situation are simply the reverse of those under increasing exposure to trade. Let us first consider the situation of the highly developed (and therefore by definition capital-rich) economies.

In an advanced economy with a high land-labor ratio (the upper left-hand cell of Figure 1.1), we should expect intense *class conflict* precipitated by a newly aggressive working class. Land and capital are both abundant in such an economy; hence, under declining trade owners of both factors (and producers who use either factor intensively) lose. Moreover, they can resort to no such simple remedy as protection or imperialism. Labor being the only scarce resource, workers and labor-intensive industries are well positioned to reap a significant windfall from the "protection" that dearer or riskier trade affords; and, according to our earlier assumption, like any other benefited class they will soon endeavor to parlay their greater economic power into greater political power. Capitalists and landowners, even if they were previously at odds, will unite to oppose labor's demands.

---

[22] Feis 1965, chap. 1; and my discussion in chapter 2.

[23] Emigrants from the United Kingdom to areas outside Europe totaled 5.1 million between 1871 and 1890 (Mitchell 1978, table A-5). For labor-land ratios, see my Table 2.4.

[24] Sheehan 1978.

Quite to the contrary, declining trade in an advanced economy that is labor rich and land poor (the upper right-hand cell of Figure 1.1) will entail renewed *urban-rural* conflict. Capital and labor are both abundant, and both are harmed by the contraction of external trade. Agriculture, as the intense exploiter of the only scarce factor, gains significantly and quickly tries to translate its gain into greater political control.

Urban-rural conflict is also predicted for backward, land-rich countries under declining trade; but here agriculture is on the defensive. Labor and capital being both scarce, both benefit from the contraction of trade; land, as the only locally abundant factor, is threatened. The urban sectors unite, in a parallel to the "radical" coalition of labor-rich developed countries under expanding trade discussed previously, to demand an increased voice in the state.

Finally, in backward economies rich in labor rather than land, class conflict resumes, with labor this time on the defensive. Capital and land, as the locally scarce factors, gain from declining trade; labor, locally abundant, suffers economic reverses and is soon threatened politically.

Observe again, as a first test of the plausibility of these results—summarized in Figure 1.3—how they appear to account for some prominent disparities of political response to the last precipitous decline of international trade, the depression of the 1930s.[25] The U.S. New Deal represented a sharp turn to the left and occasioned a significant increase in organized labor's political power. In Germany, a depression of similar depth (gauged by unemployment rates and declines in industrial production)[26] brought to power first Hindenburg's and then Hitler's dictatorship. Landowners exercised markedly greater influence than they had under Weimar;[27] and indeed a credible case can be made that the rural sector was the principal early beneficiary of the early Nazi regime.[28] Yet this is exactly the broad difference that the model would lead us to anticipate, if we accept that by 1930 both countries were economically advanced—although Germany, after physical reparations and cessions of industrial regions, was surely less rich in capital than the United States—but the United States held land abundantly, which in Germany was scarce (respectively, the left- and right-

[25] This discussion prefigures the more complete one of chapter 3.
[26] Landes 1969, 391.
[27] Gessner 1977; Abraham 1981, 85–115 and chap. 4.
[28] See, inter alia, Holt 1936, 173–74 and 194ff.; Gerschenkron 1943, 154–63; Schoenbaum 1967, 156–63; and Gies 1968. Certainly peasants and landowners had been among National Socialism's earliest and strongest supporters: virtually every study of late Weimar voting patterns (e.g., Lipset 1960, 138–48, and sources there cited; Brown 1982; Childers 1983) has found a large rural-urban difference, controlling for such other variables as religion and class, in support for National Socialism.

FIGURE 1.3

Predicted Effects of Declining Exposure to Trade

Land-Labor Ratio

	High	Low
Economy Advanced	CLASS CLEAVAGE: Labor assertive, Land and Capital defensive U.S. New Deal	URBAN-RURAL CLEAVAGE: Land assertive, Labor and Capital defensive W. European Fascism
Economy Backward	URBAN-RURAL CLEAVAGE: Labor and Capital assertive, Land defensive South American Populism	CLASS CLEAVAGE: Land and Capital assertive, Labor defensive Asian & East European Fascism

hand cells of the upper half of Figure 1.3). Only an obtuse observer would claim that such factors as cultural inheritance and recent defeat in war played no role; but surely it is also important to recognize the sectoral impact of declining trade in the two societies.[29]

As regards the less developed economies of the time, it may be profitable to contrast the depression's impact on such South American cases as Argentina and Brazil with its effects in the leading Asian country, Japan. In Argentina and Brazil, it is usually asserted, the depression gave rise to, or at the least strengthened, "populist" coalitions that united labor and the urban middle classes in opposition to traditional, landowning elites.[30] In Japan, growing military influence suppressed representative institutions and nascent workers' organizations, ruling in the immediate interest—if

[29] Some historians have recognized the sectoral impact of declining trade in Weimar's final convulsions; the controversial essay of Abraham (1981) is only the best-known example. They may, however, have exaggerated agriculture's woes: see Holt 1936 and Rogowski 1982.

[30] Skidmore and Smith 1984, 59–60; Sunkel with Paz, 1973, 352–54; Cardoso and Faletto 1979, 124–26 and chap. 5. In Argentina, of course, the populist regime of Perón did not assume full power until 1946; but the cleavage (and the growing strength of the labor-bourgeois forces) was evident from the early 1930s.

hardly under the domination—of landowners and capitalists.[31] (Similar suppressions of labor occurred in China and Vietnam.)[32] In considering these contrasting responses, should we not take into account that Argentina and Brazil were rich in land and poor in labor, while in Japan (and, with local exceptions, in Asia generally) labor was abundant and land was scarce?[33]

RED-GREEN COALITIONS

Let us now relax the assumption that the land-labor ratio informs us completely about the relative abundance of these two factors and admit that a country may be rich or poor in *both* land and labor. Four new cases arise, in theory if (as I suspect) rarely in practice (see Figure 1.4): economies may be, as before, advanced or backward (i.e., capital rich or capital poor), but they may now be rich in both land and labor, or poorly endowed in both factors.

Two cases, that of the advanced economy that is rich in both factors and of the backward one that is poor in both, are theoretically improbable[34] and politically uninteresting: if all factors were (temporarily) abundant relative to the rest of the world, the society would unanimously embrace free trade; if all were scarce, it would agree on protection. Let us consider, then, the remaining two possibilities.

In an advanced economy where both land and labor are scarce, expand-

[31] Reischauer 1974, 186–87 and 195–99; Kato 1974.

[32] Clubb 1972, 135–40; Popkin 1979, xix and 215.

[33] For precise labor-land ratios, see Tables 3.1 and 3.2.

[34] Surprisingly enough, both are possible under one widely employed definition of abundance and scarcity in the multifactor case. If we say (as does for example Leamer 1984, 15) that a country is abundant in a factor to the extent that its share of world endowment in that factor exceeds its share of total world consumption, then a country would abound in all three of our factors if and only if all of the following inequalities held:

$$K_i/K > GNP/WP$$
$$T_i/T > GNP/WP$$
$$L_i/L > GNP/WP,$$

where K, T, and L are respectively world endowments of capital, land, and labor; the analogous indexed terms are the ith country's endowments of those same factors; WP is the sum of all nations' GNPs; and the *GNP* is that of country i. It should be evident that, for any given endowments of country i, a low enough GNP—i.e., a low enough level of consumption and production—will insure the satisfaction of all three inequalities. (Analogously, of course, a country can be "scarce" in all factors if only its GNP is high enough.) Such universal abundance or scarcity, however, is inconsistent with balanced trade and implies simultaneous inefficiency (or, in the case of scarcity, efficiency) in the use of all factors. Hence such a situation is initially improbable and inevitably transitory. Cf. Leamer 1984, 8–10.

FIGURE 1.4

Predicted Effects on Economies That Are Rich, or Poor, in Both Land and Labor

	Land and Labor Both Abundant	Land and Labor Both Scarce
Economy Advanced	ϕ	EXPANDING TRADE: Capital assertive, free-trading; Land and Labor protectionist, defensive DECLINING TRADE: Land and Labor assertive; Capital "internationalist," defensive
Economy Backward	EXPANDING TRADE: Land and Labor free-trading, assertive; Capital defensive, protectionist DECLINING TRADE: Capital assertive; Land and Labor "internationalist," defensive	ϕ

ing trade will benefit only capital. Agriculture and labor—"Green" and "Red"—can be expected to unite. Only capitalists will unreservedly embrace free trade; to the extent that such policies are objectively possible, farmers and workers will support protection and, if need be, imperialism. Either a "progressive" capitalist dictatorship, pursuing trade and development, or an economically retrograde but more participatory regime may ensue.[35] When trade contracts in such a case, the scarce factors of land and labor gain economically at capital's expense; and the alliance of Red and Green, likely demanding expanded mass participation in politics and a radical curtailment of capitalist power, grows markedly more assertive.

In a backward economy with abundant land and labor, change in exposure to trade again mobilizes a coalition of Red and Green, but with diametrically opposed positions. Expanding trade now *benefits* farmers and workers but harms capitalists; and the mass coalition—or, where agriculture is dominated by a few large landowners, a coalition of gentry and labor—pursues a wider franchise, free trade, and a general disempowerment of capital. Contracting trade, in such an economy, benefits only the owners of capital and injures both workers and farmers; again intense conflict between capital and both other sectors is predicted, ending in either a capitalist dictatorship or an anticapitalist revolution.

Can either situation arise in reality? Myint has argued cogently that the backward economy with abundant land and labor may not be rare.[36] Primitive economies are often thinly populated, with vast reserves of untilled land; at the same time, as Lewis (1954) argued in a seminal essay, they are frequently so plagued by underemployment (e.g., in peasant families and in servile or clientelistic relationships) that, for immediate purposes, labor in them can be regarded as unlimited in supply.[37] More precisely, labor can be withdrawn from its present use with almost no marginal loss of productivity.[38]

Although it has been less widely noticed, Myint has also suggested that an "artificial" *scarcity* of labor may arise in densely populated societies.[39] Where, far from there being any hidden unemployment, people have "had to devote the whole of their time and resources to obtain a minimum subsistence," any turn to alternative enterprise or employment carries substantial risks and costs. To plant an export crop, or to work in the new mill, is inevitably to forgo some part of subsistence production. And what if the crop fails, export prices collapse, or the mill closes in midseason?

Myint's point, I believe, can be taken further. If in some traditional land-abundant economies there is hidden unemployment and much leisure, in some traditional land-scarce societies there is equally *over*employment and

---

[35] A third possibility, of course, is that capitalists may buy the acquiescence of one or both other groups.

[36] Myint 1958, 323; Myint 1980 (originally published 1964), esp. chap. 3.

[37] Barber (1961), Hopkins (1973), and other students of Africa have suggested a third source of hidden unemployment in the simple paucity of available goods, which causes people to value leisure more. See chapter 2.

[38] For this reason the Myint-Lewis model is often described, borrowing a phrase from Adam Smith, as one that regards exports as a "vent for surplus."

[39] Myint 1980, 38.

a hidden *taste* for leisure. The phenomenon of the "self-exploiting" family enterprise, either as small farm or as small business, is well known. Such circumstances may create an additional barrier to the recruitment of labor, for family members often conceive, with reason, that the comparative laxity of factory or large-farm discipline will "ruin" the wage earner for the rigors of work on the homestead.

We expect, then, that a simultaneous scarcity of labor and land is likeliest to be encountered precisely in those densely populated societies whose pretrade economy is most characterized by small, extremely marginal, self-exploiting family enterprises.

Again, only to suggest the plausibility of applying these categories to actual cases,[40] we may ask to what extent the Red-Green coalitions of Sweden and Norway in the 1930s[41] were a predictable response to trade contraction of (by then) capital-rich but land- and labor-poor economies; and, analogously, in what measure the anticapitalist alliance of peasants and workers in Russia in the later nineteenth and early twentieth centuries derived from the growing exposure to trade of a backward but land- and labor-rich economy.

POSSIBLE OBJECTIONS

Several objections can plausibly be raised to the whole line of analysis that I have advanced here.

1. Most fundamentally, one can question the empirical accuracy of the Stolper-Samuelson theorem, or of the Heckscher-Ohlin-Vanek (HOV) model that underlies it. That was attempted chiefly by Leontieff in two seminal papers (Leontieff 1953 and 1956); his survey of the evidence was updated by Baldwin (1971). In essence, Leontieff purported to show that the United States exported labor-intensive goods and imported capital-intensive ones; Baldwin obtained the same result for later and more complete data. Because the United States was almost universally accounted to be abundant in capital and scarce in labor, this finding was the opposite of what the theory would predict; and Leontieff went on to observe that the conventional Stolper-Samuelson conclusion about the effects of protection must also be wrong: rather, "protectionist policies are bound to weaken the bargaining position of American labor and correspondingly strengthen that of capital."[42]

The "Leontieff paradox" is widely known. Less familiar, unfortunately, is Leamer's (1980) conclusive demonstration that Leontieff's entire mode of analysis was erroneous, and that Leontieff's own data show the United

[40] These cases are treated in greater detail in chapters 2 and 3.
[41] Hancock 1972, 30–31; Rokkan 1966, 84.
[42] Leontieff 1953, 349.

States as "revealed by its trade to be relatively well-endowed in capital compared with labor."[43] Moreover, a wider investigation of recent patterns of international trade (Leamer 1984) demonstrates the HOV model to be surprisingly accurate.

2. It may be argued that the effects sketched out here will not obtain in countries that depend only slightly on trade. A Belgium, where external trade (taken as the sum of exports and imports) roughly equals gross domestic product (GDP),[44] can indeed be affected profoundly by changes in the risks or costs of international commerce; but a state like the United States in the 1960s, where trade amounted to scarcely a tenth of GDP, will have remained largely immune.

This view, while superficially plausible, is incorrect. The Stolper-Samuelson result obtains at any margin; and in fact holders of scarce factors have been quite as devastated by expanding trade in almost autarkic economies—one need think only of the weavers of India or of Silesia, exposed in the nineteenth century to the competition of Lancashire mills—as in ones previously more dependent on trade.[45]

3. Given that comparative advantage always assures gains from trade, it may be objected that the cleavages described here need not arise at all: the gainers from trade can always compensate the losers and have something left over; trade remains the Pareto-superior outcome. As Stolper and Samuelson readily conceded in their original essay,[46] this is perfectly true. To the student of politics, however, and with even greater urgency to those who are losing from trade in concrete historical situations, it remains unobvious that such compensation will in fact occur. Rather, the natural tendency is for gainers to husband their winnings and to stop their ears to the cries of the afflicted. Perhaps only unusually strong and trustworthy states, or political cultures that especially value compassion and honesty, can credibly assure the requisite compensation (for the case of Sweden in the 1930s, see chapter 3)[47] and even in those cases, substantial conflict over

---

[43] Leamer 1980, 502. Leamer (502n.) concedes, however that Baldwin's findings "cannot be explained away so easily." Even if closer analysis should sustain the "paradox," it would mean little. As Baldwin's (1971, 127–32) extensive discussion of the intervening literature indicates, economic opinion holds almost universally that the "paradox," if it exists, must be an artifact of some excluded variable; human capital or natural resources, both possibilities mentioned even by Leontieff (1953, 344 and 348), are among the most frequently mentioned candidates.

[44] For figures for all its member states, see the Organization for Economic Co-operation and Development 1982, 62–63.

[45] Cf. Thomson 1962, 163–64, on the vast dislocations that even slight exposure to trade occasioned in many previously isolated areas of nineteenth-century Europe.

[46] Stolper and Samuelson 1941, 73.

[47] As trade comes to have more devastating and destabilizing effects, however, states' incen-

the nature and level of compensation will usually precede the ultimate agreement.

4. Equally, one can ask why the cleavages indicated here should persist. In a world of perfectly mobile factors and rational behavior, people would quickly disinvest from losing factors and enterprises (e.g., farming in Britain after 1880) and move to sectors whose auspices were more favorable. Markets should swiftly clear; and a new, if different, political equilibrium should be achieved.

To this two answers may be given. First, in some cases trade expands or contracts so rapidly and surprisingly as to frustrate rational expectations. Especially in countries that experience a steady series of such exogenous shocks—the case in Europe, I would contend, from 1840 to the present day—divisions based on factor endowments (which ordinarily change only gradually)[48] will be repeatedly revived. Second, not infrequently some factors' privileged access to political influence makes the extraction of rents and subsidies seem cheaper than adaptation: Prussian *Junker*, familiarly, sought (and easily won) protection rather than adjustment.[49] In such circumstances, adaptation may be long delayed, sometimes with ultimately disastrous consequences.

At the same time, it should be conceded that, as improved technology makes factors more mobile (see the subsequent discussion) and anticipation easier, the theory advanced here will likely apply less well. Indeed, this entire analysis may be a historically conditioned one, whose usefulness will be found to have entered a rapid decline sometime after 1960.[50]

5. Exactly to the contrary, it can be asserted that some factors are less mobile within nations than the Stolper-Samuelson model assumes; this is the crux of the so-called specific factors model of tariff effects.[51] In essence, it can be shown, a factor trapped in a specific sector and not readily put to other uses may lose in the short run from policies that will benefit it over the longer term, and vice-versa. Thus capitalists in America, where capital is abundant, will benefit from free trade in the long run; but capital that is invested in a labor-intensive sector and that cannot readily be redeployed

---

tives to develop credible systems of compensation increase; and, to the extent that they succeed, the analysis pursued here may be made obsolete. See chapter 6.

[48] The chief exception to this rule arises from extensions of trade to wholly new areas with quite different factor endowments. In 1860, for example, Prussia was abundant in land relative to its trading partners; as soon as the North American plains and the Argentine *pampas* were opened, it ceased to be so. Cf. chapter 2. (I am grateful to my colleague Arthur Stein for having pointed this out.)

[49] I remain unpersuaded by the hypothesis of Hardach 1967, that the Junker supported halfheartedly, or actually opposed, protection. See the more conventional account of Lambi 1963.

[50] I owe this suggestion to an anonymous referee.

[51] Mussa 1974.

may be harmed over the near term. Some have accepted this approach as explaining apparent anomalies in groups' positions on trade issues.[52]

Three points deserve emphasis. First, as Mussa (1974) made clear in his seminal essay, no one doubts that the Stolper-Samuelson theorem holds for the long run; at most, the specific-factors model describes a short-term exception, or lag, in the operation of the Stolper-Samuelson predictions.[53] Second, much would suggest a priori that this "short run," or lag, should be growing steadily shorter. Surely capital has become more mobile within nations over time; so, one suspects in light of more frequent migrations and career changes, has labor; even land is more readily shifted among uses, as improved transportation and communication have permitted the siting of factories and headquarters in areas that once would have seemed too remote. Third, as Magee (1978) rightly emphasized, the question is an empirical one, which is appropriately addressed by the evidence of historical coalition formation on issues of trade. The central chapters of this volume advance a much broader array of such evidence than did Magee's essay, which confined itself to a single country (the United States) in a single year (1973). I submit that, on balance, that evidence speaks unambiguously in favor of the Stolper-Samuelson position and against the specific-factors model.

6. This analysis, some may contend, reifies such categories as "capital," "labor," and "land," assuming a unanimity of preference that most countries' evidence belies. In fact, a kind of shorthand and a testable hypothesis are involved: a term like "capital" is the convenient abbreviation of "those who draw their income principally from investments, plus the most capital-intensive producers"; and I indeed hypothesize that individuals' political positions will vary with their derivation of income—or, more precisely, of present value of all anticipated future income—from particular factors.

A worker, for example, who derives 90 percent of her income from wages and 10 percent from investments will conform more to the theory's expectation of "labor" 's political behavior than one who depends half on investments and half on wages.[54] An extremely labor-intensive manufacturer will behave less like a "capitalist" than a more capital-intensive one.[55] And a peasant (as noted previously) who depends chiefly on inputs of his

[52] See particularly Magee 1978.

[53] Mussa 1974, 1192.

[54] An interesting subsidiary hypothesis is this: as a worker approaches retirement, and as more of his anticipated future income stream derives from pension-plan investments and less from wages, he will behave politically more and more as a capitalist. Has the growing conservatism of American workers been adequately explored in relation to the aging of the post–baby-boom American work force?

[55] The intensity of factors in production is ascertained by their relative contribution to value added. Hence a manufacturer may own little capital himself but may, through equity or debt, raise much capital and use it intensively in his processes of production.

own labor will resemble a "worker," whereas a more land-intensive neighbor will behave as a "landowner."

7. Finally, it may be objected that I have said nothing about the outcome of these conflicts. I have not done so for the simple reason that I cannot: history makes it all too plain, as in the cases of nineteenth-century Germany and America, that the economic losers from trade may win politically over more than the short run. What I have advanced here is a speculation about *cleavages*, not about outcomes.[56] I have asserted only that those who gain from fluctuations in trade will be strengthened and emboldened politically; nothing guarantees that they will win. Victory or defeat depends, so far as I can see, both on the relative size of the various groups and on those institutional and cultural factors that this perspective so resolutely ignores.

CONCLUSION

It is essential to recall what I am *not* claiming to do in this volume. I do not contend that changes in countries' exposure to trade explain all, or even most, of their varying patterns of political cleavage. It would be foolish to ignore the importance of ancient cultural and religious loyalties, of wars and migrations, or of such historical memories as the French Revolution and the *Kulturkampf*. Other cleavages antedate, and persist through, the ones I discuss here, shaping, crosscutting, complicating, and indeed sometimes dominating their political resolution.

Neither will I be able to offer, despite the detail of the remaining chapters, anything like a conclusive empirical demonstration of the hypotheses that this chapter has advanced. At most, the empirical regularities that I shall note may serve to suggest the plausibility of the model and the value of further refinement and testing of it.

In the main, I am presenting here a theoretical puzzle, a kind of social-scientific "thought experiment" in Hempel's (1965, chap. 7) original sense: a teasing out of unexpected, and sometimes counterintuitive, implications of theories already widely accepted. For the Stolper-Samuelson theorem *is* generally, indeed almost universally, embraced; yet, coupled with a stark and unexceptionable model of the political realm, it plainly implies that changes in exposure to trade must profoundly affect nations' internal political cleavages. Do they do so? If they do not, what conclusions shall we draw, either about our theories of international trade, or about our understanding of politics?

[56] On the other hand, particularly clear-cut outcomes can reveal something about cleavages. The near-unanimity with which nineteenth-century Britain eventually embraced free trade tells us much about the strength and solidity of the labor-capitalist alliance that originated and sustained that policy. See chapter 2.

CHAPTER TWO

The Revolutionary Expansion of Trade, 1840 to 1914

CHANGES IN TRADE

TABLES 2.1, 2.2, and 2.3 describe, in the dispassionate language of statistics, what up to then was by far recorded history's swiftest and most comprehensive expansion of international commerce.[1] Between 1840 and 1895, world trade roughly sextupled in nominal terms;[2] from then to 1913 it more than quintupled.[3] In real terms—that is, taking into account price movements[4]—it appears that international trade increased by between 135 and 150 percent between 1800 and 1840, more than quadrupled between 1840 and 1870, more than doubled between 1870 and the end of the century, and grew by about half again between 1901 and 1913.[5] As the tables reveal, in no decade after 1820 did the average annual real increase in world trade fall below 2.3 percent; and in the peak years between 1840 and 1870, it averaged around 5 percent (i.e., over 60 percent per decade).[6]

The main sources of this startling growth have long been clear: railroads (see Table 2.4 below) reduced the costs of land transportation by between 85 and 95 percent;[7] better ships, including from the 1880s onward significant numbers of seafaring steamships, brought the average cost of oceanborne transport to less than half its former levels;[8] canals opened formerly

---

[1] Rostow's estimates, which rest on plausible efforts to correct Mulhall's and to link them with ones advanced by Hilgerdt in 1945, should probably be taken as authoritative. (For the technical details see Rostow 1978, appendix B.) I present them together with the older efforts for purposes of comparison.

[2] Mulhall 1896, 39.

[3] Woytinsky and Woytinsky 1955, 38.

[4] Mulhall's indexes (1896, 399 and diagram XVII) suggest that, except for a slight uptick between 1835 and 1845, prices fell steadily from about 1810 to the early 1850s; they then rose (by perhaps 15 percent) to a level that was maintained for about twenty years; and, in the depression of the early 1870s, resumed a continual decline that was reversed only after 1900 (see Tables 2.1 and 2.2). At the end of the nineteenth century, prices were on average less than half of what they had been in its first decade.

[5] Cf. Landes 1969, 366. The price deflators that underlie these estimates are those of Mulhall and the Woytinskys: see Tables 2.1 and 2.2.

[6] Less technically inclined readers should bear in mind that compound interest is involved here; hence the annual rate of increase is not simply the decennial rate divided by ten.

[7] Mulhall 1896, 46; Woytinsky and Woytinsky 1955, 310.

[8] Mulhall 1892, 300–1, estimates the average cost of "freight by sea" at forty shillings per ton in 1850, "or more than double what it is now." As an example, the cost of shipping a ton

TABLE 2.1
World Trade, 1720–1870 (Mulhall Estimates)

Year	Merchandise: Exports and Imports	Price Index[a]	Annualized Growth Nominal	Real
1720	88	—	—	—
1750	140	—	1.5%	—
1780	186	—	1.0	—
1800	302	246	2.5	—
1820	341	186	0.6	2.0
1830	407	166	1.8	3.0
1840	573	180	3.5	2.6
1850	832	153	3.8	5.5
1860	1489	178	6.0	4.3
1870	2191	166	3.9	4.8

Source: Mulhall 1892, 128; trade expressed as millions of current pounds sterling. Price indexes are also those of Mulhall (1896, 399: five-year averages of "aggregate price-level of twenty articles"), and my estimates of real growth are based on them.
[a] 1895 = 100.

TABLE 2.2
World Trade, 1867–1913 (Woytinsky Estimates)

Year	Merchandise: Exports and Imports	Wholesale Price Index	Annualized Real Growth
1867–1868	$10,533 m.	137	—
1872–1873	13,760	151	3.5%
1880	15,204	122	4.0
1890	16,823	100	3.0
1901	22,291	97	2.9
1911	36,761	111	3.7
1913	40,600	117	2.4

Source: Woytinsky and Woytinsky 1955, 38–39. Calculations of real growth are mine and employ as deflators Woytinsky's indexes of wholesale prices.

landlocked areas to navigation and—notably in the Suez and Panama—shortened ocean routes; improved communications (especially telegraphy) and banking reduced information and transaction costs; and, as a generation of students has emphasized perhaps to excess, British hegemony on the seas and in finance guaranteed security of international commerce, stability of exchange rates, and, to a lesser extent, reliability of international contracts.[9]

of grain from New York to Liverpool had fallen from twenty-three to twelve shillings between 1868 and 1884 alone.
[9] The pioneering argument on this point was that of Kindleberger 1973.

TABLE 2.3
World Trade, 1720–1913 (Rostow Estimates)

Year	Volume Index[a]	Annualized Real Growth
1720	1.13	—
1750	1.90	1.75%
1780	2.18	0.46
1800	2.3	0.27
1820	3.1	1.50
1830	4.3	3.33
1840	5.4	2.30
1850	10.1	6.46
1860	13.9	3.25
1870	23.8	5.53
1876–1880	30	2.94
1881–1885	38	4.84
1886–1890	44	2.97
1891–1895	48	1.75
1896–1900	57	3.50
1901–1905	67	3.29
1906–1910	81	3.87
1911–1913	96	4.34

Source: Rostow 1978, 67 and 669.
[a] 1913 = 100.

These innovations changed not only the amount but the character of international trade. For centuries, principally "preciosities" had been exchanged—bullion, spices, jewelry, textiles, tea, sugar, and similar goods of a low weight-to-value ratio. Now, such bulky commodities as iron, grain, coal, timber, and (with the advent of refrigerated shipping in the 1880s) meat could be routinely shipped profitably across borders and oceans. In 1893, sixty-five times as much coal and thirteen times as much grain were carried in ocean shipping as in 1840; together, these two commodities alone accounted for just under half of total seaborne tonnage in 1893, as against about 20 percent in 1840.[10] Inevitably, this qualitative change exposed to international competition local monopolies, particularly in agriculture, that distance and terrain had long sheltered.[11]

Moreover, by opening wholly new regions—in the Americas, Russia, Oceania, and Africa—to international trade, the new technologies in effect altered relative factor endowments. Within the limited ambit and expensive freightage of "world" trade in 1800 or even 1850, parts of eastern and

[10] Mulhall 1896, 40–41.
[11] Cf. Landes 1969, 196–97, on the effects of the railroad.

TABLE 2.4
Rate of Railway Construction: Percentage of 1930 Trackage Laid by
Various Dates, 1840–1910

Region	1840	1850	1860	1870	1880	1890	1900	1910
World	0.6	3.1	8.7	16.8	29.8	49.0	63.3	82.5
North America	1.1	3.1	11.1	18.8	34.1	60.4	72.0	90.4
Central America[a]	—	—	1.9	2.7	6.6	30.9	43.0	79.7
South America[a]	—	—	0.5	2.9	10.5	28.9	45.1	68.5
Europe	1.0	7.6	16.3	30.4	47.1	62.6	76.4	89.0
Russia	0.03	0.8	1.9	13.5	28.8	38.8	61.0	79.2
Asia	—	—	1.1	6.2	12.2	24.4	44.2	72.1
Africa	—	—	0.7	2.6	6.8	13.9	29.5	54.2
Oceania	—	—	0.7	3.8	16.7	40.3	51.2	65.9

Source: Woytinsky and Woytinsky 1955, 341.

[a] Only estimates that combine Central and South America are available for 1840 and 1850: 0.1 and 0.4, respectively.

southern Europe still seemed abundant in agricultural land; but these regions could not begin to compete with the expanses of fertile land that railroads and steamships opened to world markets after 1870 in the Americas and Oceania. Almost overnight—and, as we shall see, with radical political consequences—even Europe's thinly populated areas were transformed, relative to the rest of the (now wider) world, from relative abundance to relative scarcity of land.[12]

The changes, then, were sudden and deep; but they did not occur everywhere at the same time. Whereas "core" Europe, and particularly those coastal and riverine regions that had long enjoyed access to wider markets, felt the impact almost at once (i.e., during the great expansion of the 1840s), other areas were opened more slowly than the global figures of Tables 2.1, 2.2, and 2.3 suggest. One measure of the pace is presented in Table 2.4, which indicates, for each major region of the world, the extent to which modern railway trackage (i.e., that of 1930)[13] had been achieved at the end of each decade of the nineteenth century after 1830. Observe that roughly a quarter of the modern railway network had been constructed in Europe by the mid-1860s, a date named by some authorities as showing the first unmistakable impact of railroads on the European economy.[14] A similar level was attained in North America and Russia by the

[12] See preliminarily Kindleberger 1951; and Gerschenkron 1943, chap. 1.
[13] Woytinsky and Woytinsky 1955, 341.
[14] E.g. Landes 1969, 153.

middle 1870s; in Oceania and Central and South America by the mid-1880s; in Asia by about 1890; and in Africa, by shortly before 1900. We should expect the political responses to be similarly graduated.

In these circumstances, if anywhere, owners of abundant factors should have sought to expand, and owners of scarce factors to defend, their share of political power. Before we can investigate whether that indeed happened, we must know something of the endowments that the various regions of the world brought to this unexampled new bazaar.

FACTOR ENDOWMENTS

Land

Although the available data for the early part of our period are fragmentary and approximate, they suggest strongly (Table 2.5) that, as of roughly the 1840s, western Europe contained the globe's most densely populated regions; Japan, India, and China ran it a close second. Even the most land-scarce regions of the New World (e.g., Haiti and El Salvador) were thinly populated by comparison with the European average. Southeast Asia (e.g., Siam) and the Middle East had a lower labor-to-land ratio than any of these. Russia, the Americas, Africa, and (we may infer from later data) Oceania were almost absurdly abundant in land.

For a point almost at the end of the nineteenth century, the indefatigable Mulhall ventures more informative figures on the ratio of population to productive land in selected countries (Table 2.6); and here the gap between land-poor Europe and Asia and land-rich Russia, the Americas, and Oceania emerges even more clearly. Within Europe, plainly the industrial heartland encompassing Belgium, England, and the Netherlands is most thickly settled. It is followed by the central European countries of Germany, Italy, Switzerland, and Austria; by northern Scandinavia and France; and, at some distance, by Europe of the periphery, including Scotland, Spain, Denmark, Ireland (whose population density was almost halved, by famine and emigration, between the 1840s and the 1890s),[15] Greece, and the Danubian states.

Throughout the period of expanding trade, then, we can safely regard the economies of northwestern Europe and of eastern and southern Asia as land scarce. In relation to them, some of the accessible regions of peripheral Europe—notably Denmark, the Baltic, and eastern Europe—still enjoyed a relative abundance in land that was already fading and that disappeared utterly with the opening of the American grain trade in the

---

[15] Against the figure of 252 per square mile (equal to 92 per square kilometer) reported for Ireland in 1846 by Bowden, Karporich, and Usher 1937 (see my Table 2.5), Mulhall 1892, pl. 8, reports for 1890 a density of 148 persons per square mile (57 per square kilometer).

TABLE 2.5
Population Per Square Kilometer of Inhabited Land: Representative Countries and Regions, 1846

EUROPE

Belgium	142	Sicily	63
Lombardy	119	Bavaria	58
England/Wales	107	Austrian Empire	56
Ireland	97	Switzerland	56
Parma	94	Holstein	53
Netherlands	88	Prussia	48
Baden	86	Hannover	46
Württemberg	85	Portugal	40
Neuchâtel	85	Schleswig	38
Bohemia	82	Denmark	33
Saxony	77	Scotland	33
Piedmont	77	Rumania	30
Tuscany	72	Spain	24
Naples	72	Sardinia	23
Luxembourg	67	Greece	21
Papal States	66	Sweden	7
France	63	Norway	4

ASIA

Japan	68	China	45
India (1881)	63	Siam	7

CARIBBEAN AND CENTRAL AMERICA

Haiti	18	Santo Domingo	3.3
El Salvador	12	Costa Rica	1.6
Guatemala	5		

MIDDLE EAST

Ottoman Empire	6	Persia	1.4

RUSSIA 3.5

NORTH AMERICA

United States	3.2	Mexico	2.2

AFRICA

Liberia	2.7

SOUTH AMERICA

Chile	2.7	Peru	1.5
Ecuador	2.5	Bolivia	0.9
Colombia	1.9	Brazil	0.8
Paraguay	1.9	Uruguay	0.8
Honduras	1.8	Venezuela	0.8
Nicaragua	1.8	Argentina	0.3

Source: Bowden, Karpovich, and Usher 1937, 3; Banks 1971, table 1; for India, Mulhall 1892, 55.

TABLE 2.6
Population Per Square Kilometer of Productive Land:
Representative Countries, 1896

Belgium	287	Scotland	86
England	277	Spain	82
India	247	Denmark	77
Netherlands	232	Ireland	74
Germany	148	Greece	66
Italy	145	Danube States	64
Switzerland	142	United States	49
Austria	126	Russia	44
Sweden/Norway	113	Canada	36
France	105	Argentina	3.9
Portugal	100	Australia	1.3

Source: Mulhall 1896, 22 and 381; for India, Mulhall 1903, 631. Includes as "productive" all land in crops or pasture; forests are excluded.

1870s.[16] Thereafter, the relative scarcity of land in even the less densely populated parts of Europe was exposed: the Americas, Russia, Oceania, and southeast Asia[17] became the cost-efficient purveyors of food and fiber to the rest of the world.

Capital

Lacking reliable data on countries' endowments of capital for this period,[18] we must proceed by inference—as was suggested in chapter 1—from indicators of economic modernity, productivity, and industrialization. By such measures, Britain enjoyed throughout the first half of the nineteenth century by far the greatest abundance of fixed capital investment of all the world's economies. In 1850, it had per capita twice the number of cotton spindles, twice the output of pig iron, and three times the steam horsepower of its nearest European rivals.[19] Bairoch's overall index of per capita levels of industrialization, reproduced in Table 2.7, provides one measure of how Britain stood in 1860 against its closest competitors. On the whole, as Landes has written, even the more advanced Continental economies were at midcentury "still about a generation behind Britain in industrial development."[20]

[16] Partial figures on grain exports in this period are given by Mitchell 1978, 164–65.

[17] On the very rapid growth of the rice-export sector in Cochinchina after 1867, see Popkin 1979, 134–35.

[18] Mulhall counted as "capital" only the sums invested in stocks and bonds; otherwise, he offers only estimates of national wealth.

[19] Mitchell 1978, 215–16 and 258; Banks 1971, segment 1; Landes 1969, 221.

[20] Landes 1969, 187.

TABLE 2.7
Bairoch Indexes of Per Capita
Industrialization, 1860[a]

United Kingdom	64
Belgium	28
Switzerland	26
United States	21
France	20
Germany	15
Sweden	15

Source: Bairoch 1982, 281.
[a] 100 = level of United Kingdom in 1900.

Nonetheless, as Bairoch's numbers suggest, two economies could bear comparison with Britain even at this early period—and, therefore, almost certainly were abundant in capital relative to the rest of the world: first Belgium, "the most industrialized nation on the Continent,"[21] with a railroad system substantially complete by midcentury, a per capita annual output of pig iron about 40 percent and of steam power about one-third of Britain's, and a machine-building sector that surpassed all others in Europe;[22] and second Switzerland, whose cotton spindleage per capita, based on abundant waterpower, was half Britain's and three times that of France, the world's next most intensive producer.[23] Additionally, it seems likely that a few regions of France—above all the North, with its early adoption of steam power, and slightly later the area around Lyon—enjoyed a level of investment that was obscured by the country's general backwardness.[24]

In comparison with these few oases, we shall probably be right to see the entire world around 1850 as scarce in capital, particularly because (as Bairoch has observed) the inequalities among the less developed economies at this time were almost certainly smaller than they have since become.[25] By the period just before World War I, the situation had obviously changed considerably. By consistently sustaining higher rates of capital formation, many Continental economies—including preeminently Ger-

[21] Landes 1969, 187.
[22] Mitchell 1978, 3–8 and 215–16; Banks 1971, segment 1; Landes 1969, 141, 153, and 221. The figures for pig iron output and steam horsepower per capita among the leading economies in 1850 are given in appendix Tables A2.1 and A2.2.
[23] Mitchell 1978, 3–8 and 258; Landes 1969, 168. For cotton spindles per thousand of population in 1852 among the major economies, see appendix Table A2.3.
[24] Landes 1969, 159–61. Smith 1980, 76, observes that "in the 1860s and 1870s the Lyonnais was France's most important industrial region in terms of total product and total work force."
[25] Bairoch 1982, 282.

TABLE 2.8
Bairoch Indexes of Per Capita Industrialization, 1913[a]

United States	126	Austria-Hungary	32
United Kingdom	115	Norway	31
Belgium	88	Netherlands	28
Switzerland	87	Italy	26
Germany	85	Spain	22
Sweden	67	Finland	21
France	59	Russia	20
Canada	46	Japan	20
Denmark	33	All others	< 20

Source: Bairoch 1982, 281 and 330.
[a] 100 = level of United Kingdom in 1900.

many's[26]—had been able to approach Britain in per capita productivity and capital endowments; the United States had clearly surpassed it.[27] Bairoch's summary estimates of per capita levels of industrialization for 1913, given in Table 2.8, make the point vividly.

Although it would be otiose to try to draw an exact line between the developed and the underdeveloped economies in this set, one can reasonably conclude that all those from Canada upward in Bairoch's list were abundant in capital by 1913.[28] Denmark, given its large per capita investment in agriculture,[29] may also qualify as capital rich. With equal certainty, we can label all of the economies from Spain downward—and, a fortiori, the even less advanced economies of Asia, Africa, and Latin America[30]—as still scarce in capital: their level of industrial production remains in this period well below that which Belgium and Switzerland had attained sev-

[26] In the last years before World War I, Germany's net domestic capital formation amounted to 15.6 percent of net national product; Britain's, to 6.7 percent. Landes 1969, 329.

[27] Even by 1900, per capita production of raw steel among the major European economies was a close race. The leading producers were the United Kingdom at 135 kilograms per capita; Germany at 115; and Belgium at 98 (Mitchell 1978, 3–8 and 223). By 1913, total German production of steel was more than double that of the United Kingdom (i.e., per capita production was higher). See also Mulhall's 1895 estimates of the per capita value of aggregate manufactures, reproduced in appendix Table A2.4.

[28] Feis (1965, 69ff.) observes that Germany began to export capital in considerable quantities in the late 1880s.

[29] Mulhall (1896, diagram VIII) gives Denmark's per capita agricultural investment as 115 pounds sterling; the next highest level is Australia's, at about 92 pounds.

[30] Even in agriculture, Latin American investment was low: Mulhall (1896, diagram VIII) estimates Argentina's in 1895 at 50 pounds sterling per capita; that figure may be usefully contrasted with the contemporaneous one of 92 per capita (see immediately above) for equally land-rich Australia.

enty years earlier.[31] The remaining four European states—Austria-Hungary, Norway, the Netherlands, and Italy—are less certainly categorized; like France in the earlier period, they are probably best regarded as largely capital-poor societies that encompass some islands of more intense investment.

Labor

The regions of northwestern Europe that were conspicuously scarce in land were also abundant in labor: ten million souls emigrated from the United Kingdom alone in the latter half of the nineteenth century.[32] Paradoxically, however, some of the land-rich areas of the Old World may also have been abundantly endowed with labor, for reasons that flow from the analyses of Lewis (1954) and Myint (1958 and 1980; cf. the discussion in chapter 1): outmoded structures of servile labor, familial subsidization, and clientage kept large numbers of workers underemployed; and these reserves could be rapidly mobilized once those structures were subverted. Hence labor could be obtained in these regions at almost zero marginal cost. This appears to have applied most clearly to still semifeudal Russia, which experienced quite a high rate of emigration despite its high land-labor ratio.[33] The situation was exacerbated by Russia's very rapid population growth in the later nineteenth century: the number of inhabitants multiplied by 2.5 between 1850 and 1913.[34] What we may call "Myint-Lewis labor abundance" seems also to have prevailed in much of Africa and southeast Asia in these years.

I shall accept provisionally, then, that labor was genuinely scarce in the later nineteenth century only in the areas of new settlement: the Americas (exclusive of the Caribbean), Australia, and New Zealand. It was certainly abundant in the most land-scarce regions of Europe and eastern Asia; it is likely also to have been plentiful, at least in the near term, in the more land-rich areas of Russia, Africa, and southeast Asia.

CATEGORIES AND EXPECTATIONS

The analysis of chapter 1 leads us to anticipate, in general, that the rapidly expanding trade of the nineteenth century will, as it affected each country and region, have united and radicalized the owners and intensive users of

[31] In Bairoch's (1982, 281) analysis, for example, Brazil and Mexico both have indexes of seven in 1913; China's is three.
[32] Mitchell 1978, 47. On the general subject of nineteenth-century migration, see Hobsbawm 1979, chap. 11.
[33] Rates of emigration in Mitchell 1978, 47.
[34] Mulhall 1896, 135 and 156; Mitchell 1978, 4; Banks 1971, 48.

abundant factors and brought them into opposition to the owners and intensive users of scarce factors. Our three-factor model implies six possible cases, of which—on the basis of the sketch of factor endowments just concluded—five appear to have had real application in this period.

Abundance of Labor and Capital; Scarcity of Land

At the outset of our period, this category comprises only the few advanced European economies: Great Britain, Belgium, Switzerland, and parts of France. In the ensuing seventy years, more European states edge into it: Germany, Sweden, most of France, Denmark, and perhaps a few others. Here we expect expanding trade to have united capitalists and workers—and, indeed, the entrepreneurs who use either factor intensively[35]—against landowners and agriculturists. (Ordinarily, this implies an urban-rural cleavage in politics.) The former will have supported free trade; the latter, protection and imperialism.[36]

Abundance Only of Labor; Scarcity of Capital and Land

Into this category fall the backward and densely populated economies: that is, at the outset of our period (with the minor and transitory exceptions noted earlier), all of Europe except Britain, Belgium, Switzerland, and northern France; at its end, still almost all of southern and eastern Europe; throughout it, eastern and southern Asia. In these regions, we expect, labor will have been mobilized in support of free trade and a wider share of political power; capitalists and landowners will have united against labor and in support of protection and imperialism. Social class will thus be the basic political cleavage.

Abundance Only of Land; Scarcity of Labor and Capital

Under this rubric we encounter all of the "frontier" societies of the nineteenth century: Latin America; until their industrial maturation, the United States and Canada; and Australia and New Zealand. In these regions, expanding trade should have augmented the political demands of landowners, who will have embraced free trade; capitalists and workers, as

---

[35] So long as capital remains scarce, industries will be more protectionist the more capital intensive they are. As capital becomes abundant, the relation should reverse: sectors become more *free-trading* the more intensely they use capital.

[36] See again the discussion in chapter 1 at n. 14.

well as intensive users of either factor, will have united in support of protection and, in some cases, imperialism. The chief political conflict pits rural against urban forces.

Abundance of Land and Capital; Scarcity of Labor

Only the United States and Canada begin, both near the end of the nineteenth century, to move into this category. As they do so, we expect owners and intensive users of capital[37] to unite with landowners to oppose labor and to support freer trade; labor remains protectionist and imperialist. Class conflict intensifies.

Abundance of Land and Labor; Scarcity of Capital

If we accept the hypothesis of Myint, these conditions will have characterized those land-rich regions of the globe in which highly traditional societies or servile forms of labor had perpetuated large-scale underemployment. Hypothetically affected in the nineteenth century are Russia, much of Africa, and at least some parts of southeast Asia.[38] Here, workers and peasants can be expected to unite in support of freer markets and a greater share of power; capitalists will oppose them and embrace protection and, often, imperialism. The coalition of Red and Green against capital dominates political competition.

Abundance Only of Capital; Scarcity of Land and Labor

Even in the early twentieth century, the only plausible candidate for this category is Sweden, which alone among the emergent capital-abundant states exhibited the kind of marginal agriculture that might give rise to rural overemployment.[39] (Norway, with a similarly bleak agriculture, remains economically underdeveloped.) Sweden's continuing massive emigration, however—over 6 percent of its population left the country between 1900 and 1910[40]—speaks against any hypothesis of labor scarcity in

---

[37] See above, n. 55 in chapter 1.

[38] Cf. my discussion in chapter 3. Popkin's discussion (1979, chap. 4) of Cochinchina strongly suggests the kind of simultaneous abundance of land and labor that Myint postulates.

[39] See, on Norwegian and Swedish agriculture respectively, Esping-Andersen 1985, 45–46 and 49.

[40] Of a total population of 5.1 million in 1900, 324 thousand emigrated to points outside Europe between 1900 and 1910. Mitchell 1978, 7 and 47.

this period. Barring unexpected discoveries, we must regard this theoretically existent class as empirically empty in the years between 1850 and 1913.

EVIDENCE

In one of the classic works of modern comparative sociology, Barrington Moore, Jr. (1967) focused attention on a particularly malignant—indeed, protofascist[41]—developmental coalition, namely the protectionist one of capitalists and landowners against labor.[42] If the present approach is correct, such an alliance was likeliest to arise in the formative nineteenth century in countries where land and capital were both scarce and only labor was abundant—that is, countries in our second category, which comprises virtually all of Europe save its economically advanced northwestern corner, and all of eastern and southern Asia. There capital and land could be expected to unite in support of protection and imperialism; only labor, and the most labor-intensive agricultural and manufacturing enterprises, will normally have supported free trade and a less expansive foreign policy.

What Moore saw—rightly, in my estimation—as the far more hopeful coalition of capital and labor should have arisen, according to the present theory, principally in two quite different circumstances: where both of those factors were abundant, and only land was scarce (essentially northwestern Europe, our first case; and where both labor and capital were scarce, and only land was abundant (the "frontier" societies of the third case). In the former case, workers and capitalists alike will have favored free trade and a foreign policy of restraint; in the latter, both will have embraced protection and imperialism. In either of the two cases, however, the fatal alliance of land and capital is circumvented and, in Moore's perceptive telling, the path to a tolerably free society remains open.

A third coalition, however, with quite different consequences, is predicted in certain circumstances by the theory adopted here. If not inevitably socialist, it is by definition anticapitalist; and it arises when land and labor are united by either a common scarcity or a common abundance. I suggested that simultaneous scarcity of the two factors did not arise in the nineteenth century; but simultaneous abundance probably did, in Russia

---

[41] As I shall try to indicate in chapter 3, the approach adopted here may also shed a light somewhat different from Moore's on why the societies of this category were particularly prone to fascism in the 1930s.

[42] Although I am persuaded that coalitions are more protean than Moore's view of them would allow, I admit that a successful protectionist one can, as in Germany, have lasting effects. By sustaining less capital-intensive and more land-intensive enterprises even into an era of abundance of capital and scarcity of land, protection artificially maintains support for yet greater protection, and for imperialism.

and in Africa, with results that I shall examine more closely. In any event, factor endowments of this type, if we assume that they actually occur, should in theory prohibit the protofascist developmental alliance of land and capital.

While saying all of this, we must bear in mind the many hesitations and reservations of the general analysis (as outlined in chapter 1): that trade cannot possibly offer a complete account of any nation's or any period's political cleavages, and that the pressures described here will always be channeled and amplified by such other variables as culture and institutions. Moreover, the evidence that I shall be able to advance in this and subsequent chapters, coming as it does from a great range of cases, necessarily permits only preliminary and suggestive conclusions. Much more work will be needed before the theory can be regarded as even provisionally confirmed. With all of these caveats before us, let us nonetheless attempt to explore the resemblance between nineteenth-century political reality and the theory advanced earlier.

Economies Abundant in Labor and Capital,
Poor in Land: Great Britain, Belgium, Switzerland,
and Parts of France

Most clearly in Britain, expanding trade was associated with the triumph of a liberalism that united capital and labor, guaranteed free trade, and curtailed landed power. Agitation against the protectionist Corn Laws, led by capitalists and capital-intensive manufacturers, began as early as the 1820s. By the early 1840s, the Anti-Corn Law League had attracted a mass following among urban and, to some extent, rural workers.[43] In 1846 Peel, the Conservative prime minister, embraced repeal of agricultural protection and split his party: under Bentinck and Disraeli, the landowning Tory elite in effect expelled the "Peelite" faction; and the division insured a generation of Whig and Liberal rule, the Tories returning to power with an assured majority only in 1874.[44]

By the middle 1860s at the latest, Liberal rule rested on a firm alliance of the urban working and middle classes, of labor and capital;[45] and Liberal governments steadily pursued even freer trade, lower taxes and transaction

---

[43] Thomson 1962, 161. Cobden, the principal spokesman of the movement, was himself a cotton manufacturer. Some leaders of the largely working-class Chartist movement, however, supported the Corn Laws: Magnus 1964, 65–66.

[44] Perhaps the best single account of these events is Blake 1968, chap. 10. On the political sequel, see Thomson 1978, 119 and 238–39. Ironically, the thirty years following repeal of the Corn Laws brought a new "golden age" for British agriculture, which remained competitive by becoming more capital intensive: Bowden et al. 1937, 582.

[45] Magnus 1964, 163; Thomson 1978, 37.

costs, expansions of the franchise,[46] and diminutions of the remaining powers of local landowners, the Crown, and the House of Lords.[47] So entrenched did Liberal principles become in Britain that Conservatives could regain power only by equaling or exceeding the Liberals' liberalism[48]—as Disraeli, in a minority Conservative government, did with regard to the franchise in 1867 or, supported by a parliamentary majority, with respect to trade union rights in 1875.[49] One of the few significant differences between the parties came to be imperialism: most Liberals opposed it; almost all Tories, predictably, endorsed this "system of outdoor relief for the upper classes."[50]

Most astonishingly, when landowners began to suffer from imports of American grain after 1875, Disraeli—who had made protection his byword in the 1840s—flatly refused to help: the mass franchise and the state of public opinion made protection politically hopeless, he observed in the House of Lords, his own "rusty phrases of forty years ago" notwithstanding.[51] Under a Conservative government, landowners and farmers were permitted to go to the wall. Among the profound consequences were a new wave of bitterness and violence in Ireland (still almost wholly agricultural); the bankruptcy and reform of the Oxford colleges (whose endowments were largely in land); and, over the next generation, the final *embourgeoisement* of the English aristocracy.[52]

Despite these blows, religion and tradition kept most of the old Whig aristocracy loyal to the Liberal party until 1886, when Gladstone's endorsement of Irish Home Rule drove them, as well as such former Radicals as Chamberlain, out almost in a body.[53] From this point the Liberals were

---

[46] Gladstone announced, almost offhandedly, his conversion to the principle of universal manhood suffrage as early as 1864; in 1861, he reformed budget procedures to curtail the powers of the House of Lords. By the passage of the Third Reform Act in 1884, the electorate had reached five million, or about a seventh of the population and perhaps two-thirds of adult males; from this point universal manhood suffrage was inevitable. Magnus 1964, 151–52 and 160–61; Ensor 1936, 88.

[47] The peers' opposition to the Liberals' Third Reform Act (1884) first raised ministerial suggestions for the abolition of the chamber: Ensor 1936, 88–89. Among the other major battlegrounds were the powers of, and the franchise for, municipal government: Thomson 1978, 63–73.

[48] Later parallels suggest themselves.

[49] Thomson 1978, 120. On Disraeli's handling of the suffrage, see Blake 1968, chap. 21, and Magnus 1964, 185–88; on the trade unions, Ensor 1936, 132–33.

[50] Thomson 1962, 464; Thomson 1946, 164; Doyle 1986, 296.

[51] Blake 1968, 664; cf. Ensor 1936, 54.

[52] Ensor 1936, 56–57, 115–21, and 284–86; Engel 1983, chap. 5; Thompson 1963, 308–26. On the last point, one should also recall Lady Bracknell's trenchant question in *The Importance of Being Earnest*: "Was he born to the purple of commerce, or did he rise into it from the aristocracy?"

[53] Ensor 1936, 206–7. Even before 1886, however, the Liberal peers were a small minority of the entire House of Lords.

a party of urban capitalists and workers, supplemented—again religion and culture play their part—by the "Celtic fringe" of Wales and Scotland. And once that realignment was accomplished, the final disempowerment of the House of Lords and the Crown—that is, of the remnants of the old landed elite—by Lloyd George's Budget of 1909 and the Parliament Act of 1911 was probably inevitable.[54]

In Belgium, the urban-rural struggle took the different form of a secular-clerical controversy. After the decline of the "union of oppositions" that had made the Revolution of 1830 against the Dutch, Liberals contended directly with Catholics for parliamentary majorities.[55] The Liberals dominated from 1846 to 1884; the Catholics, from 1884 to 1914. While their controversies, centering on such familiar issues as education and civil liberties, were bitter, the underlying economic conflict was more mundane: the Catholic party represented the great landowners and the rural Flemish masses; the Liberals, "the industrial, commercial, and professional bourgeoisie," especially of Wallonia.[56] As in Britain, the tariff, imperialism, and the suffrage were important questions. Reversing the consistent protectionism of their previous Hapsburg, French, and Dutch overlords, and of the early postindependence regime, the Belgian Liberals achieved complete free trade by 1861;[57] and, as in Britain, their opponents did not dare subsequently to challenge that decision.[58] Belgium remained in the later nineteenth century a thoroughly export-oriented economy, and conservatives—as, again, in Britain—sought solace in colonization.[59] By 1893 universal male suffrage, albeit with some plural votes, had been achieved.[60]

In Switzerland liberalism and free trade triumphed even earlier. A civil war in 1847 against the attempted secession of seven Catholic (and largely rural) cantons sustained and transformed the confederation: it became a national, if still federal, state on the U.S. model, as firmly dominated by its urban-based Liberal and Radical parties as the United States was by the Republicans after its Civil War.[61] The strategy of free trade and export-led growth, which some cantons had pursued as early as the late eighteenth century, now guided the nation, with highly favorable economic results.[62] Universal male suffrage was achieved by 1874.[63]

---

[54] Ensor 1936, 386–88 and 414–32.
[55] Lorwin 1966, esp. 149–61; Kossmann 1978, 206–10 and 229–59.
[56] Lorwin 1966, 155.
[57] Mokyr 1976, 222–28.
[58] Emerson 1979, 131. Indeed, once tariffs on agricultural imports were lowered, Catholic leaders sought to abolish industrial protection and became pragmatic adherents of free trade. Kossmann 1978, 232.
[59] Katzenstein 1985, 175; Thomson 1962, 464–66.
[60] Thomson 1962, 324.
[61] Codding 1961, 30–34; Bonjour 1948.
[62] Katzenstein 1985, 174–75; Thomson 1962, 189–90.
[63] Thomson 1962, 324.

In France, divisions over religion and regime were genuine and independent; they did not coincide with, and indeed usually overshadowed, conflicts between factors.[64] Nonetheless, it seems clear that traditional large landowners, here as in Britain, strongly endorsed protection: the Bourbon Restoration (1815–1830), which epitomized their rule, imposed the highest tariffs in modern French history.[65] Most industrial workers, as well as the most labor-intensive peasants (in such lines as viniculture and silk growing), strongly favored free trade.[66] Capitalists, as one would expect in a country on the verge of capital abundance, were shifting and divided. During most of the July Monarchy (1830–1848), the powerful and semiofficial chambers of commerce remained largely protectionist.[67] By the mid-1840s, however, free trade was gaining strength; and, contrary to the assertions of some older historians,[68] the Second Empire's radical reductions of tariffs in 1860 were widely endorsed by, and substantially benefited, business.[69]

After 1860, as Smith's (1980) brilliant and detailed study has shown, the bankers and industrialists of "the large, cosmopolitan centers"—Paris, Lyon, Marseilles, Bordeaux—favored free trade; so did the capital-intensive commercial farmers of the Northwest; so, as before, did the silk growers and, until phylloxera devastated them in the 1880s, the viniculturists. On the other hand, the manufacturers of "the provincial cities and the mill towns," including especially backward ironmasters, shipbuilders, and spinners and weavers of cotton, were protectionist.[70]

On the issue of trade, then, workers, capitalists, capital-intensive industrialists, and the least land-intensive farmers held common ground against less modern and less capital-intensive industry, land-intensive peasant holdings, and, perhaps above all, large landowners. Free trade, under the Second Empire and in the first two decades of the Third Republic, helped (along with other policies),[71] to reduce aristocratic power and to cement the alliance of workers, smallholding peasants, and advanced capital that ultimately expanded democracy, tamed the military, and separated church

[64] Gilbert 1970, 47; Smith 1980, 51n.

[65] Caron 1979, 95–97. Between 1827 and 1836, tariff revenues amounted to 22 percent of total imports; between 1837 and 1846, to 17 percent.

[66] Thomson 1946, 51; Brogan 1967, 405.

[67] Caron 1979, 96; Thomson 1946, 56.

[68] E.g. Zeldin 1979, 181–82; Bowden et al. 1937, 616–17. Landes (1969, 244) goes so far as to claim that "in a sense, the Empire began to die in January 1860" with the crucial Cobden-Chevalier Treaty that reciprocally lowered tariffs with Britain.

[69] Smith 1980, chap. 1; Caron 1979, 100–5. Even Zeldin (1979, 188–93) is at pains to emphasize the general prosperity that the empire brought.

[70] Smith 1980, 90 and chap. 2 generally.

[71] In this respect, Zeldin (1979, 137–75) has argued, the Second Empire was both innovative and important; it lastingly undermined the influence of traditional rural elites.

and state.[72] After about 1880, growing imports of foodstuffs, by turning most peasants protectionist, forced the Republican parties to abandon strict free trade.[73] Even so, only moderate tariffs—again, in contrast to what historians long claimed—were imposed.[74]

As in Britain and Belgium, the traditional landowning classes sought compensation in colonies and in military expansion.[75] Although some staunch Republicans, such as Ferry, advocated and practiced imperialism, they were treated as apostates by most radicals for doing so;[76] and the actual proconsuls of the new empire—Lyautey, for example—were drawn largely from the old aristocracy.[77] As one of the most perceptive students of recent French history has put it, the empire reflected "less the Republican and democratic nature of modern France than the nationalist, authoritarian character of the social classes which [were] most concerned with its creation."[78]

Other, often more significant, conflicts cross-cut those of factors and trade: devout workers voted with conservative landowners, and anti-clerical landowners (above all in the South) retained their ties to urban "reds." Yet the impact of expanding trade, and the issue of how to adjust to it, failed crucially in more advanced France to create the monolithic union of land and capital that it aroused in Germany (see the next section). Indeed, expanding trade in France—except, perhaps, in the most backward districts—is associated with an advance of Liberalism, an alliance of labor and capital, and a decline in the influence of large landowners.

Economies Abundant Only in Labor,
Poor in Capital and Land: Less Developed
Europe, East and South Asia

In sharp contrast to the pattern displayed by the few islands of capital abundance that we have just considered, almost all of the rest of Europe

[72] Cobban 1965, chaps. 2 and 4; Zeldin 1979, chap. 9. It is essential to recognize that the foundations of an effective parliamentary democracy were laid in the "Liberal Empire" between 1860 and 1870: Thomson 1962, 242–45; Zeldin 1979, 184–88.

[73] Smith 1980, chaps. 4 and 5. Caron (1979, 110) emphasizes the importance of the phylloxera epidemic, which cost the free-trade cause "its chief parliamentary support, that of the representatives from the wine-growing regions."

[74] Even after the tariff increases of 1892 and 1910, French duties amounted to 8 percent of the total value of imports (in 1849 they had been 17 percent, in 1869 4 percent); for the United States in 1910, the comparable figure was 23 percent. Caron 1979, 97 and 111.

[75] On the aristocratic domination of the officer corps until after 1900, see Brogan 1967, 380–82.

[76] Zeldin 1979, 266–67.

[77] Thomson 1946, 61–62, relates the delicious tale of Lyautey's grandmother, at the age of ninety and surrounded by some sixty descendants, announcing that "I thank God that not one among you is a Republican." Cf. Brogan 1967, 628–29.

[78] Thomson 1946, 167.

responded to the increasing trade of the nineteenth century with class conflict: labor, embracing free trade, opposed a protectionist coalition of capital and land. This was of course quintessentially the case with Germany's militant socialism and its "marriage of iron and rye"; but similar alliances of land and capital, and a similarly irreconcilable working class, can be observed in Spain, Italy, and Austria-Hungary; and, with significant variations, in Sweden and Norway.

In Germany, it is important to recall, the areas east of the Elbe had actually been abundant in land, relative to their available trading partners, up to the opening of the American prairies in the 1870s. Prussia exported grain; and the Junker latifundists endorsed free trade quite as strongly, and for the same reasons, as did antebellum planters in the U.S. South.[79] In this phase of expanding trade, roughly from the 1830s to the early 1870s, the natural alliance in Germany was between free-trading workers and Junker, in opposition to protectionist industry. As Hamerow's (1966) insightful analysis contends, just such a coalition actually arose and explains the collapse of the essentially middle-class German revolution of 1848: Friedrich Wilhelm IV finally found the courage to follow the long-proffered advice of such conservative thinkers as Wagener, Huber, and von Radowitz "to turn to the masses, . . . [our princes'] natural allies" and (as another royal adviser reported Radowitz's views in the heat of the 1848 crisis) to "champion the working class, the so-called proletarians, against the bourgeoisie."[80] From the other side of the divide, the working-class leader Lassalle in the 1860s advocated, much to Marx's disgust, collaboration with the "feudal" Junker to extort concessions from the industrial bourgeoisie; and Bismarck, with whom Lassalle sustained a cordial correspondence, may be seen to have moved toward such a policy with his endorsement of universal suffrage for elections to the Reichstag of the North German Confederation in 1867, and of the empire in 1871.[81]

In 1875, however, American grain began to undersell Germany's in all markets, exposing the latter country's real paucity of land; yet Germany remained at this time also underdeveloped (i.e., poor in capital). Now the natural alliance, which however might well have taken some time to consummate, was one of the two scarce factors, capital and land, against the only remaining abundant resource, labor. In the event, as everyone knows, the realignment was accomplished in four short years.[82] The Junker, who had long fervently advocated free trade, were swiftly converted to protec-

[79] Moore 1967, chap. 3.

[80] Hamerow 1966, 73 and 176.

[81] Passant 1962, 91; Marx and Engels 1978, 532–33; Gilbert 1970, 65.

[82] Among the classic studies of these dramatic events are Gerschenkron 1943; Rosenberg 1943 and 1967; Kindleberger 1951; and Lambi 1963. Related, and even more penetrating and caustic, is Kehr 1973, 273–86. A dissenting and ultimately unpersuasive treatment is Hardach 1967.

tionism; the heavy industrialists, who chronically sought tariffs, had done so more desperately since the onset of a business depression in 1873; and Bismarck, seeing a chance both to undermine the free-trading National Liberals and to put the Reich's finances on a sounder footing, united the two powerful factions on a platform of protection for both industry and agriculture, plus antisocialist laws to offset the inevitable push for higher wages that food tariffs would bring. The smaller-scale peasants of western and southern Germany, whose livestock and dairy farming gave them an interest in cheap fodder and thus, plausibly, in free trade, were for the most part still land-intensive enough that they allied with the Junker in support of protection.[83]

At the same time, as Rosenberg (1967) has emphasized, workers greatly benefited from trade: their new wealth and leisure, rather than any poverty, was the basis of a powerful socialist movement in Germany; and German labor strongly and consistently endorsed free trade.[84] Admittedly, the costs of protection fell almost entirely on the urban workers and weakened— intentionally, some authors assert—their social and political position;[85] but the tariffs could not deprive labor of all its gains from trade. As world trade expanded, German workers gained in numbers and influence.

As Germany's accelerating economic growth raised it into the ranks of the capital-abundant countries after 1890,[86] the "marriage of iron and rye" began to fray, exactly as the theory would predict. Caprivi's "New Course" of lower tariffs and toleration of the Left (1890–1894) was a first sign, albeit one that ultimately revealed only the force of agrarian resistance.[87] More significant were the secession in 1895 from the high-tariff *Central-verband deutscher Industrieller* of the most capital-intensive new industries, above all in chemicals and electrical equipment, to found the more free-trading *Bund der Industriellen;*[88] the wider industrial rebellion against high tariffs that underlay the formation of the *Hansabund* a few years later;[89] and, finally, the victory of the low-tariff forces in the Reichstag elections of 1912, which may even have helped impel the threatened Junker elite into the saving patriotic flames of World War I.[90]

In the countries of Europe that remained economically backward, the

---

[83] Some northern German peasants, including those of Schleswig-Holstein whom Heberle (1963 and 1970) studied so intensively, remained free-trading. On the issue of intensity of factors in production, see my discussion in chapter 1, esp. n. 55.

[84] Rosenberg 1967, 47–51; Gerschenkron 1943, 33–36.

[85] Kehr 1973, 291–93.

[86] Landes 1969, 329. Feis 1965, 68–69, suggests that Germany began to export capital in significant volume in the late 1880s.

[87] Passant 1962, 118–20.

[88] Stegmann 1970, 33–34; Ullmann 1976.

[89] Mielke 1976.

[90] Stegmann 1970, 33–34; Calleo 1978, 39–40.

coalition of land and capital survived. In Spain, the industrialists of Barcelona accepted an alliance with the great landowners of the Center and South; one result was the agreed rotation in office of Conservative and Liberal governments that endured from the monarchist restoration in 1874 into the first decade of the twentieth century and that, beginning in 1877, pursued a policy of protection.[91] (A similar "rotativism" between Progressive and Regenerator parties characterized Portuguese politics in this period.)[92] At the same time, both urban and rural labor became steadily more radicalized: peasant risings in the 1850s and 1860s (including, in Andalusia, substantial support for anarchism), general strikes in Barcelona in 1902 and Cordova in 1905, and the savagery of Barcelona's Tragic Week of 1909 prefigured the Civil War of the 1930s.[93]

In Italy, the industrial and financial elites of Milan and Turin dominated the new national government but conceded control of the South to local latifundists; from 1887 on, capitalists and landowners agreed on a policy of high tariffs.[94] Labor in the countryside and the towns, benefited by trade but excluded from the gains that even wider exchange might bring, grew rebellious: rural unrest, officially labeled "banditry," had arduously to be suppressed in the South after unification, Milan experienced riots and barricades in 1898, and a general strike was attempted in 1904. Socialism grew ever stronger and ever more radical.[95]

In what had been until 1867 the Austrian Empire, capitalists and landowners carried a similar compromise to its logical extreme: Austrian industrialists conceded full home rule to Magyar latifundists, instituting what was henceforth the Dual Monarchy of Austria-Hungary.[96] High tariffs, enacted in 1875 and put into effect on the expiration of a constraining treaty in 1878, were for both parties an agreeable side benefit of the bargain.[97] Labor, as the sole beneficiary of expanding trade, was again free-trading, again radical, and again the excluded partner.[98]

In Sweden and Norway, somewhat as in France, conflicts of culture,

[91] Gilbert 1970, 58–59; Bowden et al. 1937, 617; Hobsbawm 1979, 340; Landes 1969, 245; Ullman 1968, 10–11. On protection, which reached new heights in 1891 and again in 1907, see particularly Carr 1966, 393–96, and Ullman 1968, 11 and 21.
[92] Kurth 1979a, 336.
[93] Thomson 1962, 236 and 379; Hobsbawm 1979, 209; Gilbert 1970, 58–59. The leading student of the Tragic Week shows clearly that its anticlerical outbursts were a diversion from the deeper issues of secret wealth, wage cutting, tariffs, and conscription. Ullman 1968, esp. p. 22 and chaps. 2, 9, 14, and 15.
[94] Gilbert 1970, 60 and 62–63; Landes 1969, 244–45.
[95] Hobsbawm 1979, 209; Gilbert 1970, 61–63.
[96] Thomson 1962, 272–73; Gilbert 1970, 77.
[97] Landes 1969, 245; but Bowden et al. 1937, 617, impute to the Magyar estate owners a continuing free-trade orientation.
[98] Thomson 1962, 371.

regime, and even language crosscut and intermingled with those inspired by trade.[99] Nonetheless large landowners and capital-intensive industrialists[100] were generally protectionist and conservative; workers and more labor-intensive farmers and manufacturers inclined toward free trade.[101] As Gourevitch (1986) has written, "In the later nineteenth century, . . . Sweden had its own iron-rye coalition."[102] In both countries, workers, as trade's clearest beneficiaries, mobilized early, cohesively, and radically.[103]

In sum, as James Kurth has accurately observed, the protectionist "marriage of iron and rye" (or, in some contexts, of "cloth and wheat"), which Moore anathematized, and a radicalized working class were not phenomena unique to Germany in the latter half of the nineteenth century.[104] Rather, they appear to have emerged widely, as the theory would predict for this period, among Europe's less developed economies.

A question that will repay a closer investigation than can be undertaken here is the extent to which similar manifestations arise, as the theory leads us to expect, in the densely populated and backward Asian societies as they are exposed to trade in this period. It appears, for example, that the massive Taiping Rebellion (1851–1866) found its strongest support in the most land-scarce and most trade-penetrated regions of southern China and, within those regions, among landless peasants and the urban poor.[105] In Japan after 1853, the landowning *bushi* class suffered economic losses and rallied to the slogan of *joi* (oust the barbarians!);[106] by contrast, by the 1860s peasant movements in such heavy silk-producing (i.e., labor-intensive) and export-oriented areas as Nagano and Gumma prefectures were demanding among other things "the right to free sale of agricultural produce."[107] The 1880s saw a new wave of tenant revolts that took up the ideology of the newly founded *Jiyuto*, or Liberal, party; a principal complaint was the subsidies to industry (tariffs being forbidden by the "un-

---

[99] Gourevitch 1986, 111–12; Rokkan 1966, 73–89.

[100] Recall that, so long as a factor remains scarce, expanding trade harms owners *and intensive users* of that factor.

[101] Esping-Anderson 1985, 46; Gourevitch 1986, 112.

[102] Gourevitch 1986, 113.

[103] Esping-Anderson 1985, 59–62, 79–81, and 83–85; Rokkan 1966, 81–82; Lipset 1970, 30.

[104] Kurth 1979a, 337. Occasionally in Europe, and more frequently in Asia, trade did not emerge as an explicit issue; or it did so only in the covert form of a demand for wider access to markets. The cleavages, however, are almost always as predicted; and we may anticipate that the importance of trade will often have been obscured (see chapter 1, n. 14).

[105] Scalapino and Yu 1985, chap. 1, esp. 12–13 and 17–19; Feuerwerker 1975, 47–49 and 54–55; Hobsbawm 1979, 140–41.

[106] Scalapino 1953, 26–27 and 30–31.

[107] Woodside 1976, 32–33.

equal treaties") and the heavy taxation that financed them.[108] Needless to say, these movements excited only the united opposition of landholding and urban elites.

India also experienced a series of antilandlord and anticapitalist peasant revolts in the second half of the nineteenth century.[109] Historians have connected these to an increasing prosperity of the lesser peasantry and to demands for improved access to markets.[110] Shortly after the turn of the century landless and land-poor peasants revolted also in the most densely populated parts of a Vietnam that was being rapidly integrated into world markets.[111] As in the Chinese case, landlords united with (often foreign) capitalists to suppress the threat.[112] To what extent were these stirrings a response, not of those threatened by modernity, but of at least potential beneficiaries of expanding trade, who sought to remove parasites and impediments and to gain direct access to markets? The question is made acute by the evidence of Asia's response to a later period of expanding trade,[113] which we shall address in chapter 4.

Economies Abundant Only in Land,
Poor in Capital and Labor:
The Americas and Oceania

Most clearly in the United States, but also in Australia, New Zealand, Canada, and much of Latin America, we see quite a different pattern than in either of the two regions discussed earlier: a thrust for political power by agriculture, resisted by a protectionist alliance of labor and capital.[114] As in northwestern Europe, the conflict is largely between the cities and the countryside; but here, farmers are the aggressive and free-trading element, while both capitalists and workers embrace tariffs and, particularly in the United States, imperialism.

The details of the U.S. experience are too familiar to require extensive

---

[108] Scalapino 1953, 101–6 and 112.

[109] For overviews, see Desai 1979, chap. 4 and pt. 2.

[110] Sen 1982, chap. 1; Seal 1968, 210.

[111] Popkin 1979, xvii and 153–58; Woodside 1976, 32–33.

[112] Seal 1968, 239–40; Scalapino and Yu 1985, 27–29 and 33. Note also the counterrevolutionary appeal to merchants in a proclamation of February 1854 by the government general Zeng Guofan: Feuerwerker 1975, 83.

[113] Popkin (1979) argues persuasively that the Vietnamese revolution was grounded in peasants' demands for freer access to markets.

[114] An interesting parallel analysis is that of Denoon 1983, esp. chap. 1, who points to the similarities of development in the land-rich economies of New Zealand, Australia, South Africa, Uruguay, Argentina, and Chile up to World War I. Denoon, however, emphasizes the differences between these "dependent" cases and the North American ones. I owe this citation to an anonymous referee.

discussion.[115] Beginning with the railways' penetration of the Great Plains[116] and fueled as well by the effects of the post–Civil War deflation on indebted farmers, agrarian discontent threatened both major parties. After initial efforts in the Granger and Greenback movements, by the late 1880s agriculturists had formed the Farmers' Alliances that in 1892 called the People's, or "Populist," party into existence. Among the new party's chief demands were direct access to markets, by way of public ownership of railways and shipping facilities, an inflation of the currency, and (although their platform insisted that the issue was secondary)[117] free trade. Despite efforts to enlist urban workers in the cause, these demands proved fundamentally unacceptable to both capital and labor.[118] The Populists' fusion with the Democrats in 1896 under the presidential candidacy of William Jennings Bryan severed the older party's ties not only to Eastern financiers and industrialists but to the urban working class and the less land-intensive farmers of the East and Middle West.[119] In a realignment of American politics that endured until the late 1920s, workers joined owners in support of a triumphant, highly protectionist, and increasingly imperialist Republican party.[120] Most industrial areas became as firmly one-party Republican as the South had been one-party Democratic; and the Democrats became for thirty years a party of the southern and western fringe, whose only hope of national office lay in a Republican split like that of 1912.

The parallel movement in Canada came somewhat later but had a similar

[115] See any standard U.S. history of the period—e.g., Williams, Current, and Friedel 1969, 171–78, 194–201, and 222–33.

[116] The railroads made world markets available to the farmers and thus benefited and strengthened them; at the same time, the railway companies extracted substantial monopoly rents and, as federal grantees, had sold much of the land that the farmers occupied. Hicks 1961, 2–17 and 60–74.

[117] Platform of the People's party, 4 July 1892, Omaha, reprinted in Hofstadter 1958, 2: 147–53. Cf. Hicks 1961, 81. The movement's foes, however, were not deceived: the *San Francisco Chronicle* denounced Bryan as "a free trade office seeker" (cited in Mink 1986, 131n.). Sundquist (1983, 164) argues that the tariff was decisive for "the urban workingman." Admittedly, a few farmers in this era were protectionist, most notably the labor-intensive small woolgrowers of the Midwest and Northeast: see for example Lake 1988, 103–4.

[118] Mink 1986, chap. 4, contends that union, and predominantly native, labor moved to the Democrats; the Republicans harvested most of the votes of urban immigrant labor. Unfortunately, her analysis lacks the quantitative work that would demonstrate such an assertion; and Sundquist (1983, 162–68) sees any such trend as slight and ephemeral.

[119] The fundamental studies of the realignment of 1896 are those of E. E. Schattschneider (1960, esp. 78–85), James L. Sundquist (1983, chaps. 6 and 7), and—particularly for the effects at the local level—Walter Dean Burnham (1970).

[120] Bryan, renominated by the Democrats, chose to fight the election of 1900 chiefly on the issues of imperialism and the tariff; he was soundly defeated. The urban electorate, in particular, evidently supported both. Williams et al. 1969, 255–56.

outcome.[121] Although it was enacted in 1879 largely in response to a crisis of declining Federal revenues, industrial protection—touted by its Conservative supporters as the "National Policy"—soon became popular enough with urban workers and owners not only to sustain its authors in power for a decade and a half but to induce the Liberal opposition (in power after 1896) to accede to it. By 1910, however, western farmers were insistently demanding lower tariffs and public ownership of grain elevators—not, as one study of the period puts it, because they were impoverished, but because "their present income was only a shadow of what was possible." Laurier, the Liberal prime minister of the day, yielded to the extent of negotiating graduated free trade with the United States; he succeeded, as Bryan had done in the United States, only in driving away much of his party's business and working-class support. His parliamentary party split, new elections had to be called, and Laurier lost in a landslide. Canada remained committed to protection.

Australia and New Zealand present an interesting variation on this common pattern, because much of their work force was rural and landowners were a small, if powerful, minority.[122] In contrast to the United States or Canada, Australasian lands had been settled by "squatters" in enormous tracts that were used at first almost entirely for the grazing of sheep. Especially in Australia, the brute labor of sheep farming, including especially shearing, devolved onto a sizable rural proletariat, which, isolated from the larger society and continually interacting with itself, had early developed a fierce class-consciousness and a militant trade unionism.[123] The Australian miners, and the slaughterhouse and dockworkers of the cities, did not lag far behind; and Labor parties became an important force in the separate colonial parliaments in the 1890s and, after federation in 1901, in the Commonwealth. In 1910, Australian Labor achieved the world's first parliamentary majority for a socialist party.

On the central issues of the day, however, including the tariff,[124] Australian working-class representatives found common ground with urban employers and a common enemy in the large landowners.[125] In 1885, the

[121] This paragraph draws on the account of Finlay and Sprague 1979, 191–96, 213, and 229–33.

[122] Except where otherwise indicated, this account is drawn from Gollan 1974; Greenwood 1974b; and Alexander 1980b, chap. 2.

[123] See, on the rapid growth of the Australian Shearers' Union and its great strikes of 1890, Greenwood 1974b, 157–65.

[124] Even before federation, land reform—the enforced sale and dispersion of the large estates—had been a recurring issue in the individual colonies. See, e.g., Alexander 1980, 10.

[125] This account compresses a longer process, in which some unions and some manufacturers originally were more favorable to free trade, and a few agricultural sectors were protectionist. Opinion did not solidify until shortly before 1906. See, on the mature pattern, Denoon 1983, 191–92.

Third Intercolonial Trade Union Congress endorsed protection;[126] and in 1906, a minority Liberal prime minister, Alfred Deakin, won Labor's unanimous support for the policy that came to be called "the New Protection":[127] a tariff and a domestic excise, in exactly the same amounts, were levied on most manufactures; but the excise was to be refunded (and thus the benefits of protection granted) only to those firms that paid, in the judgment of the existing Court of Conciliation and Arbitration, "a fair and reasonable wage." This the Court defined, in its famous "Harvester Judgment" of 1907, as one sufficient to support a worker with a (nonremunerated) wife and three children; and that standard it translated into direct monetary terms: in the area where the agricultural implements manufacturer at issue was located, forty-two shillings per week.

By this cunning device,[128] the interests of the two scarce factors, labor and capital, were directly tied to each other and to the common cause of protection, which, needless to say, the landowners heartily opposed. Labor, and indeed a strong majority of the electorate, became wedded to high tariffs (and to the related policy of whites-only immigration).

In New Zealand, the link between labor and capital was simpler and more direct.[129] Labor, the urban middle classes, and even the smaller and more labor-intensive farmers united in the appropriately named Liberal-Labor party, which was swept to power in the elections of 1890. It succeeded in breaking landowner power, increasing the protective tariff (first enacted in 1888), expanding the legal protection of the trade unions, and laying the foundations of a substantial welfare state. Here as in Australia, the "squatters" fulminated but were too few, and too unprotected by London,[130] to oppose effectively these inimical measures.

[126] Gollan 1974, 155.

[127] Such a system had been proposed before federation by a hat manufacturer in Victoria, one Samuel Mauger. Alexander 1980, 26.

[128] Too cunning, as it turned out: Deakin's legislation was found unconstitutional in 1908, and its goals had later to be attained by less formal means. Alexander 1980, 26–27; Greenwood 1974b, 218.

[129] This discussion is drawn from Condliffe and Airey 1954, chaps. 15–17.

[130] The crucial battles had been lost earlier, when the powers of nominated upper houses were curtailed, responsible government was achieved, and manhood—or, in New Zealand from 1893, universal—suffrage was achieved. McNaughtan 1974; Condliffe and Airey 1954, 83–88 and 161–62. It remains to me something of a puzzle why British imperialism was more effective in supporting landowner power in Latin America than in its own white colonies; cf. Denoon 1983, 60. Among the conjectures are that Latin American landowners were more powerful, particularly through their ties to the military; that British financiers actually favored the breakup of the Australian latifundia (I owe this claim to an anonymous referee); and, least persuasively, that many Latin American industrialists were foreign born and hence without political influence (Cornblit, cited by Denoon 1983, 158). For some helpful, if only collateral, speculations, see Moran 1970.

In all of these cases, then, landowners—although they were strengthened and benefited by expanding trade—were ultimately defeated, and protection was imposed. In Latin America, however, the landowners won: pushing aside or capturing the military *caudillos* who had previously dominated postcolonial politics, farmers, ranchers, and miners pursued a liberalism and free trade that maximized their returns from the growing world market in primary products.[131] The notoriously weak capitalists of South and Central America, the region's inarticulate and, often, racially oppressed workers, and—perhaps not least—the powerful influence of Great Britain as principal trading partner, all contributed to the political monopoly of the landowning class in this period.[132] Only when trade was interrupted by World War I and the depression of the 1930s (see chapter 3) did the suppressed conflict between city and countryside fully manifest itself.

In general, then, the land-rich and less developed economies of the nineteenth century also avoided Moore's fatal union of land and capital, inclining instead to a "progressive" alliance of capital and labor, which however was always protectionist and frequently imperialist. That alliance won with almost trivial ease in Australia and New Zealand and against only slightly stronger opposition in Canada, triumphed in the United States only after the apocalyptic struggle of 1896, and failed throughout Latin America.

Economies Abundant in Land and Capital,
Poor in Labor: The United States and
Canada just before World War I

As the United States and Canada attained capital abundance in the last years of our period—the United States probably about the turn of the century, Canada somewhat later as noted previously—we can expect that capitalists and capital-intensive industrialists, with some lag for social learning, will have come to support free trade. In the United States, we can point tentatively to evidence of such a trend. Soon after the turn of the century, some leaders of American business began to see in foreign markets the

[131] See, among others: Sunkel with Paz 1973, 50–69 and 306–43; Hobsbawm 1979, 128–32; Skidmore and Smith 1984, 43–51; and Cardoso and Faletto 1979, chap. 3.

[132] The urban middle classes of course demanded some share of power earlier (see, inter alia, Cardoso and Faletto 1979, chap. 4); but even where, as in Argentina, an urban-based party managed to win power before World War I, it failed to challenge the landowners on the issues of tariff policy and national development—i.e., free trade was retained. Indeed, it appears, contrary to what the present theory would predict, that most Argentine industrialists and workers supported free trade. See Moran 1970 and Solberg 1987, 22 and 47. Earlier, failed efforts at protection in Argentina are detailed by Rock 1987, 149–52, and Denoon 1983, 158–59. Uruguay, where Batlle enacted as early as 1911 a meaningful measure of protection (Cardoso and Faletto 1979, 95), may be a more significant exception.

answer to stagnating and fluctuating domestic demand. In particular, manufacturers of such technologically advanced products of the period as farm machinery, electrical equipment, telephones, sewing machines, and automobiles began to agitate for tariff reduction.[133] In addition, the largest, most mechanized, and best integrated firms—for example, in cigarettes, matches, milling, meatpacking, petroleum products, soap, and plumbing fixtures—notably sought overseas expansion and a reduction of trade barriers.[134] By 1908, 40 percent even of the membership of the more small-business-oriented National Association of Manufacturers (NAM), originally a protectionist group, supported lower tariffs, and the Republican presidential candidate promised to moderate protection.[135] Theodore Roosevelt's brand of progressivism emphasized tariff reform even more strongly; and his New Nationalism was intended, as he said in his 1912 acceptance speech, to prevent the United States from having "an economic system less efficient than our great competitors, Germany, England, France, and Austria."[136] On that platform, he won financial support from major business leaders and votes from the urban middle classes; and Wilson, elected on a platform that prominently promised tariff reduction, managed actually to achieve a substantial decrease in protection.[137]

In Canada, on the other hand, nothing points to such a development.[138] Industry of almost every sort appears to have remained terrified of U.S. competition and to have vigorously supported continued protection against it; the local counterpart of the U.S. NAM, the Canadian Manufacturers Association, unanimously favored high tariffs.[139] Only with respect to British and European goods were tariffs finally reduced, and then in a limited and reciprocal way. Abundance or scarcity of capital may matter

[133] Baack and Ray 1983, 82–83, and 1985, 124–27; Terrill 1973, chap. 8; Kenkel 1983, 40–44 and 51; Hody 1986, 38. Ferguson (1984, esp. 64) sees bankers and capital-intensive sectors (except chemicals) as the main advocates of trade liberalization in the 1920s but minimizes the importance of this division for the years before World War I.

[134] See esp. Becker 1982, 21–40.

[135] Williams et al. 1969, 317; Kenkel 1983, 43 and 47–54. On the origins of the NAM, see Becker 1982, 41–42. In office, Taft of course failed to deliver: Williams et al. 1969, 319–22; Lake 1988, 132–36 and 143–44.

[136] Roosevelt's speech accepting the Progressive party nomination for President, 6 August 1912, excerpted in Hofstadter, 1958, 2: 286–92, at 288. Cf. Kenkel 1983, 93.

[137] Williams et al. 1969, 325 and 327–28. Baack and Ray (1983, esp. 83–85) advance evidence to show that "tariff cuts were greatest in fast growth industries . . . for both the 1870–1914 and 1870–1910 periods."

[138] Easterbrook and Aitken 1958, 504–5.

[139] To be sure, many Canadian firms were branch plants of U.S. enterprises; but this is likely to have followed from, rather than contributed to, Canadian protection. High tariffs inevitably encourage direct foreign investment, as the only route of access to a protected market: cf. Japanese automobile manufacturers' recent establishment of U.S. plants in reponse to our "voluntary" import restrictions.

more with respect to one's nearest and most important trading partners than in relation to the rest of the world; but in this case, what the theory predicts simply does not come to pass.

Economies Abundant in Land and Labor, Poor in Capital: Russia, Southeast Asia, and Africa

Objectively, as we have seen, Russia in the nineteenth century was more abundant in land than the United States; yet the country resounded with complaints of overpopulation and land hunger.[140] The most perceptive contemporary observers, including the modernizing minister Count Witte, resolved the paradox by prefiguring the Myint-Lewis analysis as outlined in chapter 1: the legacy of serfdom, the survival of the communal village, and the rapid growth of population inflicted chronic and worsening underemployment on the Russian peasantry.[141] Archaic social structures bound labor to the village; and the spread of labor-intensive manufactures into these petty communes showed, even against severe obstacles, that this labor could be mobilized at almost no marginal cost.[142]

Russia, in short, abounded in both land and labor. It followed that the expansion of trade should have benefited both factors, and the evidence suggests that it did. Expanding access to world markets, particularly through the rapid growth of railroads between 1857 and 1876, overwhelmingly assisted Russian agriculture, in direct proportion to each region's previous isolation. Over the decade of the 1870s, the price of rye, which in western Europe was falling sharply because of new competition from American grain, rose by 30 percent in St. Petersburg, by 66 percent in Oryol (about one-third of the way between Moscow and the Black Sea), by 85 percent in Kharkov (yet nearer the Black Sea), and by 100 percent in remote Saratov (to the northwest of the Caspian Sea). By weight, grain exports more than trebled between the early 1860s and the late 1870s, rising from 1.4 to 4.7 million metric tons and from about 30 percent to about half of Russia's total exports.[143] Between 1900 and 1913, agricultural production rose by 33.8 percent, grain exports by about 50 percent, net agricultural income by 88.6 percent.[144] Rents and land prices rose correspondingly: the latter roughly doubled between the 1870s and the 1890s

---

[140] The paradox is noted by Seton-Watson 1967, 507. Cf. Kochan 1966, 40–42.

[141] "The masses of the people remain in enforced idleness. A considerable part of our peasant population does not know to what to put its hand in winter." Witte, quoted in Kochan 1966, 11.

[142] Riasanovsky 1977, 459ff.; Robinson 1932, 246–47.

[143] Seton-Watson 1967, 406 and 530.

[144] Nove 1972, 23.

and almost doubled again between 1905 and 1917.[145] Indeed, one may plausibly speculate that much of rural Russia's population explosion in these years was owed to the new margin of safety that wider markets and greater specialization afforded: not by accident was fecundity greatest in those regions, south of Moscow and along the central Volga, where exports boomed most dramatically.[146]

Urban wages rose also, if far less dramatically. In real terms, there was an increase in the final years of the nineteenth century and another just before World War I—from, admittedly, appallingly low initial levels.[147] More remarkable were the sheer scope and speed of the proletariat's growth: from a few tens of thousands in 1850, the industrial work force expanded to some 2.9 million by 1900.[148] The growth of Russia's major industrial centers in this period is detailed in Table 2.9.

Even so, nothing like all of the possible gain from increased trade flowed to agriculture and labor. What chiefly stood in the way was the state's strategically dictated policies of industrialization and protection.[149] As early as the 1820s, Russian tariff policy had become markedly protectionist,[150] and this trend accelerated under Vishnegradsky and Witte after 1887. Witte, moreover, undertook to squeeze both agriculture and consumption to generate the capital that would industrialize Russia. All imported articles of consumption were heavily taxed; the state bought from domestic suppliers even at large premiums; excises were increased especially on domestic products of inelastic demand (spirits, sugar, fuel, and matches); and cash taxes were increased and made payable just after the harvest.[151] By thus forcing the peasants to raise money when prices were lowest, the government insured that more grain would come onto the market and that export earnings would increase. As Gerald Robinson put it well in his classic study of the pre-Revolutionary peasantry, "if [these policies] had been deliberately contrived as a yoke to fit the necks of men who sold the products of

---

[145] Robinson 1932, 101; Riasanovsky 1977, 478; cf. Kochan 1966, 43.

[146] Kochan 1966, 42; Nove 1972, 22. According to official Soviet estimates, the Russian population grew from 69 million in 1850 to 133 million in 1900 and 161 million in 1910: Mitchell 1978, 10.

[147] Robinson 1932, 108 and 249–50; Riasanovsky 1977, 476.

[148] Mitchell 1978, 59. A further 3.2 million were employed in services, 1.1 million in commerce and finance. A total of 15.1 million continued to work in agriculture.

[149] Witte, in terms eerily similar to those invoked by Stalin to justify the first Five-Year Plan, grounded his politically difficult policies on strategic necessity: if it did not industrialize rapidly, Russia would suffer China's or India's fate. Kochan 1966, 12.

[150] Seton-Watson 1967, 246.

[151] Seton-Watson 1967, 517ff.; Riasanovsky 1977, chap. 23; Kochan 1966, introduction and chap. 1; Gerschenkron 1960.

TABLE 2.9
Population of Major Russian Industrial Centers, 1850–1910 (in thousands)

	1850	1885	1900	1910
Baku	14[a]	46	112	218
Ekaterinoslav[b]	12	47	121	196
Nizhne Novgorod[c]	31	67	90	109
Kazan	45	94[d]	132	188
Kharkov	25	101[e]	175[f]	236
Kiev	50	166	247[f]	505
Petrograd	485	877[d]	1267[f]	1962
Moscow	365	748[g]	989[f]	1533
Odessa	90	194[h]	405[f]	506
Tiflis	35[i]	90	161[f]	188

Source: Mitchell 1978, Table A2.
[a] 1863.
[b] Present-day Dniepropetrovsk.
[c] Present-day Gorky.
[d] 1880.
[e] 1879.
[f] 1897.
[g] 1882.
[h] 1877.
[i] 1854.

agriculture and bought those of industry, the design could hardly have been more perfect."[152] These measures were widely—and, in the view of most historians, rightly—blamed for the famines of 1891–1892 and 1898–1899, for (as Seton-Watson puts it) "they effectively deprived the peasants of any reserve to sustain them in the face of a harvest failure."[153] Certainly they aroused the fury of the peasantry, and of the landed sector generally. Increasingly, politics in prerevolutionary Russia was characterized by an unbridgeable opposition between agricultural and industrial interests.[154] Urban workers were equally alienated from the system of protection and even more hostile to the regime. According to their spokesmen, tariffs had the further disadvantages of encouraging foreign ownership, overcapitalization, and cartels.[155]

Not for the last time, a Russian government tragically misapprehended its situation. Instead of freeing up trade, the czarist regime attacked, with all its wonted violence, the antiquated structures of community and depen-

[152] Robinson 1932, 246.
[153] Seton-Watson 1967, 518; cf. Kochan 1966, 9 and 17.
[154] Robinson 1932, 245–46 and 253; Kochan 1966, 3–4 and 16–18; Seton-Watson 1967, 531.
[155] Riasanovsky 1977, 470–72 and 474–76; Nove 1972, 17–18 and 25; Kochan 1966, 17–19; Seton-Watson 1967, 529 and 531.

dence that sustained underemployment. In essence, it attempted to import capitalism without importing goods. In 1861, serfdom was abolished;[156] after 1905, Stolypin's famous reforms put the *obshchina*, or rural commune, also on the path to rapid extermination.[157]

Any modern student of property rights would recognize both institutions as formidable impediments to economic progress.[158] Serfdom was essentially a Draconian system of wage control. By giving estate owners an artificially cheap source of labor, it encouraged the gentry to overutilize labor and underutilize capital.[159] The resultant retention of labor in the rural sector kept urban wages artificially high. Of course, peasants working for nothing tended to shirk, just as landlords under rent control do not hasten to make repairs.

The rural commune, to which the regime had largely transferred the land purchased from the gentry in 1861, had all the faults of the traditional common-field system: its periodic redistribution of land, isolated plots, and coordinated cropping discouraged both investment and innovation. Why improve soil that would eventually go to another? Why buy machinery, if it must be moved among widely separated strips? Why try new crops or techniques, if the entire village must approve any change?[160] Moreover, because under repartitional tenure a family's share depended on its number of mouths, there were incentives to breed freely and to restrain children from leaving the farm. Rural labor remained artificially cheap, and landlords continued to practice labor-intensive agriculture.

True as all this was, Stolypin and his fellow reformers overestimated the short-term remedial effect that purely legal reforms, or changes in the structure of ownership, could have.[161] (Again, a persistent Russian failing emerges, which one may conveniently call "administrative hybris.") Granting peasants on demand a consolidated, permanent holding, or making their shares in the *obshchina* fully salable, could not immediately transform complex structures of mutual dependence and expectation that dated back

[156] An excellent treatment of the details of the emancipation is Zaionchkovsky 1978, chap. 3. In some areas peasants enjoyed hereditary tenure; in all areas they gained individual title to their houses and garden plots.

[157] General discussions of the Stolypin reforms and their effects are given by Kochan 1966, 124–31; Seton-Watson 1967, 649–54; Riasanovsky 1977, 459–60 and 480–81; Nove 1972, 22; and Volin 1960, 302–4.

[158] See particularly North 1981. That the Russian reformers of the period saw the evils clearly even without this perspective is demonstrated in the citations assembled by Seton-Watson 1967, 401.

[159] As a *pomeshchik* from Tambov put it with crystalline insight, if he bought a thresher, what would the peasants do all winter? Zaionchkovsky 1978, 7.

[160] Kochan 1966, 39–40.

[161] I am indebted to Peter Katzenstein, and to an anonymous referee, for pressing me to clarify my position on the importance of property rights in this context.

centuries.[162] Stolypin accurately observed that areas of *traditional* individual tenure had remained markedly loyal in 1905; but from this he falsely concluded that the *imposition* of such tenure could end peasant unrest. In essence, Stolypin's "wager on the strong" was also a wager that Russia's "artificial" abundance of labor, sustained by traditional village structures, could be quickly ended.[163] To be sure, by 1915 40 to 50 percent of all peasant households may have held their land in individual tenure, and rural wages and investment were up;[164] but this hardly dented rural underemployment (or, as it was persistently mislabeled, "land hunger").[165] Myint-Lewis effects kept Russian labor abundant, and Russian workers remained antiprotectionist, anticapitalist, and antiregime.

In these circumstances, land and labor formed their fateful antiregime alliance. It is crucial to understand that, by World War I, the peasants were Russia's real landowners: in 1916 they possessed, in communal or individual tenure, 80 percent of the land, including fully half of what the gentry had retained in 1861.[166] The gentry, having failed to follow the "Prussian model" of capital-intensive, large-scale agriculture that Alexander II had envisioned, depended increasingly on office and favor, rather than on landownership, for their status and income.[167] Gaining as a class,[168] the peasants abandoned their traditional passivity and revolted repeatedly: in 1897–1898, 1902, 1905–1906, and crucially in 1917–1918.[169] Moreover,

[162] On the impossibility of rapid change in these structures, see esp. Robinson 1932, 225–27.

[163] Indeed, Stolypin's wager could be regarded as a more visionary effort: by exposing Russia's real scarcity of labor, it might be possible to unite labor and capital in support of a protectionist coalition on the U.S. Republican model. I owe this point to Stephen McMillan.

[164] See again the sources cited in n. 157.

[165] Because the system prevented both peasants and gentry from intensifying their use of capital, and because labor could not be employed more intensively within the traditional cropping system, it appeared that output could be expanded, and labor used productively, only by gaining access to more of the only remaining factor, namely land. That, of course, was an illusion.

[166] Nove 1972, 23.

[167] Riasanovsky 1977, 469; Gerschenkron 1960, 44. On the intentions of the reformers of 1861, see the 1855 note of the new Czar's liberal adviser Professor Kavelin, quoted in Zaionchkovsky 1978, 58.

[168] To the indicator of landownership may be added that of literacy: in 1868, 8 percent of peasant recruits to the army could read; in 1882, 20 percent; in 1897, 50 percent. Kochan 1966, 45.

[169] See, on the various revolts: Kochan 1966, 37–38, 42, and 252–53; Kingston-Mann 1983, 57–58, 76, and 78; Seton-Watson 1967, 560; Robinson 1932, 138ff.; Bovykin and Kiryanov 1977, 225. That passivity, and not the long-accepted myth of recurrent revolt, accurately characterizes the pre–1860 Russian peasantry is argued convincingly by the Soviet historian Zaionchkovsky 1978, 26ff. The geographical centers of the later insurrections—the South and Southeast in 1897–1898; the lower Dnieper in 1902; central Russia, the Volga basin, and the Ukraine in 1905–1906; and again the middle Volga and the central agricultural

a detailed analysis of official reports on the best-documented disturbances, those of 1905–1907, indicates broad participation by middle and even wealthier peasants: not the landless, but the landowners, bore the struggle.[170]

Workers opposed the regime with at least equal vigor. Tightly concentrated in a few industrial centers, they organized early and struck repeatedly, often for political reasons:[171] a first major wave of strikes came in the early 1890s; a second began soon after 1900 and culminated in the general strike of 1905; and a third commenced in 1912 and peaked in 1914, when perhaps 1.25 million (out of a total industrial work force of over 3 million) went out.[172] All of these were but forerunners of the culminating wave of strikes and revolts in 1917–1918. In both 1905 and 1917–1918, workers made common cause with peasants, fatally undermining the regime.

Other factors of course played a part in sustaining this peasant-worker alliance, such as the peasant roots, and the continuing rural contacts, of many workers;[173] and the lost wars of 1905 and 1917, whose effects were borne by both rural and urban masses.[174] Still, what the Stolper-Samuelson analysis leads us to expect seems to be sustained in uncanny detail. Moreover, such a perspective permits us to explain what other approaches cannot: why the revolutionary alliance of Red and Green succeeded in Russia but failed everywhere else in pre–World War I and wartime Europe.

In analyzing sub-Saharan Africa in this period,[175] several leading students have explicitly adopted some variant of the Myint-Lewis model of simultaneous abundance of land and labor.[176] Certainly no one doubts that land was abundant: "In most of the continent," one leading historian has written, "land was free, easily taken up and as easily abandoned."[177] The very notion of ownership of land was weakly developed.[178] That labor was

---

regions in 1917–1918—suggest a correlation with market penetration and export orientation; but I do not know if the question has ever been competently investigated.

[170] Perrie (1972, esp. 138–41) offers the most detailed and perceptive analysis of social composition that I have been able to find for any of the Russian peasant revolts.

[171] Robinson (1932, 148) observes that the secret police formed and controlled labor unions in these years "in the hope of diverting the labor movement from political to economic aims." Cf. Kochan 1966, 34–36 and 73–74.

[172] Riasanovsky 1977, 476.

[173] Robinson 1932, 249; Nove 1972, 25; Riasanovsky 1977, 475.

[174] Skocpol (1979, esp. 133–36) assigns great weight to this variable; and, even more, to the ensuing incapacity of the army to suppress revolts.

[175] An excellent general introduction is provided by Tidy with Leeming 1980, chaps. 4 and 5. Also of value are Ingham 1965, chaps. 2 and 3; July 1970, chap. 13; and Birmingham 1981, chap. 3.

[176] See particularly Barber 1961, chap. 8; Helleiner 1966, 9–10 and 50–55; Elliott 1969; and Hopkins 1973, 321ff.

[177] Colson 1969, 42.

[178] Under the traditional *chitemene* system of central Africa, whoever cleared a tract of land

also plentiful is allegedly shown by the extremely rapid expansion of exports after 1840—in West Africa, they roughly tripled between 1850 and 1900 and quadrupled again by 1914—which was achieved with no evident contraction of traditional agriculture and with minimal investment of capital.[179] As Helleiner, Myint, and others have argued, if labor was neither diverted from prior uses nor replaced by capital, it must have been abundantly available, as "disguised unemployment," in the traditional economies.[180]

This conclusion, it should be said at once, is controversial. Arrighi (1970), among others, has contended that any abundance of labor was artificial and politically induced: by white seizure of Africans' lands, discrimination against African produce, levies of coerced labor, or importation of non-African workers. Moreover, in many cases subsistence agriculture did decline as (or even before) exports rose.[181] To a great extent, these arguments are economic nonsense; even where they have some economic plausibility, they can rarely withstand close historical investigation.

Abundant labor, first of all, cannot be artificially created. Suppose that labor had in fact been fully employed, and therefore in light of land-labor ratios scarce, in the traditional economy.[182] Then, even if Africans had been stripped of all their land, as was done to the indigenous peoples in many

---

was entitled to its produce; in the Ivory Coast, usufruct rather than ownership was also common. See, respectively, Barber 1961, 45–47; Hopkins 1973, 218. On the commercialization of land tenures in the cocoa-farming regions of western Nigeria, Berry (1975, chap. 4) offers authoritative detail.

[179] Newbury (1969, 77–79) estimates that the total trade of West Africa more than doubled in value (from £3.5 to £8 million) between 1850 and 1880. Palm oil imports into Britain from West Africa rose from 1000 tons in 1810 to over 40,000 tons by 1855. Total exports of peanuts from Senegal, nonexistent in 1840, were nearly 30,000 tons annually by 1890; exports of palm kernels from Lagos rose over the same period from nothing to 37,000 tons annually. Hopkins 1973, 128. In the last years before World War I, trade expanded even more explosively: West Africa's trade in 1897 was £10 million, by 1914 £41 million; in the same years, total sub-Saharan trade rose from £71 million to £188 million. Munro 1976, app. 1.

[180] Helleiner 1966, 9–10; Myint 1980, 35–36. More detailed studies have borne out these conclusions. Szereszewski (quoted in Elliot 1969, 144) found that the labor intake of the nascent cocoa industry in Ghana grew from about 100,000 man-days in 1891 to 37 million man-days in 1911 with no reduction of labor intake in other sectors and a low rate of population increase; he infers, irrefutably, that "per capita labor services must have increased."

[181] See Arrighi 1970, 213, on declining yields in African agriculture in Rhodesia. Even Hopkins (1973, 234) observes that peanut producers in Senegal eventually abandoned subsistence farming to the extent that rice was imported.

[182] Arrighi (1970, 201) argues precisely this, dismissing the extensive evidence of male inactivity in traditional African societies as a misreading occasioned by cultural bias. A useful corrective is the conclusion of Hill (1970, 24), which she bases on painstaking local research: "Many of the men were literally unemployed . . . and were looking for a worthwhile occupation."

parts of South America, labor would have remained scarce (as it did in South America); and, absent imported labor or huge investments of capital, the export surge that in fact occurred would not have been possible.[183] Because this point was discussed in detail in the book (Barber 1961) that was Arrighi's principal target, and because Barber fully recognized the impact of white settlement and of discrimination against African produce, this elementary error seems almost willful.[184] To seal the point: in fact, exports grew most rapidly in West Africa, where no white settlement occurred and where marketing was least discriminatory.[185] Neither could coercion—which, again, was almost unknown in West Africa—have affected the scarcity or abundance of labor.[186]

Two possibilities must be taken seriously from an economic standpoint: that labor was imported to a significant degree from more densely populated regions of the world, and that the surge in exports was achieved only at great cost to the domestic economy. The historical evidence supports neither claim. There was considerable migration within Africa but less importation of cheap Asian labor than occurred in the United States.[187] Summarizing the results of recent research on the British colonies in Africa, Munro (1984) concludes that "the growth of incomes from export production seems to have been accomplished at little or no cost to aggregate food supply."[188]

The case for simultaneous abundance of land and labor in Africa, and for exports as a "vent for surplus" of both factors, seems to me quite strong. It seems equally clear that expanding trade benefited these factors and threatened domestic capital. Except under the short-lived "predatory colonialisms" of the Congo and French Equatorial Africa,[189] the signal beneficiaries of wider markets were Africa's small farmers.

So long as the slave trade endured, Africa had been dominated by quasifeudal warrior elites. Their power rested on investments in the weaponry

---

[183] At most, seizure of land would have diverted African labor into wage employment and away from familial production of goods for export. That might well have lowered the wage rate and affected the distribution of incomes; but it would have affected neither the social organization of production (Coase 1960) nor the social scarcity or abundance of labor.

[184] Barber 1961, 183–84. There can be few more scathing scholarly treatments of institutionalized racism than chapter two of this volume.

[185] Munro 1976, 55ff. and 95–96.

[186] Munro 1984, 35.

[187] Munro 1984, 35.

[188] Munro 1984, 48. In Nigeria, export volume rose fivefold between 1900 and 1929; traditional output increased over the same period by 10 percent. Helleiner 1966, 7. The seeming exceptions, such as the Senegalese peanut farmers who began importing rice (above, n. 181), are likely to have arisen from natural pursuit of comparative advantage. Such events were as little evidence of damage to the domestic economy as was Britain's abandonment of grain farming after 1875.

[189] Munro 1976, 101–6.

and training of their men, and on holdings and grants of cattle—not, as in feudal Europe, of land, since in Africa land was free.[190] Their revenues derived from the capture and sale of slaves. The coming of "legitimate" (i.e., nonslave) commerce and the progressive outlawing of the slave trade swept these elites aside. Peasants, responding quickly to the opportunities that export markets provided, cleared land and raised and sold what the world demanded.[191] The profits that they earned brought them political influence; so, emphatically, did the guns that they soon were able to purchase.[192] In some cases, new sects, such as the Islamic Mourides in Senegal, provided solidarity and protection to the peasants.[193] Slaves, seeing the new opportunities and the open frontier, began to escape in large numbers.[194] Deprived of their revenues from the sale of slaves, the traditional warrior elites receded.[195] Some tried to exploit the new markets themselves, with slave-worked plantations; others attempted to ally with the rising peasantry. Neither expedient enjoyed wide success.[196] Some of the former elites themselves underwent a process of "peasantization."[197]

In many cases, the warrior elites were supplanted by literal merchant princes or by local oligarchies of traders.[198] The dominant group in each area worked out conventions with its neighbors, assigning monopoly rights to trade within specific boundaries.[199] According to one plausible interpretation, it was Europeans' (and some Africans') resentment of these arrangements, under the pressure of falling commodity prices in the world depression after 1873, that led to armed conflict, growing exclusionism, and ultimately the "scramble" for European colonies in Africa.[200] In any event, as Hopkins has concluded, "the chief purpose of colonial rule was to speed a process of economic change which was already under way."[201]

In this sense, the early phases of colonial control, again with the horrible exception of such "predatory" cases as the Congo, tended even more to

[190] Colson 1969, 41–42.
[191] The two classic instances of markedly unprimitive shrewdness and risk taking are the expansions of peanut farming in Senegambia and northern Nigeria and of cocoa farming in Ghana. Hopkins 1973, 216–22, and Copans 1980, 89–91; Hill 1970, chap. 2. On the rapidity of response, see Hopkins 1973, 138ff.
[192] Copans 1980, 91–92.
[193] Hopkins 1973, 221–22; Copans 1980, 91–93.
[194] Hopkins 1973, 228.
[195] A detailed study of one case is Reynolds 1974, chap. 4, esp. 114ff.
[196] Hopkins 1973, 142–45.
[197] Copans 1980, 91.
[198] Colson 1969, 34–36.
[199] Newbury 1969, 76.
[200] See for example Newbury 1969, 90–94; Hopkins 1973, 154–156; and Munro 1976, 72–73.
[201] Hopkins 1973, 176.

benefit the African masses.[202] By granting African farmers freer access to markets, unimpeded by the former middlemen, Jean Copans has argued, "the new [colonial] economic system made the former slave a free and independent agricultural producer."[203] European attempts to undermine the free African producer by establishing plantations failed almost without exception;[204] and, even where heavily subsidized white settlers were installed, two leading students have concluded, "[African] peasant commodity production, far from being 'destroyed,' continually expanded."[205] Even the expansion of seasonal and migrant wage labor, on settlers' and African peasants' farms, and in European-owned mines, tended to enlarge the opportunities of ordinary Africans.[206]

In this period, then, expanding trade benefited workers and increased the value of land. It harmed, and inspired political opposition to, owners of particular kinds of capital, namely the traditional cattle- and weapon-owning warrior-aristocrats and, a few years later, the monopolistic merchant oligarchs who depended on working capital.[207] What remains in dispute is the fate of a different kind of capitalist: the local craftsperson or manufacturer.[208] Although it is commonly and plausibly alleged that imported manufactures must have seriously undercut these groups, some students have observed that the actual evidence in support of this view is weak.[209] What seems certain, however, is that the colonial powers, at least up to World War I, successfully discouraged capital-intensive local manufactures.[210] In general, flourishing labor and land opposed declining capital in nineteenth-century Africa; and, aided substantially by their alliance with colonial rule, labor and land won.

Finally, let us consider briefly the much-studied case of Cochinchina (the southernmost part of present-day Vietnam, centering on the Mekong Delta) as representative of what Myint (1958, 1980) explicitly hypothesizes to have been a larger class of land- and labor-rich societies in Southeast Asia in this period. Certainly the region was regarded both before and during French colonial rule as an "agricultural frontier" in which good

---

[202] Hopkins (1973, 170), however, attributes these beneficial effects not to the abundance of African labor but chiefly to the naturally small scale of production that prevailed in most of the African exports. I see no necessary contradiction: the reason that small-scale production was advantageous in Africa may have been its abundance of labor.

[203] Copans 1980, 91. Cf. Hopkins 1973, 225, and Munro 1984, 34.

[204] Hopkins 1973, 210ff.; Copans 1980, 90.

[205] Lonsdale and Berman, quoted in Munro 1984, 57.

[206] Hopkins 1973, 222–25; Barber 1961, 188.

[207] Newbury 1969, 81.

[208] These were much more extensively developed in Africa than our usual stereotypes allow. Hopkins 1973, 48.

[209] Hopkins 1973, 250ff.

[210] Helleiner 1966, 16.

land was abundant; but especially after the French conquest there was also ample labor, as refugees found in Cochinchina relief from the more straitened and repressive circumstances of the rest of Vietnam.[211] The area had already been one of large plantations, with perhaps three-quarters of its inhabitants landless as early as 1840; the French extended this trend and opened the economy to world markets, encouraging a lucrative export trade in rice and rubber. The economic consequence, as Popkin observes, was that *both* landlords and laborers prospered, even if the former did so disproportionately. Politically, the change gave rise to villages less subject to manipulation, more sophisticated in exploiting the French institutions, and—as Gourou put it—lacking in the "peasant mentality" that one saw in the rest of Vietnam.[212] Overall within colonial Vietnam, the South came to outweigh the traditionally dominant North in influence.[213]

Over the longer run, one could perhaps have foreseen a development parallel to prerevolutionary Russia's: an alliance of laborers and smallholding peasants against inefficient large landlords and domestic and foreign capitalists. Certainly Cochinchina developed some of the earliest protests against colonial rule and, by 1945, some of the strongest revolutionary activity; but that is to get ahead of our story.[214] Suffice it to say that here, too, there is early evidence of an effective coalition of Red and Green.

Conclusion

Historians have long been aware of the central importance of the nineteenth century's developmental coalitions; and, in particular, of the baleful consequences when land and capital allied to oppose labor and to support protection. What has emerged here is a possible determinant of the crucial alliances and of their policies. The explosive expansion of trade in the nineteenth century everywhere made protectionists (or, often, only deepened the existing protectionism) of owners and intensive users of scarce factors; and, where both capital and land were scarce but labor was abundant, auspices were favorable for the fatal "marriage" of landowners and capitalists, and for a radicalization of labor: hence the currency of both phenomena throughout backward Europe and densely populated Asia.

Elsewhere, land and capital failed to unite; and their divisions over how to respond to expanding trade are an important part of the story. In densely populated but capital-abundant northwestern Europe, only landowners—and, of that group, especially those who held the most land-intensive large properties—embraced protection; capitalists, except in back-

[211] Woodside 1976, 120–21.
[212] Popkin 1979, 141.
[213] Woodside 1976, 121.
[214] Popkin 1979, 229ff. and 247.

ward, labor-intensive sectors, found their natural allies in free-trading workers and created powerful radical parties. In virtually all the rest of the world, land was abundant but capital was not; hence farmers supported freer, and capitalists much less free, trade. In the frontier societies of the Americas and Oceania, labor was also scarce; hence it coalesced readily with capitalists, and the result—where the coalition won—was as modernizing and democratic (if in this case protectionist) as in northwestern Europe. Where serfdom or the primitive village had accumulated large reserves of labor, as in Russia and parts of Southeast Asia, labor tended to ally instead with agriculture, leaving capital alone and detested.

I hasten to reiterate that, even if correct, this account can be at most a part of the story. As has been clearly observed in discussing France, Russia, and eastern and southern Africa in this period, such other conflicts as those of confession, culture, land tenure, traditional status, and race undoubtedly played an independent, and sometimes a predominant, role. What the present theory points us toward is at most another important source of coalition and opposition. The broad pattern of the evidence, however, supports the hypothesis that in this period trade was a factor of considerable significance.

CHAPTER THREE

The Interwar Period and the Depression of the 1930s: The Decline and Fall of World Trade

Changes in Trade

WORLD WAR I wrote an abrupt and fiery coda to the preceding century's unremitting expansion of trade. The blockades and embargoes of the war directly interrupted commerce; and the consequences of the peace, even if they were less dire than Keynes (1919) had predicted, inhibited any easy revival of trade on its previous scale and intensity. Russia's revolution, civil war, and economic dislocation long excluded it as a source or a market in anything like its previous extent: Russian grain exports, which had peaked at nearly 13 million metric tons in 1910, never exceeded 2.6 million in the 1920s.[1] Shifts of boundaries separated factories from their accustomed resources and outlets. The successor states of eastern and southeastern Europe, out of insecurity and a desire for autarky, imposed absurd barriers to trade on once-vital European transit routes.[2] The unequal inflations of the various belligerents' currencies, during and (even more) after the conflict, burdened international transactions with new insecurities and costs, from which all too often only barter could offer an escape.[3] And protectionism recrudesced powerfully almost everywhere—even, astonishingly, in once devoutly free-trading Britain.[4]

For some of the principal trading partners of the old international order, these new obstacles proved insurmountable: even in the relative prosperity of 1928–1929, British exports achieved only 81 percent and German ex-

---

[1] Mitchell 1978, table C7, 167.

[2] "For a time, none of the Austrian successor states was ready to allow its railway rolling stock to cross its borders for fear of seizure, and goods had to be unloaded and reloaded at every frontier station." Landes 1969, 360.

[3] Landes 1969, 361–62.

[4] Although it is often asserted that Britain only abandoned free trade in 1931, in fact it "temporarily" continued wartime duties after 1918 and then imposed *ad valorem* tariffs of 33 percent on a broad range of "strategic" products from 1921 on. On average, European duties on finished products in 1927 were about 1.5 times their 1913 levels. Landes 1969, 360 and 365.

ports 90 percent of their 1913 volume;[5] and purveyors of primary products from the Second and Third World to Europe suffered, even where the volume of their exports expanded, from rapidly worsening terms of trade.[6] Nonetheless, world trade on the whole stagnated rather than collapsed in the 1920s; by 1924 it had resumed its 1913 volume and by 1928 was 13 percent higher.[7]

After 1929, however, international trade slumped precipitously; and the inevitable loss of gains from trade and specialization, as nations fled in panic toward autarky, was hardly the least significant feature of the depression that Keynes called, with laconic accuracy, "the greatest economic catastrophe of modern times."[8] Measured in gold dollars, world trade in 1932 amounted to 39.7 percent of the amount achieved in 1928, and from there the situation worsened: by 1935, it was 35.2 percent of the levels of 1928. Even by 1938, world trade had "recovered" only to the extent of achieving 40.9 percent of its 1928 value.[9]

The causes of this collapse, which are still in dispute, do not concern us here. Certainly the policies of intensified protection that many states adopted at about this time, including not least the Smoot-Hawley Tariff of 1930 in the United States, cannot have helped.[10] Rather, we want to trace the political sequels and consequences of declining trade. To do that within the framework set out in chapter 1, we must know something of the factor endowments of the various countries that were affected.

FACTOR ENDOWMENTS

Land

Table 3.1 provides a useful starting point as regards resources of land and labor in the interwar period. It may usefully be compared to Table 2.5, which presents data from almost a century earlier. In the intervening years, plainly, central Europe had surpassed southern and northwestern Europe as the world's most densely populated region; but otherwise the rank order of the world's regions was little changed. In the 1930s no less than in the

[5] Landes 1969, 365–67. By one reckoning of value, however, German exports in 1929 were 33 percent higher than in 1913, revealing a general shift to products of higher value added. Castellan 1969, 186; Dederke 1984, 84.

[6] In more favored cases, such as Argentina, export growth continued but at a greatly reduced rate. Rock 1987, 191.

[7] Landes 1969, 366.

[8] Cited in Rosecrance 1986, 108.

[9] Calculated from League of Nations figures cited in Landes 1969, 393.

[10] Kindleberger 1973, 132. For a stout denial that protectionism played any significant role, see Strange 1985, 239–40.

TABLE 3.1
Population Per Square Kilometer in Major Regions of the World, 1930

Central Europe	118.2	Southwest Asia	8.40
South Central Asia	70.7	USSR	7.99
Southern Europe	67.6	North America	6.28
Northwestern Europe	54.1	Sub-Saharan Africa	5.21
East Asia	45.6	North Africa	4.95
Southeast Asia	28.5	South America	4.21
Central America	12.4		

Source: United Nations, *Statistical Yearbook*, 13th issue (1961), p. 41. Uninhabited polar regions and some uninhabited islands are excluded; all other territory, including deserts and wastelands, is counted.

1840s, land was far scarcer throughout Europe and Asia than in any part of the Americas, Russia, Southwest Asia, Africa, or Oceania. The difference emerges even more clearly in a finer presentation (Map 3.1): only the remotest regions of Scotland, Scandinavia, and the Alps fall below the figure of ten persons per square kilometer (twenty-six per square mile) that is roughly the upper limit of the American and African averages.

These ratios are misleading to the extent that they include unproductive land. Partial efforts to calculate population per unit of productive land for this period (Table 3.2), however, as well as more recent attempts to do so more broadly, suggest only minor, and mostly within-region, amendments.[11] We observe in Table 3.2 that the most thinly populated European state in the 1930s, Ireland, still had over twice the population per unit of agricultural land of the most densely populated North American country, the United States; but we see also that agricultural land was scarcer in the Low Countries, western Germany, and Norway than in the rest of Europe, and scarcer in Italy than in southern Europe generally. Present-day, more complete data[12] show additionally that agriculturally productive land is far less plentiful in Japan and Korea than in China; less abundant in Egypt than in the rest of North Africa; and scarcer in the Caribbean than anywhere in mainland America.

For present purposes, then, we shall not be far wrong in continuing to count Europe and Asia (except Russia) in this period as scarce in land, and the Americas, Russia, Africa, Australia, and New Zealand as abundant in land. Within Europe, the ratio of population to productive land is highest in the Low Countries, the industrial belt of central Europe, Norway, the

[11] These efforts have their own obvious pitfalls: the productivity of land varies extremely and is affected by the capital invested in it (drainage, irrigation, deep tillage, etc.).

[12] United Nations 1958, vol. 11, pt. 1, table 1; World Bank 1983, vol. 2. I have summarized these results in Table 4.4.

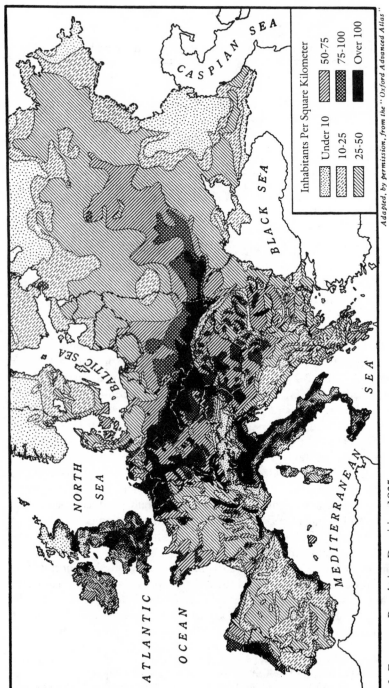

3.1 European Population Densities, 1935

Inhabitants Per Square Kilometer

Under 10	50-75
10-25	75-100
25-50	Over 100

TABLE 3.2
Population Per Square Kilometer of Agricultural Land in North America
and Europe in the Late 1930s

Belgium-Luxembourg	435.0	Sweden	131.5
Netherlands	380.3	Finland	127.5
Western Germany	294.3	Denmark	116.7
Norway	264.7	France	102.4
United Kingdom	244.3	Spain	88.8
Italy	209.8	Greece	85.9
Switzerland	192.8	Ireland	53.2
Portugal	158.1	United States	22.1
Austria	155.3	Canada	8.9

Sources: Mueller 1965, table vii-1; Banks 1971, segment 1; for West Germany (territory of the present-day Federal Republic), Mitchell 1978, 4. "Agricultural land" includes arable (whether occupied or not), meadows and pastures, and rough grazing land; it excludes forests and woodlands.

United Kingdom, and Italy; it radiates out to lower—if, by world standards, still quite high—levels in the rest of northern, eastern, and southern Europe.

Capital

At the extremes, it is equally easy to distinguish the capital-rich from the capital-poor economies. Few will doubt that capital was scarce, albeit in varying degrees, throughout Asia, Africa, the Soviet Union, and Latin America in these years, or that it was abundant in the "core" economies of northwestern Europe and in the United States, Canada, Australia, and New Zealand.[13] Only within Europe do serious problems of classification arise; and, while the primitive state of national income accounting before

[13] Admittedly, Argentina was counted by Mulhall (1903, 320) in the late nineteenth century as having the third-highest per capita income, after the United States and Britain, of all the world's countries; but it seems plain (e.g., Skidmore and Smith 1984, 75; Mulhall 1896, diagram VIII) that this bonanza rested on land-intensive rather than capital-intensive production. Certainly later students of Argentina (notably O'Donnell 1979) have bemoaned its shortage of capital and its inability to "deepen" investment. Doubts may arise from the opposite direction about Australia and New Zealand: Did their prosperity, too, not flow simply from the production of grain and meat for export? (Note particularly Bairoch's index of per capita industrial production, summarized in Table 3.4, for New Zealand.) In Australia, manufacturing employment exceeded pastoral and agricultural by 1926 (Schedvin 1970, 61); in New Zealand in 1921, primary production claimed 26 percent and industry 24 percent of employment, and 56 percent of the population was urban (Condliffe and Airey 1953, 183). On capital accumulation in Australia in the period 1900–1930, see Sinclair 1970, esp. 12, 12n., and 17.

TABLE 3.3

Per Capita Output of Major Industrial Products in European States, 1925[a]

				Per Capita Production of		
	Population	Pig Iron	Raw Steel	Sulfuric Acid	Synthetic Fibers	Electric Power
Austria	6.535	58.148	71.002	6.733	0.230	0.327
Belgium	8.092	314.261	315.002	57.093	0.618	0.271
Bulgaria	5.479	—	—	—	—	0.005
Czechoslovakia	14.730	79.158	100.136	7.739	0.068	0.133
Denmark	3.435	—	—	0.873	—	0.111
Finland	3.463	3.176	8.374	3.176	—	0.156
France	40.228	211.146	185.542	37.287	0.162	0.277
Germany	63.181	161.077	193.017	15.210	0.187	0.322
Greece	6.205	—	—	4.029	—	0.021
Hungary	8.688	10.704	26.588	5.755	—	0.051
Italy	37.974	12.693	47.032	21.067	0.366	0.170
Netherlands	7.936	14.869	—	44.103	0.340	0.168
Norway	2.814	30.917	2.843	—	—	2.488
Poland	27.177	11.591	28.774	6.807	0.022	0.061
Portugal	6.826	—	—	—	—	0.022
Romania	18.057	3.544	5.593	1.385	—	0.013
USSR	147.028	8.903	12.705	0.680	0.001	0.020
Spain	23.564	22.407	26.566	8.572	0.021	0.065
Sweden	6.054	75.818	78.461	18.831	0.017	0.606
Switzerland	4.006	—	—	7.489	0.599	0.996
United Kingdom	37.887	167.920	198.063	22.382	0.322	0.320

Source: Calculated from Mitchell 1978, tables A1, D7, D8, D16, D18, and D22.

[a] Population is in millions; iron, steel, sulfuric acid, and synthetic textiles are in kilograms; electric power is in thousands of kilowatt-hours.

World War II continues to preclude any precise cross-national measurement, figures like those in Tables 3.3 and 3.4 can help to sharpen our impressionistic judgments.

From left to right, the principal columns of Table 3.3 reflect "generations" of the industrial revolution: iron and steel, the essential products of the phase of heavy industry; sulfuric acid, the mainstay of the chemical phase[14] synthetic fibers, in these years the most advanced aspect of that phase; and electricity, which permitted a new burst of more energy-efficient and less centralized productivity.[15] Plainly the champions of the generation of iron and steel are Belgium, Britain, France, and Germany, fol-

[14] Landes (1969, 109) describes sulfuric acid as "a substance of such versatility . . . that its use has come to serve as a rough index of industrial development."

[15] Landes 1969, 431–40.

TABLE 3.4
Bairoch Indexes of Per Capita Industrialization, 1928[a]

United States	192	Austria	56
United Kingdom	122	Norway	48
Belgium	116	Finland	43
Germany	101	Italy	39
Switzerland	90	New Zealand	37
Sweden	84	Hungary	30
Canada	82	Japan	30
France	78	Spain	28
Czechoslovakia	66	Ireland	23
Netherlands	61	Poland	22
Denmark	58	USSR	20
Australia	58	Others	<20

Source: Bairoch 1982, 281 and 330.
[a] 100 = level of United Kingdom in 1900.

lowed at a distance by Czechoslovakia, Sweden, Austria, and (in steel only) Italy. Chemicals add to this group Switzerland and the Netherlands and fortify Italy's appearance of abundance in capital. Electricity, finally, brings to the fore such hydropower rich states as Norway, Switzerland, Sweden, and Austria; France and Belgium are not far behind. By way of comparison with these detailed indicators, Bairoch's summary indexes of industrialization for 1928 are presented in Table 3.4.

Taken together, these measures leave little doubt that not only the obvious cases of Belgium, France, Germany, Switzerland, and the United Kingdom, but also Sweden, the Netherlands, Austria, and Norway, by now possessed advanced, capital-intensive economies.[16] Czechoslovakia, Austria, and Italy are by some measures somewhat less developed but still, on all appearances, richer in capital investment than the world generally: Austria is strong in electricity and synthetic fibers, Czechoslovakia in heavy industry, Italy in chemicals.[17]

Labor

In general, we continue to assume that regions abundant in land were scarce in labor, and vice-versa. The possible exceptions to this general rule, however, should be recalled as outlined in chapter 1. According to Myint's

[16] Given the unusual capital intensity of Danish agriculture (Esping-Anderson 1985, 42) and its high ranking on Bairoch's scale, that country should probably also be included.

[17] On Bairoch's ranking, Finland would be included in this group; but I remain puzzled, in light of the data of my Table 3.3, by the relatively high index he assigns it. Even in production of wood pulp (Mitchell 1978, table D19), Finland remained far behind Norway and Sweden.

(1958; 1980) analysis, backward, land-rich countries may also be abundant in labor if they have, or have recently had, weak markets and transport and extensive structures of serfdom or clientelism. His principal examples were Asian and African, but we shall have to bear in mind the possibility that the USSR in this period still qualifies: certainly the rapidity of its collectivization and industrialization under Stalin suggests that labor was not in short supply.[18] (See the fuller discussion later in this chapter.) Parts of Southeast Asia can probably also be so characterized.[19]

Conversely, we should entertain the possibility that some of the advanced European economies, particularly in Scandinavia, were simultaneously scarce in land and labor. Following our discussion in chapter 1, we may conjecture that societies of this kind characterized by uncompetitive small peasant holdings, ruralist values, and strong family ties will have had agrarian overemployment and inelastic supplies of labor, and will, therefore, have reacted as if that factor were scarce.

CATEGORIES AND EXPECTATIONS

In general, we expect that declining trade of the kind that characterized the 1930s, and in some localities even the 1920s, will have augmented the power of owners and intensive users of scarce factors and will have engendered conflict between them and owners of abundant factors. Given the enormous losses that the depression inflicted on nearly all sectors, we of course do not anticipate that even the controllers of scarce factors will have gained absolutely from the collapse of trade; but they should have gained relatively, increasing their share of potential national income, and their claims to power, at the expense of more abundant factors. Following the three-factor analysis of chapter 1 and the sketch of endowments presented in this chapter, we can specify six categories.

Abundance of Land and Capital;
Scarcity of Labor

Under this rubric fall what are by now the developed economies of North America and Oceania: the United States, Canada, Australia, and New Zealand. Here labor should demand increased power, challenging landowners and capitalists; class conflict is expected to increase.

---

[18] On the USSR in this period, see Nove 1972, chaps. 6–8; on rapid economic development as presumptive evidence of simultaneous abundance in land and labor, Myint 1958, 324–25, and Myint 1980, 33ff. On the other hand the mass starvation of the Russian peasantry suggests that this growth was not achieved without a considerable contraction in the "subsistence" sector. Whether that contraction was necessary is still very much in dispute.

[19] See again Table 3.1 and chapter 2.

Abundance Only of Land;
Scarcity of Labor and Capital

This category comprises principally the less-developed economies of the Americas (exclusive of the labor-rich Caribbean), which in this period include virtually all of the states of Latin America. Here we expect efforts to shift power away from landowners and toward an alliance of capitalists and workers; urban-rural conflict ensues.

Abundance of Land and Labor;
Scarcity of Capital

This condition, according to our earlier conjecture, may have characterized the Soviet Union, most of Africa, and parts of Southeast Asia in this period. To the extent that it did, the slump should have brought to these countries an expansion of capitalist or managerial demands at the expense of landowners and workers. Red and Green are in the same camp, but that camp is under siege.

Abundance of Labor and Capital;
Scarcity of Land

We capture under this heading most of the highly developed European economies: Belgium, France, Germany, Switzerland, and the United Kingdom; and, more marginally, Austria, Czechoslovakia, and Italy. Here only landowners can benefit, at least relative to other factors, from the slump; and only they fully embrace strategies of national self-sufficiency (sometimes including, since land is an immobile factor, imperialism or conquest). Owners of land, and of land-intensive enterprises, expand their political influence; capitalists and workers (including landless or near-landless peasants),[20] and owners of the least land-intensive enterprises,[21] lose some share of political power. The chief political division is normally between urban and rural forces.

Particularly in this context, however, one proviso, which is integral to the Stolper-Samuelson theorem[22] and was discussed earlier in passing (see

---

[20] Recall that, in the sense used throughout this volume, "labor" is shorthand for "those who have principally, or only, their labor to sell" (see the discussion at n. 55 of chapter 1). Rural workers and landless peasants are thus laborers.

[21] It is worth suggesting that heavy industry, which depends on local sources of ore and energy, is more land intensive than such sectors as electrical equipment and synthetic chemicals. In this sense the frequently observed, if usually tentative, alliance between heavy industry and agriculture could make some sense. The role of the quite labor-intensive petty bourgeoisie in many fascist movements, however, is harder to explain.

[22] Stolper and Samuelson 1941, 70–71.

chapter 1), must be reemphasized.[23] The theorem applies only to economies whose endowments are such that they *do not specialize completely* and
wholly abandon the production of any major category of goods.[24] To the
extent that comparative disadvantage induces a country wholly to cease
production of, for example, agricultural commodities, all bets are off: we
can no longer predict the economic—and hence, on the reading adopted
here, the political—effects of expanding or contracting trade. To be accurate, then, we must amend the foregoing statements about the developed
European economies in the 1930s to say that landowners will have expanded their political power *to the extent that an agricultural sector had survived in the given country.* If, as may be anticipated, some states in this category had found their comparative disadvantage in agriculture to be so
great that they had largely abandoned that pursuit, our theory will draw a
blank: it will be unable to offer a prediction.

Abundance Only of Labor;
Scarcity of Capital and Land

Into this domain fall virtually all of the less developed economies of Europe, Asia, and the Caribbean in this period: Spain, Portugal, Greece, and
the successor states of eastern and southeastern Europe; Japan, China, India, much of Vietnam, and most of the territories that constitute present-
day Malaysia and Indonesia;[25] the Bahamas, Jamaica, and Haiti; and (with
a high labor-land ratio atypical for its region) Egypt. In all these regions,
we anticipate, declining trade will have augmented the power of capitalists
and landowners and will have encouraged them to attempt wholesale
repression of labor (including, as noted earlier, landless and marginal peasants). Class conflict will have been sharp, with workers losing ground more
often than not.

Abundance Only of Capital;
Land and Labor Both Scarce

As I have suggested previously, some of the smaller advanced European
economies in this period, particularly in Scandinavia, may fall into this cat-

[23] I am grateful to Ahmed Enany for having pressed me on this point in discussing earlier
drafts of this chapter.

[24] More recent economists state this condition more precisely as requiring that countries'
endowments lie within the same "cone of specialization"—e.g., Leamer 1984, 6.

[25] Indonesia, as Geertz (1963, esp. chap. 2) perceptively observed, has long been divided
into densely and sparsely populated regions, making for profound differences in social and
political development. His approach interestingly complements the one adopted here. I am
grateful to my colleague Richard Baum for having called this study to my attention.

egory. To the extent that they do, we anticipate that the collapse of trade will have encouraged workers and landowners—again, the coalition of Red and Green—to seek greater power and that capitalists will have been forced onto the defensive.

EVIDENCE

Allowing, as always, for the inevitable effects of cultural and historical variables that the present analysis excludes, we expect to find substantial regional differences of political response to the slump of the interwar years. In the developed economies of North America and Australasia, workers should in theory have become politically more assertive; in those of western Europe, landowners should have claimed more. In the land-rich backward economies of Latin America, labor and capital will have united against landowners; in the more densely settled but capital-poor regions of Asia and of eastern and southern Europe, land and capital will have joined to combat workers. To what extent do actual events conform to these expectations?

Economies Rich in Land and Capital, Poor in Labor: The United States, Canada, Australia, and New Zealand

Of perhaps greatest significance—at least by contrast with the contemporaneous experience of western Europe, which I shall shortly review—is what does *not* happen in these economies: in none of them does fascism become a serious threat;[26] in none of them does the Right ultimately gain as a consequence of the depression. Rather, their general pattern involves a substantial mobilization and strengthening of workers, a shift of policy to the left, and entrenchment of social class as a significant political cleavage.

The United States and New Zealand offer the clearest supporting evidence. In the United States, labor began to leave its long alliance with the Republican party as early as the 1920s.[27] The drastic shift of allegiances came in the elections of 1930 and 1932. By 1936, the New Deal had vastly expanded organized labor's membership and power through such measures as the Wagner Act; had sealed a new alliance between workers and the Democratic party; had laid the foundations of the welfare state in the United States; and had for the first time made class, rather than region, the principal axis of American political cleavage that it remained for some four

[26] A "New Guard," whose leaders openly admired Hitler and employed the fascist salute, flourished briefly in Australia in 1931 but collapsed in low comedy a year later: Ward 1977, 193–94 and 197.

[27] Burnham 1970, 55–58.

decades.[28] In that transformation, one recent analysis suggests, the Democrats substantially diluted their long-standing opposition to protection.[29] The Reciprocal Trade Agreements Act (RTAA) of 1934 left untouched the basic rates of the extremely high Smoot-Hawley tariff, and by 1939 tariffs were only slightly below the levels imposed by the Fordney-McCumber Act of 1922.[30]

In New Zealand, too, politics shifted decisively to the left.[31] The Labour party, supported principally by urban and rural workers and by some small farmers, won a large majority in the elections of 1935. It proceeded to enact a far-reaching program of wage increases, expanded social insurance (including family allowances and medical care), protection of agricultural workers, stronger arbitration of disputes between labor and management, and—its most controversial measure—compulsory unionism. At the same time, state export monopolies were established over agricultural products, and extensive protection was granted to industry through a system of import licenses.

In Australia and Canada, leftist pressures were strong but were ultimately defeated: in the former case, by maladroit working-class leadership; in the other, by an inchoate party system and a decentralized constitution. In Australia,[32] early declines in export markets, coupled with efforts of the incumbent Nationalist government in 1928 and 1929 to reduce wages and extend hours in a variety of industries, brought major strikes, parliamentary desertions, and new elections (precisely in October 1929) that gave the Labor party—which still represented almost exclusively workers in agriculture, industry, and transport—a landslide victory. Astonishingly, as the depression deepened catastrophically after 1929, Scullin's Labor government, taking as gospel the advice of local and British bankers,[33] pursued policies of rigid orthodoxy and deflation that worsened the slump, split the party, and, by late 1931, forced new elections. Labor's erstwhile enthusiasts deserted the party in droves. The antisocialist opposition won an overwhelming victory and, trading on Labor's tarnished reputation, retained

[28] On the achievements of the New Deal, see such standard histories as that of Williams et al. 1969, chap. 20. On the rise and significance of the class cleavage in the United States, see Burnham 1970, 30–31, and Alford 1963, chap. 8.

[29] Lake 1988, 206, concludes flatly, with abundant supporting quotation from leading Democrats, that "The RTAA was not intended to overturn the American system of protection." Rep. Fred Vinson, a Democrat from Kentucky, went so far as to assert that "no one on the Democratic side of the House" was a free-trader.

[30] Lake 1988, 205 and 207. Far more puzzling from this standpoint is the relative success of agriculture—and, in particular, of the larger farmers—under the New Deal. See Williams et al. 1969, 514–18.

[31] The account here is drawn principally from Condliffe and Airey 1953, chap. 21.

[32] The present account is based principally on Ward 1977, chap. 6. See also Cotter 1967.

[33] Kindleberger 1973, 97–99; Schedvin 1970, chap. 7.

power until 1941. (Wisely, however, it refrained from further attacks on trade union power.)[34] It now seems apparent that, but for the tactical[35] and strategic missteps of the Labor leadership, measures similar to those in the United States and New Zealand could have been enacted with good effect.[36] Nonetheless class tensions in Australia remained strong, and social class has continued to predict partisanship as clearly here as anywhere in the world.[37]

The Australian case thus emphasizes vividly the distinction between outcomes and cleavages. Outcomes yield particularly to the influence of historical accidents: the quality of leadership, the timing of events,[38] the relations among principal actors. It is not hard to imagine how the United States might have experienced an outcome similar to Australia's: had Presidential elections fallen in 1930 rather than 1932, had the Democrats won before the full effect of Hoover's policies was seen, and had the new Democratic president then pursued the policies of fiscal orthodoxy that the Democratic platform of 1932 actually embraced. Still, in both cases the class-based structure of political cleavage would have long endured as a major legacy of the depression.

In Canada, it was a *Conservative* prime minister, Richard Bradford Bennett, who initiated, and in the short term failed at, the decisive turn to the left.[39] Elected in the first shock of the depression in 1930 to replace an (if possible) even more orthodox Liberal government, Bennett by 1935 had seen all conventional remedies fail. An avowedly socialist movement founded only three years earlier, the Co-operative Commonwealth Federation (CCF), seemed to be gaining ground rapidly; Bennett feared "a Socialist avalanche."[40] His own party had split, with a dissident faction de-

[34] The limits on conservative power in these years are usefully explored by Butlin, Barnard, and Pincus 1982, 80–81.

[35] Fearing the costs of a new election, Labor in 1931 rejected "double dissolution" and permitted the opposition to retain its lopsided majority in the Senate—which then, predictably, proceeded to stymie the few palliative measures that Scullin's government could bring itself to introduce. Ward, 1977, 173 and 175–76; Schedvin 1970, 148.

[36] Cotter 1967, 263–69, offers a trenchant critique of Labor's policies in this period. Cf. Schedvin 1970, 295–99. For a contemporaneous critique of remarkable cogency, see Walker 1933, chap. 6.

[37] Alford 1963, chap. 7.

[38] Even Bismarck's "marriage of iron and rye" depended heavily for its success not only on Bismarck's tactical shrewdness but on the accident of a second attempt to assassinate the Kaiser. Stürmer 1974, 216.

[39] See, among others, Morton 1983, pt. 3, chap. 5; McInnis 1959, 440–65; and Finlay and Sprague 1979, chap. 19.

[40] Finlay and Sprague 1979, 278. The CCF, because it eventually achieved power only in the prairie province of Saskatchewan (Lipset 1971), is commonly misperceived as an agrarian party. In fact, after 1940 it enjoyed substantial working-class strength, particularly in Ontario,

manding more vigorous state intervention. Facing an election later that year, and without having consulted his cabinet or party colleagues, Bennett proclaimed in a nationwide radio address in January 1935 a Canadian New Deal, which in his words would mean "the end of *laissez-faire*"[41] north of the border. He won parliamentary support for federal unemployment and social insurance, minimum wages and maximum hours, and extensive legislation against trusts and price fixing; but his belated conversion failed to rescue him from overwhelming electoral defeat. Most of his radical legislation was later held unconstitutional by the British Privy Council, as infringing powers reserved to the provinces under the British North America Act. Bennett was right, however, in perceiving a strong demand for greater state intervention; and his successors soon had to seek amendments of the Act that strengthened the federal government.

At the same time, it must be admitted that Canada long remained peculiar among this group of states in its relative weakness of class conflict. Social class never appears as a major base of partisan cleavage,[42] nor do issues of trade union rights dominate the political agenda. The Canadian Left grew stronger in these years, but it is not obvious that Canadian labor became more militant.[43]

In all of these countries, it is safe to say, we observe a shift to the left in the terms of political debate during the 1930s. In all but Canada, we see also a marked expansion of labor militancy and a growing recognition of labor's rights of organization. In none of them does either the landowning or the capitalist Right gain strength from the depression.

Economies Rich in Land, Poor in Capital and Labor:
Latin America

In almost every recent textbook of Latin American history, one can find some parallel to the following passage:

> In the period after World War I, the traditional ruling classes in many countries of Latin America fell into disrepute. . . . In particular the Great Depression of 1929–32 had a devastating impact upon the existing power structure. As a result, old aristocratic oligarchies, whose power position was based upon land, lost control to new leaders who represented urban, industrial majorities.[44]

and formed close ties with powerful industrial unions. Avakumovic 1978, 93, 97, and 126–28; Morley 1984, 28–29.

[41] Morton 1983, 184.

[42] Alford 1963, chap. 9.

[43] Finlay and Sprague 1979, 276, report that fewer workers were affiliated with trade unions in 1934 than in 1929.

[44] Dozer 1979, 507.

Although the initial response to the "crisis of 1929" (D'Elía 1982) in almost all of the Latin American states was a military coup in defense of the landed interest,[45] the tide soon ran strongly the other way. Cut off, by the European depression and even more by the early phases of World War II, from the external markets and the manufactured imports on which they had previously relied, Latin Americans intensified an "import-substituting industrialization" that inevitably augmented the numbers and the strength of domestic workers and capitalists;[46] and, over the next fifteen years, "populist" regimes that ruled in the interests of these urban groups came to power in much of the region. Vargas in Brazil, López in Colombia, Cárdenas in Mexico, Perón in Argentina, Busch and Paz Estenssoro in Bolivia, and Betancourt in Venezuela, all represented this tendency; so did such unsuccessful but significant movements as APRA in Peru and the brief "Socialist Republic" of 1932 in Chile.[47]

There can be little doubt of the accuracy of the theoretical prediction for this region in the 1930s: labor and capital gained strength, united, and often prevailed, against landowners.[48] The basic line of political cleavage was urban-rural.

Economies Rich in Land and Labor, Poor in Capital: Russia and Sub-Saharan Africa

For reasons already advanced, Russia and much of Africa in this period may, despite their obvious abundance of land, have also been rich in unor underemployed labor.[49] By comparison with the rest of the world, these regions plainly lacked capital. Hence we expect that the slump in trade will have augmented the power of the only scarce factor, capital, and will have adversely affected landowners and workers.

[45] Skidmore and Smith 1984, 56–57.

[46] In Argentina, for example, the number of workers rose from 590,000 in 1935 to 813,000 in 1940; and, between 1935 and 1939, industry's contribution to GDP rose from 17.2 to 20.9 percent. D'Elía 1982, 25.

[47] See generally Skidmore and Smith 1984, 58–60; Sunkel with Paz 1973, 69–78 and 346–66; Cardoso and Faletto 1979, 124–26 and chap. 5; D'Elía 1982; and Mauro 1975, pt. 3, chap. 2. Perón's rise to power dates only from 1944 and was not complete until the street demonstrations of October 1945 forced his opponents to surrender. Rock 1987, 249–61. Specifics of the Peronist bias against agriculture are given in Randall 1978, chap. 5.

[48] See however the more reserved interpretation of Sunkel with Paz 1973, 75.

[49] One recent authority denies the applicability of the Lewis model (of unlimited supplies of labor in primitive economies) to Africa in this period, observing that compulsion was often required to obtain workers: Wrigley 1986, 123. As Hopkins (1973, 229) notes, however, the shortages were almost invariably the result of the absurdly low wage rates that employers tried to maintain. Even Wrigley (1986, 127) concedes that massive migrations to southern and central Africa had made these regions (borrowing Amin's phrase) "the Africa of the labor reserves."

Obviously, the post-NEP Soviet Union is the chief exhibit in support of these conjectures. Collectivization revealed, despite its undoubted costs in death and misery, vast reserves of underemployed labor in the country-side;[50] and Russia was, as both its land-labor ratio and its pattern of exports had long demonstrated, rich in land as well. Temporally, the abandonment of NEP and the switch to what an unsparing Menshevik critic called "primitive Socialist accumulation by the methods of Tamerlane"[51] were closely associated with a drastic contraction, evident as early as 1927–1928, in the already low levels of postwar exports; and with the consequent collapse of that leg of the NEP strategy that had counted on trade with the West.[52] Commercial isolation, when added to the still-prevailing political quarantine, left few alternatives to "Socialism in one country."[53]

Thus the conditions of Russia and of Russian trade in this period lead us to anticipate an assault by capital, the only scarce factor, on both land and labor; and, as such critics of Stalin as Burnham insisted at the time, and as more dispassionate scholarship has since attested, this is almost exactly what happened.[54] In effect, socialization of the means of production had made the Communist party *apparat* the "owner" of the nation's capital stocks; and the forced-draft collectivization and industrialization that began in late 1929[55] involved enormous confiscations from, and disempowerments of, both peasants and workers.[56] All was made to serve the aim of accumulating more capital, and every other group was subordinated to the party officials and managers who effectively controlled that capital.

This much of the story is familiar. Less well known are the similar, if plainly less drastic, suppressions of farmers and workers, and expansions of

[50] Cf. Nove 1972, 198.

[51] M. Bogdenko, quoted in Nove 1972, 159.

[52] Nove 1972, 112, gives the following figures for annual grain exports: 1913, 12.0 million tons; 1925–1926, 2.0; 1926–1927, 2.1; 1927–1928, 0.3.

[53] Cf. the poignant analysis of Preobrazhensky (1927), discussed briefly in Nove 1972, 127–28.

[54] Burnham 1941, esp. chaps. 4 and 14. Although Burnham rejects the label of "capitalist" for the regime, he is clear that its managers, through the state, effectively control capital. For an example of more recent scholarly opinion, see Thomson 1962, 630–32.

[55] Although the theory advanced here by no means posits a lockstep synchronization of trade and politics, it may be worth noting that Stalin's infamous article on the "great turn," which heralded collectivization and forced industrialization, was published on 7 November 1929 (Nove 1972, 163); the great Wall Street crash, which presaged the total collapse of world trade, had occurred on 28 and 29 October.

[56] A good general description of the process is Rauch 1972, 177–86 and 219–29. For the levies on agriculture and the rural famines, see Nove 1972, 138, 148, 159, 179–81, and 210–11; for the decline in urban living standards, the crushing of (already feeble) trade union autonomy, and the imposition of piece-work rates and longer hours, see Nove 1972, 206–7, and Rauch 1972, 226–28.

capitalist power, in Africa in these same years. By this period there was substantial direct investment—that is, capital, with a voice in the metropole—in many of the colonies; and now this factor often grew assertive or dominant. In response to the depression, one recent student has written, the Belgian Congo "was subjected to an essentially totalitarian regime in partnership with the *Société Générale*," the principal mining company; and, throughout Belgium's African holdings, the period was characterized by "close co-operation between government and big business."[57] In South Africa and Rhodesia, unions—including prominently ones of farmworkers—were crushed, and black farmers were expropriated to increase the holdings of whites and of large corporations.[58] Price support schemes markedly favored capital-intensive settler agriculture over more labor-intensive African farms.[59] In British East Africa, the general tendency was "an increasing official commitment to the interests of overseas, and especially British, capital."[60] In France's colonies, declining markets and rising taxes pushed African farmers off the land and led to increasing strike activity, which was ruthlessly subdued.[61]

Even in West Africa, the stronghold of export-oriented African agriculture and of African export firms, the depression revealed an unmistakable favoritism toward European interests and a collapse in the living standard of African workers and farmers. Expatriate trading firms received the bulk of government guarantees and assistance; plantation-grown products such as rubber won quotas in home markets, whereas peasant-grown commodities such as cotton, cocoa, palm kernels, and peanuts were left to fend for themselves.[62]

Again, it appears, Red and Green were jointly eclipsed by the rising power of capital; but in Africa the ensuing resentments fueled the first tentative strivings for independence from colonial rule.[63] Precisely in the African case, however, aspects other than trade must again be given their due. Racism (e.g., in the vastly different treatment even of economically similar white and black smallholders) and the distribution of political power between metropole and colony (e.g., the fact that white workers and farmers had the vote in South Africa and Rhodesia) obviously also affected coalitions and outcomes.[64]

---

[57] Jewsiewicki 1986, 482.
[58] Walshe 1986, 583.
[59] Barber 1961, 24–26.
[60] Roberts 1986a, 701.
[61] Coquery-Vidrovitch 1986, 382–83 and 388–91.
[62] Hopkins 1973, 254–67, esp. 260 and 266; Munro 1976, chap. 6, esp. 161–62.
[63] Hopkins 1973, 266–267.
[64] Walshe 1986; Roberts 1986a.

Economies Rich in Capital and Labor,
Poor in Land: Developed Europe

With the exception of Scandinavia, the advanced European economies in the 1920s and 1930s contrast sharply with the pattern of cleavages observed earlier in the land-rich industrial states of North America and Oceania. In Europe, politics shift generally to the right and workers lose some share of power. Moreover, often enough schemes of conquest are advocated or actually pursued.

Three countries—Italy, Germany, and (even from 1934) Austria—succumb to some form of fascism; and a fourth, Belgium, is significantly threatened.[65] In Britain, workers lose the General Strike of 1926; and, in 1931, Labour—which, in contrast to its Australian counterpart, had achieved only a minority government—splits and MacDonald's thoroughly conservative National Government wins an overwhelming mandate. In Belgium and the Netherlands, reflationary proposals of the labor parties are rejected or subverted.[66] In France, despite some electoral victories of the Left and the brief formation of a Popular Front, conservative forces are not dislodged; rather, the Republic experiences that seepage of corporatist and fascist sentiments that undermines defense and ultimately provides widespread support for the Vichy regime and for collaboration.

This pattern is related to, if clearly not identical with, an expansion of rural and agricultural influence. As Charles Maier has written of the early 1920s in Europe, conservative restoration ordinarily involved the subduing of "Red" cities by a "White" countryside.[67] Particularly was this true of fascism, whose support was disproportionately rural and whose policies, at least in its early periods of power, strongly favored agriculture over other sectors. Fascism of course also drew support from those small-business sectors that were least capital-intensive and least efficient in their use of labor.

In Italy, the Fascist movement achieved its initial successes in Emilia and Tuscany by breaking strikes of rural workers in 1920 and 1921; and it won its strongest early support among "the farms of the north and the big landowners of central Italy."[68] Only later, and secondarily, was it embraced by the urban petty bourgeoisie. Big industry was markedly cool toward it

[65] On the homegrown Austrian fascism of the *Heimwehr*, and on the separate Flemish and Rexist fascisms within Belgium, see Carsten 1967, 204–18 and 223–29.

[66] Hansen 1981. The Dutch however remained more rigidly deflationist, and more solicitous of agriculture, than the Belgians. Kossmann 1978, 665–66.

[67] Maier 1975, 306. R. Walther Darré, the Nazi agrarian expert, may have spoken for many European Rightists when, in a policy memorandum of August 1930, he observed that Fascist control of the food supply could give crucial advantages over "the machine-gun fire of police or army." Gies 1972, 48–49.

[68] Carocci 1975, 19–20; Maier 1975, 305–19; Carsten 1967, 56–59. (The quotation is from Carocci.)

right up to, and indeed after, the March on Rome.[69] The elections of 1924, with Mussolini already in power, revealed starkly the Fascist party's predominantly rural social base.[70] Especially after 1925, the regime displayed a "ruralism" and a solicitousness toward the landowner that distinguished it from the more industrially dominated governments of the preceding parliamentary era:[71] agricultural tariffs were raised, the state pursued agricultural self-sufficiency at almost any price in the "battle for wheat," vast resources were poured into the production of fertilizers and the reclamation of land, and—against the opposition of major industrialists and the army—colonization and conquest were undertaken in Africa.[72] In 1935, Mussolini responded to the League of Nations' sanctions by proclaiming the goal of Italian autarky; and that effort further increased agriculture's importance and undermined capitalists' autonomy.[73]

In Germany, the gains of the Right and of agriculture long antedate the Nazi electoral victories. The elections of 1920 and 1924 disclosed a startling resurgence of the monarchist and Junker-dominated DNVP: from 10.3 percent of the vote in 1919, it advanced to 15.1 percent in 1920 and 20.5 percent in 1924.[74] As Winkler (1972) has argued most cogently and as Heberle (1963 and 1970) has shown in detail for the case of Schleswig-Holstein, much of this gain must have accrued from peasant abandonment of long-standing Liberal loyalties.[75] Governments, too, shifted to the right—the SPD was in no governing coalition at the national level between late 1923 and mid-1928[76]—and substantial concessions were made to agriculture, including direct representation of their main pressure group in the cabinet and the reintroduction of tariffs on foodstuffs.[77]

Agriculture, however, including particularly the smallholding peasants, demanded more. Even in 1928, the Nazis achieved significant regional breakthroughs in such rural areas as Schleswig-Holstein;[78] and virtually every study of the Nazi vote in the decisive election of July 1932 has found a sharp urban-rural difference even when such other variables as class and religion are controlled for.[79] By late 1931, the Nazis had come to dominate

[69] Sarti 1971, chap. 1. Theoretically, we expect that in the more backward (i.e., capital-poor) European economies big business will have been much more favorably disposed toward fascism. See the section immediately following.

[70] Maier 1975, 437–39.

[71] Carocci 1975, 59–60; on the earlier period, Bowden et al. 1937, 783.

[72] Carocci 1975, 56–60 and 103–5; Sarti 1971, 126 and 137.

[73] Sarti 1971, 104–11.

[74] Detailed electoral results are in Castellan 1969, 117.

[75] Cf. Puhle 1975, 90.

[76] Castellan 1969, 120–21.

[77] Stürmer 1967, 49–58 and 98–106.

[78] Berghahn 1982, 109–10; Gies 1972, 46.

[79] See, among many others, Pratt 1948, cited in Lipset 1963, 144; Lipset 1963, 138–48;

the chief agricultural interest group, the *Reichslandbund*, to a degree that they never achieved before 1933 in any industrial association.[80] (In Germany, even more clearly than in Italy, big business came to fascism only belatedly and opportunistically.)[81] Moreover, Hitler's urban support, most analyses have concluded, can be localized in those small and usually familial enterprises that were least capital intensive;[82] but, as I have indicated already, this is not a phenomenon that the present theory can easily explain.

In power, the National Socialists raised agricultural tariffs, refinanced farmers' debts, increased and subsidized the production of fertilizers, created agricultural cartels (eventually grouped under the *Reichsnährstand*), and in the Four Year Plan pushed for self-sufficiency in foodstuffs through the so-called *Erzeugungsschlacht*.[83] They praised rural values and virtues unrelentingly. One leading student has concluded flatly that "if National Socialism had a program and a goal, [the agrarian ideology] was it."[84] Even the eastern conquests were justified, and perhaps intended, as providing new lands for settlement by German peasants.[85]

In Belgium and Austria, too, the extreme Right found its strongholds, and its sources of expanding influence, in the countryside and among the urban petty bourgeoisie.[86] In the French Third Republic, agricultural dominance seemed so secure that fascism had at first little appeal. Rural influence both among the conservative parties and the Radicals—not to mention the malapportioned Senate—was so great that it prevailed whether Right or Left ruled.[87] By 1939, the French price of wheat was three times the price in London.[88] Nonetheless, in the late 1920s and 1930s a variety of right-wing leagues made some headway, in February 1934 a coup was seriously attempted, and by 1935 a fascist "peasant

---

Gies 1972, 76; Childers 1983, 224; and, most important, Brown 1982. No class difference of similar magnitude emerges.

[80] Gies 1972, 64–70; Puhle 1975, 91–92.

[81] The myth of substantial business support for the Nazis, which had long been discredited, is further undermined by the massive researches of Turner (1985).

[82] Brown 1982; Childers 1983. The contrasting view is Hamilton 1982. But Hamilton's isolated and impressionistic local studies are hard to reconcile with the more encompassing statistical efforts cited previously.

[83] See among others Gies 1968; Holt 1936; Schoenbaum 1967, chap. 5; and Abraham 1981, 85–115 and chap. 4. None of this should be taken to imply that the peasantry benefited unalloyedly from Nazi policy: indeed, as the prewar economy overheated and peasants were drawn to urban jobs, the regime increasingly tied them to the land. Cf. Berghahn 1982, 142–43, and Schoenbaum 1967, 163–69.

[84] Schoenbaum 1967, 154.

[85] Speech of Heinrich Himmler to SS and police leadership, Shitomir, the Ukraine, 16 September 1942, excerpted in Meyer 1973, 277–84, esp. 281 and 283–84.

[86] Carsten 1967, 209 and 223–24.

[87] Brogan 1967, 174–75; Thomson 1946, 193; Kuisel, 1983, 96; Cobban 1965, 128.

[88] Cobban 1965, 156.

TABLE 3.5
Percentage of Work Force Employed in Agriculture: European States,
ca. 1935

Portugal, 1940	49.5	Austria, 1939	23.7
Poland, 1931	49.0	Czechoslovakia, 1947	23.3
Hungary, 1941	40.1	Sweden, 1945	21.4
Finland, 1940	39.5	West Germany, 1946	18.3
Ireland, 1936	37.5	Switzerland, 1941	16.4
Italy, 1936	37.1	Netherlands, 1947	14.6
France, 1946	34.7	Belgium, 1930	13.9
Norway, 1930	30.6	Great Britain, 1931	5.9
Denmark, 1940	25.6		

Source: Woytinsky and Woytinsky 1953, 363. In each case, the date is
dictated by the census or other best available source.

front"—which, in the event, quickly petered out—was sowing fear among
Republican politicians.[89] The later 1930s saw growing support for
schemes of agricultural cartelization. At a peasant congress in 1937,
Jacques Le-Roy Ladurie, leader of the powerful *Union Nationale des Syn-*
dicats Agricoles, urged replacement of the existing Parliament by a "council
of corporations," in which the peasantry would be the "first order in the
nation."[90] Peasants grew alienated enough from the Republican regime
not to defend it; and, at least in some quarters, to embrace readily the
fervent overtures of the Vichy regime after 1940.[91] It is perhaps indicative
that Le-Roy Ladurie became minister of agriculture and of food supply at
Vichy.[92]

Only in Britain do we find no connection between the conservative tide
and agriculture, and the reason seems apparent: so great was agriculture's
comparative disadvantage in Britain that it had all but disappeared there
long before the 1920s. In 1931, agriculture claimed just under 6 percent
of the British work force, by some distance the lowest share in Europe
(Table 3.5), and 4 percent of gross domestic product.[93] It is fair to conclude, as for example Kindleberger did, that in the later nineteenth century
Britain had "liquidated" agriculture.[94] In such a case of extreme specialization, as has already been observed, the approach adopted here offers no

[89] Cobban 1965, 142–45 and 149–51; Brogan 1967, 654–61 and 674.
[90] Paxton 1972, 205.
[91] Berger 1972, 134; cf. Paxton 1972, 206–9.
[92] A detailed study of Vichy agricultural policy is Boussard 1980.
[93] On shares of GDP, see Mitchell 1978, table J2. The British figure is for 1930. The next
lowest European shares were: the Netherlands, 11 percent (1940); and Sweden, 13 percent
(1930).
[94] Kindleberger 1951, 33 and 46.

prediction. We must regard the shift to the right in the United Kingdom in these years as "accidental" from the standpoint of the theory, and therefore as neither supporting nor impugning it.

More to the point, the present theory can offer no explanation whatever for the acute class conflict that characterized Britain in the interwar years. Only in 1918 did the Labour party become socialist, only in the 1920s did Labour grow to be indisputably the second major party and class to be the nation's chief political cleavage;[95] and the General Strike of 1926 revealed a depth and bitterness of confrontation that even the Continent could hardly rival. Yet both capital and labor remained abundant in Britain, and issues of trade should have kept them as allied as they had been in the nineteenth century.

Near the end of this volume, I shall offer the speculation that, as agriculture wanes generally among the developed economies, a different three-factor model may serve us better: labor; human capital (including organizational skills); and physical capital. Given Britain's anemic rate of investment in physical capital after about 1880 and its growing dependence on "invisible" (i.e., service) exports,[96] it may be that its comparative advantage had come to lie in products that used labor and human capital intensively. If so, Labour's insistence on a free-trading alliance of "workers of hand and brain," the Conservatives' growing protectionism under declining trade, and escalating conflict between these two positions could have made some sense; but all of this remains, for now, mere conjecture. The model as originally sketched fails to account for the main features of British politics in the interwar years.

Economies Rich in Labor, Poor in Capital and Land: Asia and Backward Europe

Here, we expect labor to have lost ground to a coalition of land and capital. In Japan, China, and most of Vietnam, it appears to have done so. Japan's export markets had expanded considerably during World War I, and industrialization had advanced rapidly.[97] In that period and the early 1920s—usually referred to, after the reign-name of the post-Meiji Emperor (1912–1926), as "Taishō Democracy"—capital, white-collar groups, and labor had been able to gain at the expense of traditional landed elites;

---

[95] The classic retrospective study of this cleavage, and of its present-day manifestations, is Butler and Stokes 1971.

[96] Landes 1969, 326–58, esp. 329.

[97] Between 1914 and 1919, both industrial production and the number of factory workers nearly doubled. Nonetheless, more than half of the Japanese work force continued to be employed in agriculture. Kato 1974, 218–19 and 226; cf. Scalapino 1962, 269.

among other reforms, universal male suffrage was enacted in 1925.[98] When those same markets collapsed in the later 1920s and the 1930s, however, democracy also faltered: the military, strongly supported by the peasantry, the larger landowners, and some capitalists,[99] continually expanded its influence, and labor was drastically suppressed by such measures as the "Peace Preservation" Laws of 1925 and 1928 and the outlawry of leftist parties and unions after 1931.[100] By 1937 at the latest, the Diet and the political parties had lost all influence on events.[101]

Although the principal agents of the change were clearly in the military and agriculture, business embraced this "fascism from above"[102] more eagerly and extensively than its counterparts in Italy or Germany. The liberal capitalists who had endorsed internationalism and peaceful expansion immediately after World War I—and who may, as Scalapino has argued, have been even then less committed to it and less influential than is often assumed[103]—abandoned those goals in the face of collapsing markets and rising barriers to Japanese immigration.[104] Business, and particularly the *zaibatsu*, now endorsed and profited from the policy of military conquest that the colonels had long advocated.[105]

In China, movements of land-poor peasants and urban workers were crushed, and many of their cadres slaughtered, in Hunan, Shanghai, and Canton in 1927; and Chiang Kai-Shek began, with the full support of capitalist and landowning elites, to consolidate his Nationalist dictatorship.[106] By 1934, once-powerful strongholds of Communist rural workers and peasants had also been reduced, precipitating the fabled Long March.[107] These blows dealt the Left a setback from which it only slowly recovered, and the interests of both capitalists and landowners were correspondingly advanced.[108] The French colonial regime in Vietnam simi-

[98] The dominant liberal parties of this period represented principally business and white-collar groups; labor grew more militant in such ways as strikes, demonstrations, and riots. "For the first time in modern Japan, labor conflict became a social problem of importance." Kato 1974, 218–19. Scalapino (1962, chap. 7), however, rightly emphasizes the continuing power of the landed elites and the general diffidence of the industrial and financial leaders.

[99] Reischauer 1974, 186; Kato 1974, 228 and 235; Scalapino 1962, 360, 362, and 379–80.

[100] Kato 1974, 222; Reischauer 1974, 198–99.

[101] Reischauer 1974, 195–96.

[102] The phrase is Kato's: 1974, 225.

[103] Scalapino 1962, 270–74.

[104] See the excellent analysis of Iriye 1974.

[105] Reischauer 1974, 186–87 and 198.

[106] Generally on this period, see Clubb 1972, 135–40, and Hofheinz 1977. A more detailed examination is Ch'ên 1965, chap. 5.

[107] Ch'ên 1965, chap. 8; Wei 1985.

[108] Whether the subsequent gains of the Communists correlate with expansions of world trade remains to be investigated. See chapter 4.

larly decimated the fledgling nationalist and Communist movements there in the savage "white terror" of 1931, which secured landowner and capitalist domination against incipient depression-related protests.[109]

In the backward European economies, a comparable alliance of landowners and capitalists, and a similar suppression of labor, can be readily discerned. The remarkable wave of authoritarian regimes that befell Spain, Portugal, Hungary, Poland, Rumania, Greece, Yugoslavia, Bulgaria, and Lithuania in the 1920s and 1930s seems to have had very much this character;[110] so did the powerful, but ultimately unsuccessful, fascist movement in Finland.[111] Poland and Spain, despite their arguably more advanced industrial sectors (see Table 3.3), provide perhaps the clearest European examples of a "marriage" of capitalists and large landowners against urban and rural workers.[112] Elsewhere, the dominant conflict pitted large landowners against land-poor peasants and rural laborers; but here, too, the bourgeoisie cleaved steadily to the side of the landowners.[113] Although the early eclipse of democracy in many of these areas is sometimes taken as arguing against any linkage to the depression,[114] it is important to recall that it was in eastern and southeastern Europe that the earliest and severest impediments to international trade were raised.

*Economies Rich in Capital, Scarce in Labor
and Land: Norway and Sweden?*

Theoretically, we have seen, Red-Green coalitions of workers and farmers can be expected to arise under diminishing trade when both labor and land are scarce. Given that such coalitions did arise in Denmark, Sweden, and Norway in the 1930s,[115] we are led to inquire whether, in one or more of those countries, a scarcity of labor and land might have been the source.

At first, much seems to speak against such a hypothesis. Land, to be sure, has been a scarce resource throughout Scandinavia: in the late 1930s, Norway had 265 inhabitants per square kilometer of agricultural land; Swe-

---

[109] Popkin 1979, xix and 215.

[110] See the perceptive comparative treatments of Thomson 1962, 632–34 and 665–66; and Gilbert 1970, 159–68. On the Hungarian and Polish regimes, see Carsten 1967, chap. 5, and on Spain, 194–204.

[111] Carsten 1967, 161–69. Strong fascist movements, backed chiefly by smallholding peasants, also arose in Hungary and Rumania.

[112] Gilbert 1970, 166; Thomson 1962, 633. On the collaboration between landowners and middle classes in Spain, see particularly Preston 1978, 24–25 and 209, and Payne 1970 (who however attributes the alliance to leftist excesses after 1931), chap. 9 and p. 371.

[113] Rumania, with a substantial free-trading petroleum sector, presents additional complications: Gilbert 1970, 166.

[114] Thomson 1962, 633.

[115] Gourevitch 1986, 131–32; Esping-Anderson 1985, 73–88.

den, 132; Finland, 128; and Denmark, 117 (see Table 3.2). If one compares these figures with ones from the same period for the United States (22 persons per square kilometer) or Canada (9), it is hard to see the Scandinavian countries as anything but land poor. At the same time, however, several indexes suggest an abundance of labor: people, most of them peasants, migrated in large numbers out of all three countries in the nineteenth and early twentieth centuries: Norway's rate of emigration, indeed, was second only to Ireland's in those years.[116] Nor, once industrialization was under way, did any substantial immigration occur, as one would expect if labor had been scarce. Moreover, one recent student has attributed Norway's high unemployment in the 1930s largely to an unusual expansion of the work force.[117]

Following Myint, however, I argued earlier that labor could be scarce even in a densely populated society under circumstances of "hidden overemployment"; and I suggested that such overemployment was especially likely to arise among a marginal peasantry that was culturally inclined to familial self-exploitation. From this standpoint, Denmark can almost certainly be excluded as a candidate for simultaneous scarcity of land and labor. Its peasantry, having adapted with great success to the changing markets of the 1870s, was far from marginal. Labor could be withdrawn from the rural sector without any threat to the subsistence of the peasant family; and, if an industrial work force was slow to arise in Denmark, it was in large part because peasant incomes were too high to make manufacturing wages attractive.[118] In both Norway and Denmark, however, peasant families in most regions struggled to eke out a living with labor-intensive techniques on tiny, marginal plots.[119] In both, religious and ruralist ideologies may have contributed to self-exploitation within the peasant family.[120] One can even venture the argument that the massive emigration itself may, by diminishing the work force and removing precisely its most mobile elements, have contributed in these two countries to a subsequent "bottleneck" in the supply of labor.

In various ways, people behaved as if labor was scarce. Early industry in both Norway and Sweden (but not in Denmark) was highly capital inten-

[116] Esping-Anderson 1985, 47 and 49.
[117] Hanisch 1978, 146. I owe this reference to Lars Skalnes.
[118] Esping-Andersen 1985, 42–43.
[119] Esping-Andersen 1985, 45–46 and 48–49.
[120] See Rokkan's classic sketch of Norway's rural counterculture: Rokkan 1966, 76–79. At a more global and impressionistic level, one need only contrast the norms of those African communities that originally regarded agriculture as "women's work," degrading to males, who should be supported in leisure (see again Barber 1961, 46), with the rather different ideal conveyed by Lutheranism. In the short run, the former situation encourages rural underemployment; the latter, rural overemployment.

sive and generated little employment[121]—a peculiar entrepreneurial strategy, indeed, if labor had been abundant. And in both countries (but, again, not at all in Denmark) the labor-intensive smallholding peasants came early to support agricultural protection,[122] avoiding the world markets that African and Chinese peasants welcomed. I will venture here as a hypothesis, subject to closer investigation, that labor and land were both scarce in Norway and Sweden in the interwar period, and that this shared situation helps to explain the ease with which workers and farmers united and expanded their power in the 1930s.

The pioneering Danish coalition of Red and Green, this cursory inspection of the evidence suggests, cannot have had the same social or economic basis. Indeed, the only explanation consonant with the present theory would be that Denmark's coalition was really one of abundant labor and capital; that it united workers with highly *capital*-intensive farmers.[123] This speculation admits of an easy test, which I leave to the experts on these respective countries: in Norway and Sweden, the coalition should have been most strongly supported by the least capital-intensive peasants; in Denmark, by the most capital-intensive ones.

CONCLUSION

In essence, we predicted that the contraction of international trade in the 1930s would have engendered *class conflict* in two cases: where labor was the only scarce resource (the United States, Canada, Australia, New Zealand) and where it was the only abundant one (underdeveloped Europe and Asia). In the former case, workers should have augmented their power; in the former, they should have lost ground to capitalists and landowners. The New Deal and its ideological kin seem to bear out the former expectation; and the fascist and authoritarian regimes of Spain, of eastern and southeastern Europe, and of Japan, and the "white terror" that crushed movements of workers and landless peasants in China and Vietnam, appear to confirm the latter prediction.

By way of contrast, *rural-urban* conflict should have emerged wherever land was the only scarce resource (the advanced European countries, except part of Scandinavia) or the only abundant one (Latin America). In the former case, landowners and land-intensive producers should have expanded their influence; in the latter, they were expected to have retreated before an urban coalition of labor, capital, and the most intensive users of

---

[121] Esping-Andersen 1985, 43, 47, and 49.

[122] Esping-Andersen 1985, 46 and 50; Hancock 1972, 22–23.

[123] Even this account, however, is extremely problematic. No assertive movement of land-intensive producers seems to have arisen, and it is doubtful that farmers were more capital intensive than industrialists, despite the admittedly small scale of Danish manufacturing.

those two factors. The former expectation appears to be met by the conservative and fascist movements and regimes of Italy, Germany, France, and the Low Countries; the latter, by the "populist" tendencies that simultaneously pervaded Latin America.

Finally, and most tentatively, we anticipate anticapitalist Red-Green coalitions of workers and landowners wherever capital is the only scarce factor (Africa and, still in this period, the USSR) or the only abundant one (arguably Norway and Sweden). In the former case, capital should expand its power at the expense of workers and farmers; in the latter, it is expected to lose some share of influence to those same groups. If we grant that Stalinism represented the triumph of state, or "managerial," capitalism (cf. Burnham 1941) over Russian workers and peasants, the former prediction seems fulfilled; and, with respect to Norway and Sweden, there can be doubt only about the factor endowments: the Red-Green coalitions are established history.

Obviously, many other factors contributed, sometimes decisively, to the particular outcome in each region and country: cultural and political inheritance, prevalent economic theory, incumbent rulers' experience and wisdom, and the weight of wartime losses and resentments all played a role.[124] Yet in its broad lineaments, the present theory seems also to contribute powerfully to our understanding of politics in this period of catastrophically contracting international trade. The conflict between scarce and abundant factors, and the growth in power of the former, was no small part of the political upheaval of those sad decades.

[124] A more complete account, for five of the principal advanced economies (the United States, United Kingdom, France, Germany, and Sweden), is Gourevitch 1986, chap. 4.

CHAPTER FOUR

Renewed Expansion of Trade, 1948 to the Present

CHANGES IN TRADE

WITH THE RETURN of peace in 1945 and the revival of the western European economies after 1947, the world experienced an expansion of international trade that eclipsed even that of the nineteenth century (Table 4.1). Between 1948 and 1980, the volume of world trade increased at an average rate of 6.7 percent per year, equivalent to a doubling every eleven years. In the peak decade, 1963 to 1973, trade grew at an average annual rate of 9.1 percent, doubling every eight years. In the worst quinquennium of those three decades, the average annual rate of expansion fell to 4.6 percent—still well above the *average* rate of growth, it may be recalled, of the period 1840-1913 (some 4.2 percent per year: see Tables 2.1 through 2.3). In contrast to the nineteenth century, trade in this period grew more rapidly than world output (on average for manufactured goods, about 1.4 times as swiftly),[1] with the tautological consequence that, for most countries, trade claimed an increasing share of national product: among the states of the Organization for Economic Co-operation and Development (OECD), the ratio of trade to GDP almost doubled between 1960 and 1980, rising on average from 22.8 percent at the beginning of the period to 41.4 percent at its end.[2]

Both technical and political factors contributed to the change. Transportation improved remarkably even over what had already been achieved: supertankers, pipelines, and containerization lowered freight rates; more flexible—and, for many purposes, cheaper—trucks began to displace the railroads' long monopoly of long-haul overland transport; air freight came into its own; and great advances in travel, communication, and data processing further pared transaction costs.[3] No less important, in most observers' estimation, have been such institutional innovations as the Bretton Woods monetary agreements, the General Agreement on Tariffs and Trade (GATT), the OECD, the European Community and its forerunners, and

[1] Scammell 1983, 127n.
[2] Organization for Economic Co-operation and Development 1982, 62–63. The reported average weights the OECD states by population.
[3] Kenwood and Lougheed 1971, 257–58.

Table 4.1
World Trade, 1948–1980

Year	Volume Index [a]	Annualized Growth
1948	103	—
1953	142	6.63%
1958	187	5.66
1963	269	7.40
1968	407	8.63
1970	490	9.72
1975	613 (640)	4.58 (5.49)
1980	817 (875)	5.92 (6.45)

Sources: 1948–1970, Rostow 1978, 67 and 669; values for 1975 and 1980 are extrapolated on the basis of United Nations 1984, 1225–26, and are not fully comparable since they cover only "market economies." United Nations 1986, 35, provides values, in current dollars, for *total* world trade in 1975 and 1980; deflating these by price indexes for U.S. imports (Organization for Economic Co-operation and Development 1982, 76) yields the indexes and growth rates shown in parentheses, which may comport more closely with the earlier entries.
[a] 1913 = 100.

the "Kennedy round" of multilateral tariff reductions in 1962.[4] After 1970, East-West détente—again, a political decision—played a significant role, not least in restoring intra-German and eastern European trade: between 1970 and 1975, Soviet bloc trade with the rest of the world rose in nominal value for the first time slightly more than that of the world at large: 183 percent versus 180 percent.[5]

Different regions of the world shared unevenly in this expansion. The internationally traded volume of manufactured products rose by 93 percent between 1953 and 1960; that of primary products, by only 34 percent.[6] Hence on average the more highly developed economies experienced the greater growth in trade: Europe's exports rose in volume by about 7.5 percent per year between 1948 and 1962; those of the world as a whole, by about 6.2 percent.[7] In 1955, some 56 percent of the world's trade was between developed countries; 40 percent flowed between advanced and less developed economies. By 1969, these relative proportions

[4] Scammell 1983, 67–68; Landes 1969, 504–9; Kenwood and Lougheed 1971, chaps. 15 and 18.
[5] Calculated from United Nations 1986, 42.
[6] Kenwood and Lougheed 1971, 284.
[7] Over the whole period, 275 per cent for Europe, 230 per cent for the world. The disparity in export value was even more marked: an increase of 200 per cent for Europe, 150 per cent for the world as a whole. Scammell 1983, 63.

TABLE 4.2
Average Annual Growth in Volume of Exports, Major Industrial Countries, 1950–1980

	1950–1960	1960–1967	1967–1973	1973–1980
Belgium	7.7%	7.8%	11.2%	3.5%
Canada	3.8	8.9	8.6	3.0
France	7.2	6.5	12.8	6.4
Germany	15.8	6.9	9.1	5.2
Italy	11.8	11.5	8.7	6.8
Japan	—	13.5	14.6	11.2
Netherlands	10.0	6.4	12.4	2.8
Sweden	5.5	6.9	8.7	1.8
Switzerland	7.8	6.0	8.0	3.4
United Kingdom	1.9	3.3	7.4	3.4
United States	5.0	5.4	8.2	5.5
Average	6.4	6.9	9.5	5.3

Sources: for 1950–1960, Maddison 1962, reproduced in Scammell 1983, 64; for remaining columns, Organization for Economic Co-operation and Development 1982, 51. From 1960, the reported average is that for all states of the OECD, weighted by population.

had changed to, respectively, 65 and 32 percent.[8] Chief among the plausible reasons for the disparity is simply the growing wealth of the industrialized societies, which shifted their budget shares away from primary products and toward finely differentiated luxury goods and consumer durables.[9] Nonetheless, even the backward economies became more exposed to trade in these years.

Within the group of industrial states, Japan and Italy consistently expanded exports more rapidly, Britain more slowly, than the average (Table 4.2). Germany and the Netherlands experienced a strong early spurt, then settled down to more modest levels of growth. France remained behind until the late 1960s, the United States until after 1973. We may expect that these variations will have affected the timing and intensity of trade's effects on domestic political alignments.

FACTOR ENDOWMENTS

Land

By 1960, East Asia had clearly surpassed northwestern Europe in density of population (Table 4.3; cf. Table 3.1); but the most pronounced differ-

[8] Scammell 1983, 128.
[9] Thus even a moderately wealthy consumer in an advanced economy may expect to stock

TABLE 4.3

Population Per Square Kilometer of Total Land in Major Regions of the World, 1960, and Percent Increase since 1930

Central Europe	136.9	15.8%
South Central Asia	109.2	54.4
Southern Europe	86.7	28.3
East Asia	70.7	55.0
Northwestern Europe	63.0	16.4
Southeast Asia	47.7	67.4
Central America	24.0	93.5
Southwest Asia	13.8	64.3
USSR	9.71	21.5
North America	9.25	47.3
North Africa	8.54	72.5
Sub-Saharan Africa	8.31	59.5
South America	7.87	86.9
Oceania	1.93	58.7
World	22.1	48.8

Source: United Nations 1961, 41. Uninhabited polar regions and some uninhabited islands are excluded; all other territory, including deserts and wastelands, is included.

ence continued to be that which separated the land-rich Americas, USSR, and Southwest Asia from the labor-rich rim of the Eurasian land mass.

By 1960, we have much better data on the ratio of population to agricultural land (Table 4.4). Here the scarcity of land in Asia, Europe, the Near East, the Caribbean, and—a surprising change—parts of Africa clearly emerges; so does its surpassing abundance in the Americas (except parts of Central America), the USSR, Oceania, and most of Africa. The increments shown in the right-hand column of Table 4.3 can hardly have arisen from loss of arable in this period, important as that factor has been in parts of Africa and the Caribbean; they must owe chiefly to population growth.

We shall not err greatly in taking the world average for this period—approximately eighty persons per square kilometer of agricultural land—as the dividing line between abundance and scarcity of land. By this measure, all of Asia, all of Europe save Ireland, all of the Caribbean, and all of the Levant are poorly endowed in land; Oceania, the USSR, Southwest Asia, and all of North and South America except Ecuador are land rich. Africa and Central America are regionally divided.

---

her wardrobe or her wine closet, or to select a new automobile, from the offerings of a variety of countries. Scammell 1983, 68.

TABLE 4.4
Population Per Square Kilometer of Agricultural Land, 1960

EAST ASIA		CENTRAL EUROPE	
Hong Kong	30,640	East Germany	267
Japan	1,563	Switzerland	247
South Korea	1,169	Czechoslovakia	191
China	215	Austria	176
		Poland	147
LEVANT		Hungary	140
Egypt	982		
Lebanon	663	SOUTHERN AND	
Israel	184	SOUTHEASTERN EUROPE	
Jordan	132	Italy	244
		Portugal	182
CARRIBBEAN		Bulgaria	138
Trinidad and	596	Albania	131
Tobago		Romania	126
Barbados	578	Yugoslavia	124
Bahamas	565	Greece	93.4
Jamaica	332	Spain	92.3
Haiti	305		
		CENTRAL AMERICA	
SOUTH CENTRAL ASIA		El Salvador	208
Bangladesh	562	Guatemala	160
Sri Lanka	507	Costa Rica	85.2
India	247	Panama	74.5
Burma	204	Honduras	38.7
		Nicaragua	29.9
NORTHWESTERN EUROPE			
Belgium	557	SUB-SAHARAN AFRICA[a]	
Netherlands	501	Liberia	160
West Germany	414	Kenya	145
Norway	351	Nigeria	125
United Kingdom	265	Zaire	120
Sweden	183	Ghana	104
Finland	161	Malawi	90.0
Denmark	148	Uganda	77.7
France	133	Ivory Coast	61.2
Ireland	51.5	Zimbabwe	52.6
Iceland	7.7	Ethiopia	34.6
		Tanzania	26.6
SOUTHEAST ASIA		Niger	22.6
Indonesia	356	South Africa	17.4
Philippines	277	Angola	14.9
Malaysia	248	Mozambique	14.0
Thailand	209	Zambia	8.1
Laos	136	Botswana	1.2

SOUTH AMERICA		NORTH AFRICA	
Ecuador	93.7	Morocco	61.1
Chile	53.9	Tunisia	60.7
Colombia	44.9	Algeria	24.2
Brazil	44.8	Libyia	11.3
Venezuela	43.7		
Peru	31.6	NORTH AMERICA	
Uruguay	16.2	United States	40.9
Paraguay	12.5	Mexico	37.1
Argentina	12.0	Canada	28.4
Bolivia	11.7	USSR	35.7
SOUTHWEST ASIA,		OCEANIA	
MIDDLE EAST		New Zealand	18.0
Iraq	77.2	Australia	2.1
Turkey	73.9		
Iran	36.0		
Syria	30.8		
Saudi Arabia	4.8	WORLD	79.0

Source: World Bank 1983, vol. 2. World average estimated from: United Nations 1961, 41, and United Nations 1957, vol. 10, part 1, p. 7.
ª Representative states.

Capital

While the broad contours of the distribution of capital in this period are clear, finer distinctions are required in a few regions. Beyond doubt, the United States, Canada, Australia, New Zealand, and, despite the ravages of war, the advanced economies of northern Europe remain, or become again soon after 1945, abundant in capital. Equally clearly, practically all of the states of continental Asia, Africa, the Caribbean, and Central America remain capital poor. The dubious cases are those of southern and eastern Europe, the USSR, South America (parts of which industrialized considerably during the 1930s and World War II), for the early postwar years Japan, and such regional "sports" as Ireland, Israel, and South Africa (the first much less advanced, the latter two far more so, than their neighboring economies).

A starting point for judgments on this score is again offered by Bairoch's (1982) estimated indexes of per capita industrialization for representative countries.[10] Table 4.5 presents these as rank orders for the years 1953,

[10] Bairoch (1982, 321–22), as noted earlier, counts per capita output of all "manufacturing industries" as defined in the United Nations standard statistics—i.e., the concept "embraces all forms of industry except mining [and] construction, as well as electricity, gas, water, and

1963, and 1980. For 1953, we see clearly the abundance of capital in North America, Oceania, the United Kingdom, Scandinavia (except Finland), and to a lesser extent the Low Countries and central Europe; by contrast, Japan, southern and eastern Europe, Ireland, Latin America,[11] Africa, and continental Asia remain poorly endowed in capital in this period. The USSR occupies a tenuous middle position.

By 1963, Japan, Italy, and the USSR are clearly entering the ranks of the capital-abundant economies; eastern and southeastern Europe, Iberia, Ireland, and the Third World remain outside. In 1980, virtually all of Europe save Iberia and Ireland can probably be counted as capital rich;[12] all of the continental Asian, Latin American, and African economies—note the indexes for South Africa and Brazil—remain capital poor. What matters at each time, of course, is *relative* abundance of capital; but the marked feature of the postwar period is the leveling of this endowment among the more advanced economies. The middle of the nineteenth century had been marked by Britain's almost unique position; most of the twentieth century, up to 1945, by the gulf between the very few advanced economies and all the others. Now, more and more economies begin to achieve roughly similar levels of capital abundance,[13] and continue to be separated from all others by an even more striking margin.

I must emphasize again, however, that no sharp line can be drawn. Especially between close neighbors—recall the case of Canada and the United

---

sanitary services." Leamer (1984, appendix B) offers estimates of total physical capital, based on appropriately depreciated year-to-year capital investment as reported by the World Bank, for a wide range of countries in 1960 and 1975. Leamer himself (1984, 233–34) regards these figures with some trepidation, and they prove on closer inspection to be too influenced by short-term fluctuations in exchange rates to serve us well here. (Between 1960 and 1975, for example, the United States falls in Leamer's tables from about 1.65 times Switzerland's capital per person to 0.6 times as much.)

[11] Argentina may have been the regional exception—Bairoch, unfortunately, omits it from consideration—but on balance I doubt it. In Leamer's (1984, appendix B) data for 1960, which are less affected by exchange-rate problems than his later figures, Argentina is credited with about two-thirds the capital per person of Austria, $561 vs. $826. (I take population figures for 1960 from United Nations 1961, 21–40.) Applying that rough multiplier to Bairoch's indexes for 1953 would yield an Argentine index of 60, approximately comparable with Italy's; and that, I suspect very impressionistically, would prove about right. (Leamer credits Italy with a capital of $497 per person in 1960.) On the other hand, carrying that comparison forward to 1963 would push Argentina narrowly into the ranks of the countries better endowed with capital, probably just between the USSR and Italy. By 1975, Leamer's tenuous data suggest, Argentina was clearly out of the running, with capital per head barely 60 percent of Spain's: $2741 vs. $4320.

[12] By 1980, even Poland and Yugoslavia had achieved a level that was one-quarter that of the most highly industrialized economy, the United States; they had not done so in the earlier rankings.

[13] In 1953, seventeen countries had indexes greater than one-quarter that of the United States; in 1963, twenty-one countries; in 1980, twenty-five countries.

TABLE 4.5
Per Capita Levels of Industrialization, 1953–1980 (Bairoch Indexes)[a]

1953		1963		1980	
United States	354	United States	393	United States	629
United Kingdom	210	Sweden	262	Sweden	409
Canada	185	Switzerland	259	West Germany	395
Switzerland	167	United Kingdom	253	East Germany	393
Sweden	163	West Germany	244	Canada	379
Denmark	150	Canada	237	Finland	371
Australia	146	Denmark	212	Denmark	356
West Germany	144	East Germany	207	Switzerland	354
Norway	129	Australia	201	Japan	353
Belgium	117	Czechoslovakia	193	Czechoslovakia	344
Czechoslovakia	117	Belgium	183	Hungary	333
New Zealand	117	Hungary	172	Austria	325
East Germany	100	Norway	171	United Kingdom	325
Netherlands	96	France	167	Belgium	316
France	95	New Zealand	158	France	265
Hungary	92	Finland	151	USSR	252
Austria	90	Austria	148	Australia	249
USSR	73	Netherlands	145	New Zealand	248
Italy	61	USSR	139	Norway	246
Finland	53	Italy	121	Netherlands	245
Poland	49	Japan	113	Italy	231
Ireland	47	Poland	88	Rumania	218
South Africa	46	Rumania	81	Poland	196
Japan	40	Ireland	72	Yugoslavia	174
Rumania	36	Yugoslavia	69	Spain	159
Bulgaria	32	Spain	56	Ireland	147
Spain	31	South Africa	55	Bulgaria	139
Yugoslavia	28	Bulgaria	54	Portugal	130
Portugal	26	Portugal	45	Greece	114
Greece	17	Greece	36	South Africa	79
Brazil	13	Brazil	23	Brazil	55
Mexico	12	Mexico	22	Mexico	41
India	6	China	18	China	24
China	5	India	8	India	16

Source: Bairoch 1982, tables 4, 12, and 16.
[a] 100 = level of United Kingdom in 1900.

States—relative abundance may matter more than any dichotomous categorization. Still, the difference between the least advanced economies of northern and central Europe and the most advanced ones of the Third World remains stark throughout this period.

Labor

The Myint-Lewis pattern of simultaneous abundance of land and labor, which according to earlier arguments had characterized much of Africa, Russia, and Southeast Asia in the nineteenth and early twentieth centuries (see the discussions in chapters 2 and 3), disappears rapidly after World War II, as the traditional structures of village, family, and clientage that had kept labor underemployed succumb to wider economic incentives.[14] Similarly, with the dissolution of the marginal peasantry that had likely maintained rural overemployment in Sweden and Norway (see chapter 3), those capital-abundant economies' simultaneous scarcity of land and labor fades (somewhat earlier in Sweden than in Norway).[15] Increasingly in this period, we may simply regard areas abundant in land (the Americas, Oceania, most of Africa) as scarce in labor, and ones scarce in land (East and South Asia, Europe) as abundant in labor. At the same time, sinking transportation costs make it increasingly important to draw finer distinctions within these categories: clearly Japan and Korea (not to mention places like Hong Kong and—with over 12,500 persons per square kilometer of agricultural land—Singapore) are from two to sixty times more abundant in labor than western Europe; and Australia and parts of South America and Africa are markedly more abundant in land (and poorer in labor) than North America.

CATEGORIES AND EXPECTATIONS

The very rapid expansion of trade in the post-1945 world should, according to theory, have markedly increased the political strength and ambition of owners and intensive users of locally abundant factors; should have weakened owners of scarce factors; and should have pitted coalitions of the

[14] See Barber 1961, chap. 9, for evidence that Central Africa in the 1950s was reaching the end of the previous artificial abundance of labor.

[15] Esping-Anderson 1985, 52–53, suggests the following totals for total employment ("manual labor" plus "petite bourgeoisie") in agriculture for 1950, 1960, and 1970, respectively: in Norway, 28, 18, and 12 percent; in Sweden, 18, 12, and 10 percent. The slightly different data of Mitchell (1978, table B1) indicate that in 1950 agriculture, forestry, and fishing claimed 31 percent of the Norwegian work force, 25 percent of the Swedish.

former against coalitions of the latter. More specifically, we expect to see the following four patterns.

Abundance of Labor and Capital; Scarcity of Land

From very early in the postwar period, northern and central Europe—including even Czechoslovakia, East Germany, Austria, and Hungary (see Table 4.5)—resume their previous status in this category; by the early 1960s, Japan and Italy are crossing the threshold of capital abundance; by 1980 almost all of Europe outside of Iberia, Ireland, Bulgaria, and Greece has entered it, and even these strongholds of backwardness seem about to succumb. Among this diverse group of states we expect a broad replication of the tendency of the most developed parts of nineteenth-century northwestern Europe: a neoliberal, free-trading alliance of labor and capital that is inimical to the interests of agriculture. Particularly in those capitalist societies where scarcity of capital and abundance of labor had long pitted those two factors against each other (see the next section), this may imply a startling reversal of fronts and an "end of ideology"; in the communist economies, it indicates relaxation of the Draconian controls over workers long exercised by the state capitalist elite.

At the same time, the relative equalization of capital endowments among many economies in this group and the further reduction in costs of transport may accentuate the importance of inequalities in the land-labor ratio. Specifically, the advanced Asian societies' greater abundance of labor gives them comparative advantage in the production of relatively labor-intensive industrial goods (e.g., steel and automobiles). Less labor-rich Europe has an "edge" in the manufacture of goods that require greater inputs of capital (e.g., chemicals). These facts may dictate, in increasingly open markets, the uncomfortably rapid abandonment of some sectors. Over the very short run, this may lead to difficulties of adjustment of the kind predicted by the "specific factors" model (as discussed in chapter 1);[16] but over even the medium run free trade continues to serve, and is seen to serve, the European worker's best interest.[17]

---

[16] The difference between the specific-factors and the Stolper-Samuelson models is, as I observed in chapter 1, simply that between the short and the long run; and the puzzle comes in recognizing the dividing line between these two. I am speculating here that change occurred gradually enough in earlier eras to give the long-run model general applicability; only with the extremely rapid shifts of recent years has the specific-factors model found a limited usefulness.

[17] In many of the cases in which European workers have appeared to embrace protection-

Abundance Only of Labor;
Scarcity of Capital and Land

This situation describes southern and southeastern Europe early in our period and continental East and South Asia, the Caribbean, the Levant, most of Central America[18] and Southeast Asia, and parts of Africa throughout this time (see Table 4.4). Here we expect a growing militancy of labor (including the landless or land-poor peasantry) and a defensive coalition of capital and land. Worker and small-peasant revolutions cannot be ruled out.

Abundance Only of Land;
Scarcity of Labor and Capital

In this category we encounter virtually all of South America, Mexico, the bulk of Africa and Southwest Asia, and one European "sport," Ireland, which is almost as abundant in land as the United States. In these economies, expanding trade should ignite urban-rural conflict, leading free-trading landowners and agricultural interests to oppose a protectionist coalition of capitalists and workers. Where, as in much of Latin America, previous events had strengthened populist alliances of labor and capital, the resumption and expansion of trade may be expected to weaken these groups and to augment the influence of landowners and their (often military) allies.

Abundance of Land and Capital;
Scarcity of Labor

This group comprises an odd assemblage of states: throughout our period, the former frontier societies of the United States, Canada, Australia, and New Zealand; and, from sometime in the 1960s, the Soviet Union. Here the forecast differs radically from that for the labor-rich economies of our first category: because labor's interests lie with protection, while capital and the most advanced industries favor free trade, we expect considerable class conflict and, given that expanding trade harms scarce factors, ultimately a serious assault on labor's political position. Far from an "end of ideology," these states should experience a revival of it and a significant turn to the right, that is, to greater managerial influence. On the other hand conflict *between* these states may well diminish, as their elites perceive common domestic problems and interests.

---

ism, the real goal has been the defense of various kinds of rents ("featherbedding" and over-market wages) won by specific subsectors over the years. Cf. below, n. 41.

[18] From the standpoint adopted here, El Salvador should incline far more to working-class revolution than Nicaragua: compare their labor-land ratios in Table 4.4.

EVIDENCE

Economies Abundant in Labor and Capital,
Scarce in Land: Europe and Japan

Despite some recent reversals, it can hardly be doubted that the broad trend of politics in postwar industrialized Europe and Japan has been toward an "end of ideology" (Bell 1960) and a "waning of opposition" (Kirchheimer 1957) that reflected a far-reaching reconciliation of labor and capital. Everywhere that it prevailed, this new alliance achieved a substantial liberalization of trade and, even while providing generous death benefits, presided over domestic agriculture's demise. Moreover, the timing of this reconciliation, and the attainment of its policies, seems roughly to have coincided with the given labor-rich economy's achievement of capital abundance.

Admittedly, the present approach offers no explanation for the earlier prevalence of conflicts between labor and capital in many economies that had long been abundant in both factors. Stolper-Samuelson effects can have had little to do, for example, with the rise of a class cleavage in Britain or within the secular "pillars" of Belgian or Dutch society. Although I would argue that the fundamental convergence of workers' and capitalists' interest in those societies on questions of trade mollified their opposition and prevented anything like the bitterness of central or southern European class conflict, the sources of the conflict that did arise must surely have been domestic.[19]

Regardless of the origins or extent of existing class conflict, what stands out in this period is its uniform diminution in the labor-abundant advanced economies. In one pattern, old and often bitter opponents converged on common policies. Conservative governments in Britain reversed few of Labour's innovations after 1951, and Labour after 1965 accepted much that the Conservatives had enacted; wags spoke of "Butskellism" as the policy of both parties.[20] In West Germany, conservative leaders expanded the welfare state and accepted both workplace codetermination and, after 1966, Keynesian fiscal policies;[21] on the left, Communist support evaporated and the SPD embraced both NATO and the domestic moderation of the Godesberg Program. Later, the Italian Left pursued Eu-

---

[19] See also the discussion in chapter 3 at n. 95. Lipset's hypothesis (e.g., Lipset 1983), which ties the intensity of class conflict to the prevalence of "estate" organization in the preexisting society, seems to me the most plausible explanation.

[20] Punnett 1971, 24–25.

[21] Heavy industry, as represented by the *Bund der deutschen Industrie*, strenuously opposed codetermination at first, but Adenauer and the CDU leadership overrode them; and they have since come to accept it. Berghahn 1982, 205–7; Grosser 1980, 292–94.

rocommunism and a "historic compromise," and the Italian Right sought an "opening to the Left"; French Socialists accepted the Fifth Republic, French Gaullists the European Community.

In a separate but related pattern, interclass *Volksparteien*—the various Christian Democracies, the Gaullist movement, the revamped Socialisms of Germany, Scandinavia, France, and Spain—superseded the often militant and always demographically exclusive movements of the recent past.[22] Parties of the Left (the Japanese Socialists, the French Communists) or of the Right (the French Conservatives of the old CNIP) that rejected moderation fell into the ghetto or by the wayside. By both routes, as Kirchheimer (1957; 1966) observed, the tone and content of politics changed markedly: the principled conflict of goals and world views that had long prevailed yielded to a competition over competence and technique, and corporatist institutions came so to dominate policy making as to make partisan control of government almost irrelevant.

Although this *rapprochement* was widely attributed, not least by Kirchheimer,[23] to the welfare state's subversion of working-class militancy, it owed at least as much to a fundamental alteration of *capitalists'* viewpoint and policy. In the 1920s and 1930s, German, Italian, Spanish, French, Austrian, and Japanese industrialists had often opposed democracy, denied unions' right to exist, and flirted with fascism; even British owners had willingly incurred massive strikes to gain deep wage cuts.[24] After (or, in a few cases, during) World War II, employers in Scandinavia,[25] northwestern Europe, Austria, and West Germany, embraced democracy, the welfare state, and often substantial trade union codetermination; and that pattern of capitalist accommodation subsequently spread—again, roughly with the achievement of an abundance of capital—to France, Italy, and even Japan and Spain.

A crucial aspect of the bargain between reformed Right and reformed Left, between capital and labor, was economic openness; and it is a signal

---

[22] As many students have observed (e.g., Nordlinger 1967), the Disraelian Conservative party in Britain pioneered in successfully attracting working-class votes; hence, it can be regarded as the forerunner of the European "catch-all" parties.

[23] Kirchheimer 1957, 152; Kirchheimer 1966, 247.

[24] A hypothesis that follows from the present theory would likely repay detailed investigation: namely, that employers' resistance to workers' aspirations will have varied *inversely* with the capital intensity of the particular sector in capital-abundant economies, but *directly* with capital-intensity in capital-scarce regions (cf. n. 35 in chapter 2). Hence, as capital becomes more abundant in these regions, capital's strongest voices increasingly accept accommodation.

[25] Gourevitch (1986, 134) accurately calls the 1938 Pact of Saltsjöbaden in Sweden "a model for what all of Western Europe would do after 1945." Under its terms, business accepted high labor costs, the welfare state, and full-employment fiscal policy in exchange for labor peace and economic openness.

change from earlier periods that European capital now becomes as free-trading as European labor had long been.[26] Although the impetus toward freer markets came from the United States, the Organization for European Economic Co-operation (the later OECD) that the Marshall Plan had spawned, such "Europeanists" as Jean Monnet and Robert Schumann, and, after 1957, the European Economic Community (EEC),[27] the rapid achievement of greater openness would hardly have been possible without the active support of domestic leaders of capital and industry. By one authoritative estimate, 56 percent of trade within the OEEC was free of tariffs or quotas by 1950, 84 percent by 1955, 94 percent by 1961.[28]

A second important aspect of the postwar alliance of labor and capital was the final defeat of high-cost agriculture. Although popular attention has been captured by the follies of agricultural subvention and, in particular, of the European Community's Common Agricultural Policy (CAP),[29] nothing that was attempted in these years has compared remotely with the interwar efforts of the French and German governments to maintain the peasantry at all costs. Rather, as Zysman has put it well, the subsidies and price supports "held [the peasantry] in place even as its economic and social positions were destroyed."[30] Within the European states of the OECD, agriculture's share of civilian employment fell from perhaps 35 percent in 1950 to 26 percent in 1960, 18 percent in 1970, and 15 percent in 1980. Even Japan, which is routinely condemned for its alleged agricultural protectionism, has gone from having 30 percent of its civilian employment in agriculture in 1960 to 10 percent in 1980. Germany has moved from 19 percent in 1950 and 14 percent in 1960 to 6 percent in 1980; France, from 23 percent in 1960 to 9 percent in 1980.[31] Agriculture's share of value added in GDP has receded almost as rapidly: in the European OECD as a whole, from perhaps 15 percent in 1950 to 9 percent in 1960 and 4 percent in 1980; in Japan, from 13 percent in 1960 to 4 percent in 1980.[32]

[26] The shift of German industrialists—spurred, admittedly, by the loss of much of their prewar markets and raw materials—to an almost unanimous export orientation was particularly marked. Their abandonment of cartels was much more reluctant. See, e.g., Berghahn 1982, 204, 208, and 227–28.

[27] Subsequently, of course, the European Community has assumed a somewhat more protectionist aspect toward outsiders; but on balance it has been a powerful influence for more open markets.

[28] Landes 1969, 504–13, esp. 505.

[29] The absurdities of the CAP are well sketched by Ardagh 1982, 221ff. On the Japanese subsidies, see Yanagi 1983, 196–201.

[30] Zysman 1983, 24.

[31] Figures for 1960 through 1980 are from Organization for Economic Co-operation and Development 1982, 34; estimates for 1950 are based on data for selected countries in Mitchell 1978, table J2.

[32] Organization for Economic Co-operation and Development 1982, 54; Mitchell 1978, table J2.

Indeed, in many of the advanced economies, as in Britain by the 1930s (see p. 81, by 1980 agriculture had been abandoned to an extent that began to obviate the three-factor analysis (land, labor, capital) that has been employed up to now in our discussion.

A more detailed examination of developments in a few representative countries may cast these trends in sharper relief. France,[33] which in the interwar period had manifested both extreme protectionism and considerable class conflict, became after 1945 a leader in the movement for European integration and, at least rhetorically, for more open markets. To the plans of Monnet and Schuman, however, the main peasant organization, the FNSEA, was resolutely opposed; and the *patronat* (CNPF), as chief representative of industrial capital, also rejected the treaty that established the European Coal and Steel Community (ECSC) in 1951.[34] The cause of European union found consistent support during the Fourth Republic in the SFIO and the MRP—respectively, the principal Socialist and Christian Democratic parties.[35] (European unity was rejected also by the Communists, largely for foreign-policy reasons, and by the Gaullists.)

By 1957, when the Treaty of Rome that established the EEC came up for ratification, the *patronat* was in support; only the Communists, Poujadists, peasant organizations, and Gaullists opposed approval.[36] In power after 1958, the Gaullists—despite their leader's resistance to the supranational aspects of the EEC—surprised most observers by further liberalizing trade and accelerating the departure of peasants from the land.[37] A Gaullist government also undertook, against the resistance of the *patronat* but with the support of a breakaway association of more progressive industrialists, to strengthen somewhat the very weak French version of codetermination.[38]

By 1980, a close journalistic observer of France has asserted, it was rare to meet a businessman who opposed the EEC;[39] and a 1979 survey found that 56 percent of French adults considered the European Community

[33] Where not otherwise specified, the present discussion relies on the excellent analysis of Williams 1966.

[34] Williams 1966, 406 and 412; Williams and Harrison 1973, 11; Ardagh 1982, 37.

[35] Williams 1966, 105 and 113.

[36] Williams 1966, 56 and 305.

[37] Landes 1969, 505; Williams and Harrison 1973, 14–17; cf. Grosser 1980, 453. Agriculture's share of employment had fallen between 1936 and 1954 only from 36 percent to 27 percent; by 1961 it was at 16 percent and by 1969 had fallen by over a third from its level of 1960. Williams and Harrison 1973, 15; Organization for Economic Co-operation and Development 1982, 34. In his memoirs, de Gaulle (1971, 138 and 143–44) took credit for having guided France successfully into Europe and for liberalizing French trade.

[38] Williams and Harrison 1973, 173 and 352–54.

[39] Ardagh 1982, 38.

"good" for their country, as against 8 percent who found it "bad."[40] At various junctures, however, some French workers—particularly those whose traditional rents, supported by long-standing domestic monopolies, were coming under sharpest international challenge—have vehemently opposed liberalization. The chief example was perhaps the strike of miners at Decazeville in 1961–1962, which may be compared in its "blind defense of *droits acquis*" with that of Belgian miners in the 1950s, or of their British colleagues in recent years.[41] In the main, however, French workers have supported—not least by their increasing support of the Socialist, rather than the Communist, alternative—policies of economic integration and openness.

Both Left and Right in France have tended toward unity and moderation.[42] The Communists have fallen from their customary quarter of the vote in immediate postwar elections to slightly over 20 percent after 1958 and less than 10 percent in the most recent contests; the Socialists have become the unchallenged party of the Left. Similarly, the traditional Conservatives, who had normally gained about 15 percent of the vote in the Fourth Republic, fell to 10 percent in 1962 and had merged out of existence by 1973; the Radicals—anticlerical but otherwise conservative—followed them into oblivion. The mainstream Right remains divided into various personal followings, but all are moderate; old-fashioned right-wing extremism can survive only as an excrescence of racism, in the volatile National Front.[43]

In West Germany, the alliance of labor and capital in support of free trade has been even clearer and firmer. Labor accepted from the earliest postwar days the compelling need for wage restraint and the pursuit of export markets; and the DGB, the main trade-union confederation, supported the ECSC early and enthusiastically.[44] The Social Democratic party, although at first critical of the ECSC for foreign-policy reasons, by 1955 fully backed European unity: Erich Ollenhauer, as leader of the party, was formally received by Jean Monnet into the "Action Committee for a United States of Europe."[45] Big business's doubts evaporated with

[40] The comparable British figures at the same date were, respectively, 33 and 34 percent; the Dutch ones were 84 percent "good," 2 percent "bad." Ardagh 1982, 466.

[41] Williams and Harrison 1973, 14; Landes 1969, 507. As the telling phrase about "*droits acquis*" in Williams and Harrison suggests, some part of labor's (and other groups') resistance to economic openness rests not on factor endowments but on the naked pursuit or protection of rents extracted earlier. One need only consider the analogous behavior of U.S. automobile workers.

[42] This paragraph is based chiefly on Williams and Harrison 1973, chaps. 6–8, and Cook and Paxton 1986, 140–41 and 198–200.

[43] Cf. Ardagh 1982, 466.

[44] Heidenheimer and Kommers 1975, 44–45; Feld 1981, 30.

[45] Grosser 1980, 452–53.

similar rapidity, and the Treaty of Rome was negotiated and approved with almost no domestic dissent.[46] In same survey of 1979 that elicited the French responses already mentioned, West Germans approved of the EEC by a margin of 66 to 5 percent.[47]

In Britain, as is well known, labor and the Left have been far more hesitant and divided in their attitude toward Europe, and indeed toward free trade. A Labour government declined to join the ECSC at its founding in 1950–1951; and in 1961 and 1962, when a Conservative cabinet first proposed to enter the EEC, Labour advanced conditions that amounted to rejection.[48] Thereafter Labour described a dismal course of vacillation and division resolved only by the appeal to a national referendum in 1975.[49] At that point the leadership of the Trades Union Congress and a majority of the Labour cabinet favored continued membership, but on the crucial vote in the House of Commons only about forty percent of Labour MPs, most of them from the party's right and center, approved; a special Party Conference was overwhelmingly opposed.[50] Throughout the fifteen years' controversy, it was clear that Europe's strongest supporters were in banking, industry, commerce, and the Treasury.[51]

Since 1975, and even more since Margaret Thatcher's rise to power, Labour's left wing has continued to repudiate Europe and indeed has moved into open endorsement of protection.[52] This policy, almost self-evidently suicidal to workers in so labor-rich a country as Britain,[53] makes sense only as a last-ditch defense of the various rents that privileged groups within British labor have long been able to extract and that cannot withstand international competition: it is Decazeville on a national scale.[54] The policy has earned its predictable reward in the massive turn of workers in new industries, and especially in the white-collar sector, first to the antiprotec-

[46] Grosser 1980, 453; Berghahn 1982, 208.

[47] Ardagh 1982, 466.

[48] Childs 1986, 61 and 135.

[49] Childs 1986, 190–91 and 232–34.

[50] Of 319 Labour MPs, 135 voted in favor of the renegotiated terms of membership. Childs 1986, 252–53 and 339.

[51] Childs 1986, 135 and 253.

[52] An example is Conference of Socialist Economists 1980, chap. 8. See also the discussion in Gourevitch 1986, 194 and 197.

[53] A few academic economists have also endorsed protectionism as the answer to Britain's woes. The Cambridge Economic Policy Group, most notably, has urged initial across-the-board tariffs of 30 percent on manufactured goods, to rise to as much as 70 percent by 1990. Conference of Socialist Economists 1980, 95.

[54] This case, like that of Australian Labor in the 1930s (see chapter 3), raises the principal-agent issue of how a given factor's political representatives can misapprehend its interests or misspecify its tactics. In the short run, they can certainly do so, just as a corporation's management may refuse, or fail, to pursue profits; but in both cases the principals, aware that they are being badly served, will change or desert their agents.

tionist Social Democrats[55] and then to the Tories. Labour runs every risk of joining the French Communists on the ash heap of history.[56] By way of contrast, the Italian Left quickly reversed its originally negative judgment of the European Community.[57] In Italy as in Britain, big business—and particularly the most modern sectors—eager for access to the rich markets of northwestern Europe, provided early and strong support for an intra-European free market. The Communists and Socialists opposed ratification of the Treaty of Rome in 1957, but only after a bruising struggle in which the (largely Communist) leadership of the main trade union confederation, CGIL, pushed strongly for acceptance and worked to overturn the party's decision. In September 1962 the PCI openly reversed its earlier decision and pronounced the EEC a boon to Italian, and to European, labor. By the early 1970s, PCI deputies in the European Parliament were pressuring their colleagues of the PCF and of Labour's left wing to reconsider their opposition to the European Community. This fundamental agreement between Italian labor and capital on a central aspect of trade policy has facilitated cooperation across once-deep political divisions and has eased the admission of the Left to a substantial degree of power sharing.

A second useful contrast to British developments is the evolution of the postwar Japanese labor movement. Although the Occupation reforms left a residue of powerful formal rights for trade unions—the closed shop, for example, is the rule—and both the level of unionization (roughly 35 percent of the work force) and the incidence of strikes are higher than is often assumed, there is in fact a powerful strain of collaboration between capital and labor in the most modern, capital-intensive, and (usually) export-oriented sectors.[58] The major federation of private-sector unions, Dōmei, which enjoys its strongest representation in the most advanced industrial sectors, even mentions "raising productivity" in its charter as a principal goal and emphasizes in practice the need to adapt to "the realities of the

[55] Labour's continued advocacy of withdrawal from the European Community in 1980 was, it should be recalled, the principal issue on which Owen, Rodgers, and Williams—the "gang of three"—split off to form the Social Democratic party. Childs 1986, 306.

[56] Some stark facts: in 1983, Labour won precisely 27.6 percent of the popular vote, as against 42.4 percent for the Conservatives and 25.4 percent for the Alliance of the Social Democratic party and Liberals. Even among trade unionists, only 39 percent voted for Labour. Throughout southern England—the region of modern, internationally competitive industry—the Alliance replaced Labour as the principal opposition party. Labour, in the words of one dispassionate scholar (Childs 1986, 316–17 and 340), "looked like becoming a ghetto party of the inner cities and areas of high, long-term unemployment; a party of the unskilled, council-house tenants." Despite the decline of the Alliance in the most recent elections, largely to the benefit of the Conservatives, that verdict on Labour shows little sign of being reversed.

[57] This paragraph relies on Kogan 1983, esp. 98, 100, 177, and 280 and chap. 21.

[58] Kōshiro 1983, 151; Buckley 1985, 118–19; Ayusawa 1966, 349–51, 361, and 364.

national and international economy"; it is closely linked to the reformist and urban-based Democratic Socialist party.[59] Bitter and violent strikes to resist adaptation—most notably, here as elsewhere, in coal: the Mikke strike of 1959[60]—have been known, but the majority of the labor movement has abandoned such tactics. There is little support for protection,[61] but that is less of a foregone conclusion than one might think: exports represent a considerably smaller share of Japanese than of British GDP (on average between 1974 and 1980, 12.9 percent in Japan; 28.8 percent in the United Kingdom).[62]

In fact, however, a shared commitment to economic liberalization has helped importantly to bind capital and labor together in postwar Japan. Despite repeated accusations of "protectionism" from Western firms that simply fail to compete, Japan's tariffs *and* nontariff barriers are today lower than those of either the United States or the European Community;[63] and, since at least 1980 and probably earlier, the Japanese economy has tended steadily toward greater liberalization.[64]

Movements in the same direction of economic openness and labor-capital collaboration have manifested themselves in the advanced eastern European economies: Hungary, Czechoslovakia, East Germany, even Rumania and Poland. In these cases, factions of the governing managerial elite compromise with workers to pursue domestic liberalization and an opening to world markets. Typically this ignites conflict with rent seekers and controllers of scarce factors at home, and with the Soviet Union, whose ruling elite (as I shall argue) has quite different incentives.[65] It also demands a level of economic expertise that few Communist leaderships possess: Rumania, for example, is a case of liberal economic (if by no

[59] Kōshiro 1983, 149–50; Ayusawa 1966, 328 and 377. Dōmei represents 2.04 million private-sector workers; its larger rival, Sōhyō, whose strength is in the public sector, claims 1.56 million private-sector members.

[60] Ayusawa 1966, 336–40.

[61] Stockwin 1982, 137–38; cf. Yanagi 1983, 196. A more negative view is presented by Kevenhörster 1973, 49 and 110.

[62] Organization for Economic Co-operation and Development 1982, 62.

[63] No less an authority than the U.S. International Trade Commission has concluded that Japan's average tariff level is lower than that of either the United States or the European Community. In 1982, Japanese nontariff barriers in manufacturing industry were estimated as between 5 and 7 percent; those of the European Community were 20 percent, of the United States 34 percent. Schmiegelow 1985, 288. Protection continues in a few sectors deemed to be strategically or politically essential, e.g. advanced electronics and rice; but it is consistently overrated by Western politicians and journalists.

[64] In 1980, a new law on external economic relations, described as among the most liberal in the OECD, was adopted; as early as 1971, Japan's trade policies were as liberal as West Germany's. Schmiegelow 1985, 288.

[65] Both the rent-seeking aspect and that of Soviet "interpenetration" are sensitively treated by Comisso 1986, esp. 206–12 and 230–35.

means political) experimentation felled by colossal misinvestment.[66] Only in Hungary, it appears, has a coalition parallel to that of postwar western Europe largely succeeded.[67]

Economies Abundant in Labor, Scarce in Capital and Land: Asia, the Caribbean, and Parts of Africa and Central America

In these regions, cheaper and easier trade should according to theory have benefited workers, urban and rural, and such labor-intensive enterprises as small peasant holdings.[68] While at first the resultant gains may have been largely captured by traditional landowning or bureaucratic elites (or, more rarely, by nascent capitalists), political entrepreneurs will have moved quickly to organize the newly advantaged groups and to seize for them a larger share of political and economic power.[69]

Samuel Popkin's (1979) analysis of the Vietnamese revolution conforms in its major aspects to this portrait.[70] The Vietnamese economy, according to Popkin, had become fully integrated into world markets during the period of French colonial rule: particularly the rice and rubber plantations of southern Vietnam (Nam Bo, or what the French called Cochinchina) were oriented entirely toward exports. Moreover, the colonial regime's heavy impositions of taxes, and its insistence that these be paid in cash, had forced peasants away from subsistence and into cash-crop agriculture. Traditional elites, the gentry and mandarinate, who had acted paternalistically only in the romantic imaginings of some Western observers, now used their inherited positions and their good ties to the colonialists to capture much of the gain for themselves.

Far from rejecting markets and seeking a return to traditional life, however, the peasants had sought, as Popkin put it, "to tame markets and enter them on their own."[71] A series of organizations—the Roman Catholic

[66] Crowther 1986, Linden 1986.

[67] Comisso and Marer 1986 is a useful survey but focuses too narrowly on the party elite; more general social forces and coalitions are treated as secondary, if not irrelevant. The centrality of trade is, however, clearly recognized: e.g., Comisso and Marer 1986, 427.

[68] Along with the benefits will have come significant short-term losses, e.g. the decimation of traditional village handicrafts in China by imported textiles and other goods: Clubb 1978, 186; Hinton 1966, 44. On the extraordinary labor intensiveness of traditional Chinese agriculture, see Barnett 1963, 114; Bianco 1971, 92–94; and Hinton 1966, 22–23.

[69] The problems of political collective action in such a case are analogous to those of exploiting a market that requires prior organization of an infrastructure. Automobiles can only be sold in quantity after service stations and adequate roads are available; personal computers require software, training, and support. In the political as in the marketing cases, entrepreneurs have incentives, and can raise capital, to circumvent these bottlenecks.

[70] The following discussion rests on Popkin 1979, chaps. 4–6.

[71] Popkin 1979, 187.

Church, the Cao Dai, the Hoa Hao—attempted, and partially succeeded, to create the infrastructure of property rights and legal defense that would permit peasants to produce and trade independent of the increasingly parasitic gentry.[72] The Communists, however, did far better, not least because they more ruthlessly opposed the depredations of the old elite;[73] and their greater success brought them correspondingly greater support.

In Asian circumstances, paradoxically, much collectivism was required to break old ties of dependence and to guarantee direct access to markets: peasants had, for example, to organize livestock cooperatives, tend irrigation canals, and arrange their own systems of credit—all services that the elite had long monopolized. Yet Popkin is adamant, and ultimately persuasive, in projecting market access as the goal of the peasants' strivings and as the secret of their new-found strength.[74] I would supplement Popkin's account only by pointing to the importance, for this whole process, of expanding world markets after 1945. These multiplied the potential gains of access.

I propose, indeed, to suggest that Popkin's perspective may be useful for the study of the Chinese Revolution as well. Even more obviously than in Vietnam, the traditional Chinese village had been profoundly conflictual: Hinton describes it as "harbor[ing] a never-ending 'war of all against all,'" in which enormous man-hours had to be invested simply in protecting ripe crops from theft.[75] It had also long been integrated into a dense and extensive structure of interregional trade, which indeed seems to have defined such other aspects of social structure as religion and endogamy: persons knew, married, and worshiped with those with whom they regularly traded.[76] It also appears that expanding interregional and international trade contributed substantially to the enormous growth of China's population after 1650 (perhaps 120 million at that point, it rose to 150 million by 1700, 313 million by 1794, over 350 million by 1850, and 750 million by 1950).[77] Certainly the dispersal of crops from previously isolated regions (millet and barley from northern China) and from the Americas (maize, potatoes, yams) literally fed the expansion;[78] so, we may speculate, did imports of sugar, which eventually became part of the regular diet even

[72] The case of the Hoa Hao is particularly instructive: Popkin 1979, 211.

[73] For some of the concrete measures employed, see Popkin 1979, 225–29 and 236–42.

[74] Villages that had overcome the problems of infrastructure and collective action and had gained direct access to markets were markedly more prosperous, and yielded considerably higher tax revenues, than their traditional counterparts: Popkin 1979, 191, 210–11, and 227.

[75] Hinton 1966, 38 and 53.

[76] Skinner 1964–1965.

[77] Bianco 1971, 91.

[78] Bianco 1971, 91n.

of rural Chinese and may have played the same important role as a source of calories here as it did in Europe.[79]

Long-range trade and exports grew with particular intensity from the middle of the nineteenth century, and Skinner has detailed well the route by which its impact was felt in Chinese society.[80] As steam transport on major rivers, railroads, and all-weather roads between major cities were extended, the price of manufactured goods fell, and that of raw and semi-processed materials rose, throughout the system.

> Sharp differentials in the buying price of cotton [for example] within the system—highest in the city, markedly lower in the first ring of market towns around it, lower still in towns of the third ring, and so forth—still obtain, for there has been no change in the high cost of local transport. However, since the price level has risen right down the line, as far out as the second or even third ring of rural markets the price offered for cotton may have risen sufficiently to stimulate cotton culture. Similarly, the potential selling price of machine-loomed textiles will fall not only in the city but also in all markets within its trading system, with the result that imported textiles, formerly priced out of even the first ring of market towns around the city, may now achieve ready sale as far out as the second. In the case of manufactured items less bulky than textiles, the reduction in selling price brought about by [for example] the new rail line may suffice to give them a sale even in the most distant part of the system. The degree, then, to which agriculture is commercialized, cottage industry suffers, and consumption patterns alter decreases as one moves from marketing subsystems close to the city to those farther away; some degree of commercialization is possible even in subsystems at the farthest reaches of the trading area of a city which is linked to the outside world by modern transport.[81]

By the later years of the nineteenth century, imported goods were driving traditional handicrafts from many local markets, as many historians have emphasized;[82] but rising trade was also creating important new export markets: the port city of Tientsin, for example, shipped egg products, sausage casings, beans, shelled walnuts, furs and skins, straw braid, raw wool, wool rugs, and pig bristles.[83] Agriculture, except in the most remote areas, was becoming more commercialized and more specialized; and the resultant gains from trade permitted further expansion of population.

As in Vietnam, however, most of the gain was seized by traditional elites, and traditional structures severely limited the gains that could be achieved. The Chinese gentry—landowners of very moderate means by

---

[79] Barnett 1963, 113; Wallerstein 1974, 43.
[80] Skinner 1964–1965, pt. 2.
[81] Skinner 1964–1965, 213–14.
[82] Clubb 1978, 123 and 186; Hinton 1966, 44; Bianco 1971, 104n.
[83] Barnett 1963, 54–55.

Western standards, typically possessing two to fifty acres, but able in this land-scarce society to live off their rents[84]—jealously monopolized the crucial trades of grain marketing and moneylending; in addition, groups within the gentry often farmed the taxes, remitting to the state as little as a third of the total collected.[85] A vicious pattern thus emerged in the typical village: to pay taxes, or to tide him over a failed harvest, the peasant borrowed, at annual real rates that insecurity and local monopoly drove as high as 20 percent in the best of times; to repay the loan, he sold much of his crop immediately after harvest, when the market was glutted, again often to a local monopsonist; then, to survive another year, he went further into debt.[86] Clearly both individual peasants and the village economy would have fared better under solider and more competitive credit and marketing arrangements; and political entrepreneurs had large incentives to organize such better arrangements. Clearly, too, the existing system induced a spiraling concentration of landownership that was very far from encouraging an economically optimal mix of factors.[87] By 1945, according to one authoritative estimate, land-poor and landless peasants constituted 68 percent of rural families in China proper but owned only 22 percent of the land; the gentry made up 3 percent of the families but owned 26 percent of the land.[88]

The Kuomintang regime endeavored to square the circle by increasing rural productivity without challenging the local monopoly of the gentry.[89] It built, for example, only railroads and long-range highways, rejecting the local roads that would have given peasants independent access to markets. It was generous, at least by contrast with immediate past rulers, in support of irrigation, reforestation, and rural hygiene and education; but it recoiled from even the most modest and opportune reallocations of land or restrictions of landlord power. Under these constraints, rural productivity hardly budged. By contrast the Communists, experimenting as they went, were able to induce rapid increases in production even by quite timid reforms: curtailing the gentry's monopolies of marketing and credit, guaranteeing honest government, and overcoming traditional obstacles to collective action.[90]

[84] Bianco 1971, 94. Rents were usually in kind, and averaged 45 percent of the harvest; so high were land prices, however, that the landlord's net return on investment averaged only 8 to 11 percent. Bianco 1971, 96 and 99.

[85] Bianco 1971, 100–3.

[86] Bianco 1971, 102–3.

[87] Above all, here as in nineteenth-century Ireland and Russia (on the latter case, see my discussion in chapter 2), neither landlords nor tenants had much incentive to invest in capital improvements: Hinton 1966, 35–36; Bianco 1971, 94.

[88] Ch'en, *The Chinese Peasant*, cited in Bianco 1971, 95.

[89] This paragraph is based on the invaluable analysis of Bianco 1971, 64–65, 109–115, and 158–59.

[90] To the extent that this occurred in the 1930s and early 1940s, when external trade had

It is little wonder that the Communists attracted growing popular support or that, when the Japanese invasion revealed all the more starkly the contrast between Communist vigor and Kuomintang incompetence and corruption, the Communists inherited the Nationalist cause.[91] What made the Communist strength possible, however—what translated peasant discontent, this one time in Chinese history, into social revolution instead of mere banditry or millennialism—was the growing economic strength and potential of the poor peasants and the rural proletariat,[92] which in turn depended on the growth of the markets available to them.[93] The final nail in the coffin of the Kuomintang was, in this light, probably the post-1945 hyperinflation, which simultaneously erased the peasants' indebtedness and, when attempts to stem it created an internationally overvalued currency, destroyed their export markets.[94]

Further evidence for these contentions can be found in the policies that the Communists pursued after their attainment of power in 1949. Until the folly of the Great Leap Forward in 1958, and soon again after its evident failure, the new regime assiduously extended *local* transport networks including canals, motor roads, and feeder railways, encouraged the expansion of markets, and indeed aligned administrative boundaries with those of "natural" market areas.[95] They also drastically expanded international trade: exports, by one reckoning, rose from the equivalent of $0.47 per capita in 1947 to $2.66 per capita in 1953. (Exports' normal level in the 1920s had been about $1.50 annually per capita; in the catastrophic 1930s, less than $0.20.)[96]

It is a plausible hypothesis, then, that Asia's greatest social revolution—and, as indicated in chapter 2, that revolution's nineteenth-century forerunners—was facilitated by expanding international trade, which both

---

largely collapsed, its benefits will have depended mostly on interregional gains from trade. Only after 1945 can booming world markets have contributed again to revolutionary resources.

[91] That mere "nationalism" does not explain the Communists' victory, however—*pace* Johnson 1962—is proved by the peasants' frequent treatment of Kuomintang soldiers as an invading army as hostile as the Japanese, and by their occasional welcoming of the Japanese as liberators from the Kuomintang. Bianco 1971, 148–59; Clubb 1978, 239.

[92] Interestingly, and as the theory would predict, the more well-to-do peasants (i.e., ones whose income flowed more from land and less from labor) sided in China increasingly with the gentry (Bianco 1971, 188). Contrast this experience with that of Russia in the nineteenth and early twentieth centuries (see chapter 2), where the wealthier peasants often were in the vanguard of the revolutionary movement.

[93] Bianco 1971, 104–5, observes that we cannot be sure that peasant incomes were declining immediately before the revolution; they may well have been rising. Certainly the Communist economic successes demonstrated that their *potential* income had increased.

[94] Clubb 1978, 291ff.; Barnett 1963, 19, 55–56, and 71–74; Bianco 1971, 160 and 193–97.

[95] Skinner 1964–1965, 366–71.

[96] Banks 1971, 177–78.

sharpened the conflict between scarce and abundant factors and strengthened and emboldened holders of the lone abundant factor, i.e. workers and land-poor peasants.[97] Similar factors, one speculates, may have underlain the Communist insurgencies in Indonesia[98] and the Philippines.

These cases however raise anew the recurrent mystery of India: Why, under an equally low land-labor ratio and, at least in many regions, an even more concentrated pattern of landownership, have Indian peasants remained so quiescent?[99] There have of course been significant rebellions and guerrilla movements even in the postindependence period:[100] the Telangana rising in Hyderabad between 1946 and 1948, crushed only after the Indian army interned some fifty thousand peasants; the revolt of the Andhra Communists between 1966 and 1971; and the Naxalite insurgency of the late 1960s and early 1970s, to name only the prominent examples. On the whole, however, Indian peasant movements have been distinguished by their weakness. Among the reasons that have been advanced are peculiarities of the Indian village and caste structures;[101] the misguided policies of Indian revolutionaries, and in particular of Indian Communists;[102] the relative benevolence of the Indian landlord;[103] and (perhaps most intriguingly, and as an obvious contrast with prerevolutionary Russia) the weakness of the "middle," modernizing peasant in the Indian economy.[104]

The present approach suggests, if only as a hypothesis, the importance of another variable: Indian peasants' early independent access to markets, as guaranteed both by the transportation network and by the structure of property rights that British imperialism erected. Certainly India was far

[97] Two subsidiary issues deserve fuller discussion than I have been able to give them here: the position of capitalists, and that of the urban workers. Bianco (1971, 125 and 160) is quite clear that the Kuomintang regime was borne by a tight alliance of rural gentry and urban bourgeoisie, although the loss of the coastal regions to the Japanese during the war considerably weakened the importance and influence of the latter group. A greater mystery is the widely noted passivity, indeed apparent contentment, of the urban industrial work force, which despite its small size—never, before 1949, more than 1 percent of the population—might have contributed significantly to the revolution: Clubb 1978, 189ff; Barnett 1963, 19–20 and chap. 7; Bianco 1971, 83; Thomas 1983, esp. chaps. 2 and 8. Barnett's (1963, 76–80) answer, that urban labor policy was one of the few areas in which the KMT showed great tactical skill, may well be right; the slaughter of the urban cadres in 1927 (see chapter 3) may also have had a lasting effect. (I owe the latter point to an anonymous referee.)

[98] Hindley 1964, chaps. 1, 5, and 14 and pp. 40–42.

[99] I am not addressing here the question of outcome, but of political cleavage and direction of change—not "Why has there been no Indian revolution?" but "Why has the Indian class cleavage been so weak and Indian labor so unassertive?"

[100] A useful general discussion is Sen 1982, chaps. 4–7. Cf. Gough 1979, 112ff.

[101] Moore 1967, chap. 6.

[102] Mehta 1979, 748–50.

[103] Chaudhuri 1979, 368–69.

[104] Alavi 1979.

more densely covered by rail and by surface roads than China: in 1948, India had 2.68 miles of rail per 100 square miles of territory; China had 0.3.[105] In the same year, India could claim 20.5 miles of road suitable for motor traffic per 100 square miles of territory (and 7.5 miles per 10,000 inhabitants); China, 3.4 miles per 100 square miles of territory, or 2.7 miles per 10,000 inhabitants.[106] Following the analyses of Skinner and Bianco, summarized previously, we may reasonably suppose that Indian peasants had readier and cheaper access to distant markets.[107]

Equally, there is evidence that Indian justice and administration under the *raj* were less ready than their Chinese counterparts to side with local elites. In many of the twentieth-century movements of peasant protest, and routinely in those of the nineteenth century, there is an almost touching legalism: peasants appeal to statute law and contend, at least at first, that judges and administrators have misunderstood, or have failed to enforce, the relevant provisions.[108] Often enough, such protests actually achieved results: the British were wise enough to yield, or to pressure client rulers into yielding, before violence became widespread.[109] Nothing comparable appears in accounts of Chinese unrest; there, peasants appear rather to have assumed—rightly, for the most part—that the law and its agents would simply enforce the landlord's wishes.[110]

What I am suggesting is the perhaps elementary point that the Indian peasants may have revolted less because they had less to revolt about. In many ways, they had already won. They did not require a violent break-through to markets or the revolutionary construction of mechanisms of collective action, because British rule had already gone far toward giving them both. Rails and roads spread physical access to markets; British rule, whether direct or indirect, set limits to the arbitrary power of local elites and thus undermined local monopolies of marketing and credit; and the colonial and postindependence legal system permitted, at least more reliably than traditional Asian structures, the execution and enforcement of contracts.

This hypothesis can of course be tested, although it would perhaps take a major effort of collation to do so: if it is correct, peasant revolts in India should occur disproportionately in regions where access to markets was

---

[105] Banks 1971, 106 and 115. (Banks's scaling appears to err by a factor of one thousand; I have corrected his figures to conform them with the 1950 figures reported by Woytinsky and Woytinsky 1955, 360.)

[106] Woytinsky and Woytinsky 1955, 406.

[107] Gough 1979, 91–92, makes this point explicitly for the period after 1850 and credits improved transportation with the virtual absence of famine in India after 1908. (The Bengali catastrophe of 1943 was an anomaly, caused by wartime interruption of Burmese rice imports.) Local famines persisted until much later in China.

[108] Sengupta 1979; Chaudhuri 1979, 338–39.

[109] Ranga and Saraswathi 1979, esp. 52.

[110] Hinton 1966, 49–52.

most impeded and where traditional elites were least constrained in their exercise of power. The revolt of 1946–1948 in Hyderabad, one of the most traditional of the princely states; the Naxalite warfare against the *zamindari* of West Bengal, large and politically powerful landlords; and the strong representation of tribal people in all of the post-1945 revolts[111] are suggestive evidence in support of such a conjecture; but they are only that, and more research would be required to sustain or repudiate the present interpretation.

If this supposition is correct, power should still have flowed to Indian labor—the rural proletariat, the poorer peasantry, and urban workers—as trade expanded; but it should have done so peacefully and by way of reform rather than revolution. In some obvious senses, the masses did gain: the princely states disappeared, a broadly democratic regime was installed and retained, and a substantial (if frequently evaded) land reform was enacted.[112] On the other hand the dominant Congress party, in all of its significant factions, has consistently represented the interests of India's urban and rural elites[113] and has steadily advocated protectionism.[114] The Congress can be fairly portrayed as the coalition of land and capital that a trade-based theory would lead us to expect; what has yet to emerge, and what by its absence challenges the present theory, is the kind of radical movement of labor that, in similar circumstances, so uniformly appeared in the backward economies of nineteenth-century Europe.[115] The speculation of some Indian observers—that such a development has been retarded by widespread ownership of land among the peasantry, again with regional exceptions, and therefore awaits attainment of a level of rural proletarization comparable with that of prerevolutionary China—may well be correct.[116]

The experience of the Caribbean and of the densely populated regions of Central America appears to underline this point. Prerevolutionary Cuba, it is frequently observed, had the highest levels of urbanization and of rural proletarization in Latin America;[117] present-day El Salvador is

[111] Gough 1979, 114.

[112] Sen 1982, 175–76 and 181–83.

[113] "Congress adapts itself to the local power structure. It recruits from among those who have local power and influence." Weiner 1967, 15.

[114] Krueger 1974, 292–94; Bhagwati and Desai 1970, chaps. 15–17.

[115] The industrial unions and the parties of the Left are fragmented and impotent (Ghose 1971, 69–73 and chaps. 7 and 8). Regionally, agricultural workers have achieved some strength of organization (Sen 1982, 196–209).

[116] A Dr. Ahmad, in a perceptive report of 1973 to the principal Communist peasants' association, estimated that workers constituted no more than 30 percent of the agricultural population; the Green Revolution, he observed, had actually strengthened rural landownership. Sen 1982, 197.

[117] Skidmore and Smith 1984, 261–62.

both Central America's most densely populated state (see Table 4.4 and n. 18) and one with unusually concentrated landownership and a high and growing proportion of landless or land-poor peasants.[118]

In the densely populated regions of Africa, Robert Bates suggests in an important work in progress,[119] labor was similarly radicalized in the course of the postwar expansion. Colonial rule in Kenya, by partitioning the country into native "reserves" and "white highlands," had given rise to overpopulation in the former and to a substantial rural proletariat in the latter. Pushed to the wall by a shift in production techniques (the abandonment of grain farming in favor of dairying) that threatened their livelihood, the rural workers exploded—for the most part against black landowners on the reserves—in the rebellion known as Mau-Mau. Redistribution of the white settlers' lands after independence damped down this conflict; but some students suggest that, given high and growing population density (Table 4.4), it is bound to reappear.

Economies Abundant in Land, Scarce in
Capital and Labor: South America,
Most of Africa, and Most of Southwest Asia

The postwar expansion of trade renewed tension between the urban and rural sectors of the Latin American economies and, sooner or later, doomed the populist experiments of the depression and the war years. In some cases—Peru, for example, under Odría after 1948[120]—landowner power was nakedly reasserted, capital and labor were crushed, and primary exports were again pursued to the neglect of almost all else. In Bolivia, analogous efforts to restore the traditional dominance of a particular narrow "landowner" elite, the proprietors of the great tin mines, ignited a workers' revolution in 1952; it was tamed and finally reversed by a countermobilization of landholding peasants.[121] In the more advanced economies of the region, however—some of which, as we have seen earlier (see n. 11), were at the threshold of capital abundance—subtler and more complex changes ensued.

Everywhere, political conflict involved three trade-related issues: tariffs and quotas; wage rates and trade union power; and inflation. The populist coalitions had enacted, and still favored, protection and high wages; and

---

[118] Skidmore and Smith 1984, 310–11. Nicaragua, as a thinly populated state, should have experienced a radicalization of land rather than labor: see also Skidmore and Smith 1984, 306.

[119] Bates, "The Agrarian Origins of Mau Mau," chapter of book in progress on Kenya, mimeo, Duke University, 1987.

[120] Skidmore and Smith 1984, 213–14.

[121] Spalding 1977, 217–22.

they had accepted inflation as the price of these policies and, within limits, as a political good: classically, it transferred wealth from creditors and *rentiers* to wage earners, entrepreneurs, and debtors;[122] and, by leading to externally overvalued domestic currencies, it permitted the regime to ration imports and thus gave it important levers of patronage and control.[123] To the traditionally export-oriented sectors—including, above all, agriculture—all three policies were anathema: tariffs raised the costs of equipment and of many consumption goods; high wages and overvalued currencies made exports uncompetitive; and rationing of hard currency and imports entailed, whether through corruption or red tape, the extraction of significant rents, which in turn further raised the price of what they exported.[124]

Now repeatedly since 1945 throughout Latin America, military-backed (and some other)[125] regimes have imposed the "antipopulist" options in these three areas: they have halted inflation, suppressed wages and unions, and reduced tariffs and quotas. This formula fairly characterizes the dictatorships in early postwar Peru and subsequently in Argentina, Bolivia, Brazil, Chile, and Uruguay.[126] These governments have not, however, all served as mere tools of the landed interest. In contrast to earlier military regimes, some—particularly in the most advanced economies of the region[127]—have pursued shrewd and often successful schemes of rapid, export-led economic development. In doing so, they have been perfectly willing to curtail the traditional prerogatives of agriculture and to ally themselves with capitalists (particularly with multinational corporations and banks) and technocrats.[128] This distinctiveness has led to a spate of scholarly interest in what has come to be called "bureaucratic-authoritarianism" (O'Donnell 1979) or the "new authoritarianism" (Collier 1979).

Although many plausible explanations of these regimes have been advanced,[129] the present theory suggests a somewhat different perspective.

[122] Wage earners, particularly if they are well organized or well connected to the incumbent regime, win indexation in times of inflation; businessmen gain as inventories appreciate. See the seminal analysis of Keynes 1933.

[123] I owe this insight to my colleague Barbara Geddes.

[124] The pioneering treatment of this entire issue is Krueger 1974.

[125] This is an important reservation, for it indicates that "B-A" (bureaucratic-authoritarian) rule was far from being the only possible solution to some universal crisis of the Latin American economies in this period. As even O'Donnell (1979, 91n.) conceded, the Mexican regime of the PRI bore (and still bears) many similarities of policy to the "B-A" governments; Cardoso and Faletto (1979, 39) assert the same of Venezuela and Costa Rica.

[126] The "Nasserist" military regime in Peru after 1968 is the signal exception (Skidmore and Smith 1984, 218–21). For excellent sketches of the common properties of the other dictatorships in this period, see Cotler 1979, 260–61, and Skidmore and Smith 1984, 61–63.

[127] O'Donnell 1979, esp. chap. 1; more eloquently, Hirschman 1979, 61–65.

[128] This point is almost universally conceded: see, e.g., Cardoso and Faletto 1979, 50.

[129] To mention only the most notable examples: O'Donnell (1979) attributed the rise of

Particularly in countries that are near the threshold of capital abundance, and given the military importance of economic development and the natural eagerness of international banks to find lucrative investments, the temptation may arise to try to "jump" a stage of development: by suppressing wages, borrowing massively from abroad, importing expertise, and cooperating closely with technologically advanced multinational firms, these regimes induce managers to behave *as if* capital were already abundant—that is, to renounce protection and to pursue exports.[130] If that can be done, and it appears that it can be, at least in the most advanced and capital-intensive sectors, then the traditional export-oriented alliance of landowners and the military can be expanded and altered to include (perhaps, even, to be dominated by) capitalists and technocrats. Abundant land and capital, in the ascendant because of expanding world trade, confront scarce labor.

It would follow from this analysis that the whole scheme, risky enough to begin with, might collapse if the international banks' zeal to lend, and international capitalists' eagerness to invest, flagged before a real abundance of capital could be created. Lacking the plentiful capital that direct pipelines to New York and London had temporarily created, South American capitalists would revert to form, rediscovering the virtues of the populist alliance, of democracy, and of state protection and subsidy. Only the military, the agro-exporters, and the landowners would remain fully committed to free trade.[131] Much of the recent revival of South American democracy—and of its essential precondition, a renewed acceptance by local capitalists of that form of rule—can, I suspect, be explained in exactly these terms. On the other hand, the continued expansion of international trade can only strengthen the landowning and land-intensive sectors of most South American societies; hence the continued advance of the urban, neo-populist coalitions is far from assured.[132]

"bureaucratic-authoritarianism" to an inevitable crisis of "deepening"—i.e., of moving into heavy industry and the production of capital goods—in the major South American economies. (This thesis, inventive and compelling as it first seemed, has been subjected to telling criticism: see, inter alia, the essays of Hirschman, Serra, and Kaufman in Collier 1979.) Schmitter (1971 and 1973) advanced a variant of Marx's thesis from the *Eighteenth Brumaire*: "due to internal fragmentation and/or external dependence, none of the warring classes is capable of imposing its model of political order upon the others" (Schmitter 1973, 188). Kurth (1979a), drawing inventive comparisons with earlier European development, suggested a market-conditioned correlation between phases of industrialization and types of rule.

[130] I emphasize again that this tactic is open only to economies that are already near the threshold of capital abundance. No amount of borrowing could raise a Paraguay or a Bolivia into even a semblance of capital abundance.

[131] Present-day Chile demonstrates how narrow and fragile a base this coalition can provide, even when it inspires some prosperity.

[132] At the time of this writing, the ongoing Brazilian crisis seemed almost to epitomize the deep conflicts sketched out here.

In the land-rich regions that constitute the majority of the African continent, politics since World War II and, even more sharply, since independence has revealed a fundamental cleavage between the peasantry and an urban coalition of labor and capital (see especially Bates 1981). Almost everywhere so far, the urban alliance has gained the upper hand, dividing and exploiting the rural sector for its own benefit. Local manufactures have gained massive protection; urban workers have won high wages, cheap food, and a bloated public sector; agricultural exports have been taxed almost out of existence; and inflation and overvalued currencies have prevailed as widely, and have achieved the same results, as in Latin America.[133] The overall consequences of this bias have been spectacular: in Zambia in one representative period, for example, wage earners' returns increased by 32 percent between 1964 and 1968; peasants' earnings, by 3.4 percent.[134]

Cohen (1974), Markovitz (1977), Nelson (1979), Bates (1981), Olson (1982, 167–82) and others have advanced cogent reasons for the success of the urban sectors: distance and illiteracy make the peasantry hard to organize; urban firms are normally oligopolistic or monopolistic, whereas peasants compete; the volatile urban sectors are near enough to the state's centers of power (ministries, army barracks) to threaten them continually. Still, the constantly increasing potential returns to land-intensive pursuits, and the uniformly disastrous consequences of the pro-urban policy, must sooner or later offer a tempting target to political entrepreneurs. The rural-urban cleavage in Africa is unlikely to wither away, and the rural forces are likely to gain in boldness and strength over the next decades.[135]

Such a sea change, I suspect, is one force behind the fundamentalist Islamic revolutions of Southwest Asia, and particularly of Iran. In many of these land-rich countries (see Table 4.4), as in much of Africa, urban-based "developmental coalitions" of labor, capital, and the military have generally held sway since World War II.[136] The peasantry and the marginalized ur-

---

[133] On protection, see Bates 1981, chap. 4; on wages, Cohen 1974, chap. 6, and Markovitz 1977, 266–71; on food prices and subsidies, Bates 1981, chap. 2, and Nelson 1979, 393; on the taxation of agriculture and the resultant economic dislocations, Markovitz 1977, 271–73, and Bates 1981, chap. 6.

[134] Markovitz 1977, 272. In the light of such abundantly documented facts, the persistent efforts of some observers to see in Africa's urban work force an exploited, selfless, and potentially transforming proletariat leave one bewildered. See, for particularly egregious examples, Gutkind 1974, Gutkind, Cohen, and Copans 1978, and Cohen's (1974, 187–89) heroic attempt to show that urban workers actually do not earn more than peasants. At most—see the Iranian evidence immediately below—one could regard as victims the displaced peasants who now inhabit urban slums.

[135] The policies and ruling coalition of the Ivory Coast (Bates 1981, 131–32; Markovitz 1977, 301–2) may foreshadow such a development.

[136] The regime of the Shah in Iran, exactly like the African ones studied by Bates, imposed controls and subsidies that favored urban dwellers, paid domestic farmers less than world

ban workers (the latter usually the wreckage of the declining rural economy) have paid the price of "modernization" and of urban prosperity.[137] Now, organized by a convenient elite of mullahs and by a traditionalist ideology, and perhaps sensing the opportunities that expanding trade offers to land-intensive production, the peasants have struck back, sweeping aside the urban elites and their entire vision of modernity.[138] A similar threat of traditionalist revolution, the present theory suggests, looms not only over such other land-rich economies of the Middle East as that of Syria (Table 4.4), but over much of Africa.[139]

Economies Abundant in Land and Capital,
Scarce in Labor: The United States, Oceania,
Canada, and The USSR

The two leading cases in support of our theoretical expectations in this category are, surprisingly, the United States and the USSR. The parallels between the two societies—recalling, as we must, that the Soviet Union is still by far the less capital abundant of the two—go far to explain the weakness of mass support for free trade in both and lead to a very different prognosis for the Soviet Union than for eastern Europe, as outlined previously.

American business, as we have seen in earlier chapters, steadily diluted its once rigid protectionism after about 1890; by the later 1930s, the most

market prices, and squandered resources on inefficient state farms that were to serve as models of "modern" agriculture. Keddie 1981, 163 and 165–67; Katouzian 1981, 304–11.

[137] Iranian agriculture was particularly advanced in its orientation to markets and to exporting. Since the end of the last century, Iran had been a net importer of grain, its farmers having shifted to the production of cotton, fruits, and tobacco for export. As late as 1968—i.e., after the early and most successful phases of land reform, and before the rise of the "farm corporations," or quasi-state farms—the country's agricultural balance of trade was still positive; but by 1978 $264 million in total agricultural exports were countered by imports of $2.2 *billion* in food alone. The farming sector began to collapse: from 49 percent of the work force and 22 percent of GNP in 1967–1968, agriculture fell in a decade to 32 percent of the work force and 9 percent of GNP. By 1973, something like 8 percent of the population was migrating to the cities *each year*, and official policy welcomed this development. See, inter alia, Katouzian 1981, 257, 259, 304–6, and 326–27; Binder 1980, 25–26 and 35; and Keddie 1981, 164.

[138] The ruralist base of the Iranian revolution and the close ties between rural clergy and peasanty, I suggest, go far to explain the fundamentalism and conservatism that seem otherwise inexplicable. A further exacerbation was the expropriation of religious lands: Binder 1980, 26 and 35. On the role of the recent urban migrants in the revolution, see Keddie 1981, 246 and 250–51, and Katouzian 1981, 337; on the postrevolutionary shifts of policy in favor of the peasantry, Keddie 1981, 264 and 269, and Bakhash 1984, chap. 8, esp. p. 211.

[139] On the other hand, if this analysis is correct, densely populated Egypt faces little serious danger from Islamic fundamentalism.

capital-intensive branches of U.S. industry clearly favored free trade.[140] In the extraordinary situation that prevailed after 1945, with virtually every other formerly advanced economy in rubble and North America accounting for 36 percent of world exports, or twice its prewar share,[141] even organized labor in the United States enlisted wholeheartedly in the drive for wider markets and lower tariffs.[142] Only slowly did it become apparent, as the rest of the world recovered, that free trade was not in the interest of America's workers.[143] Indeed, as follows trivially from the Stolper-Samuelson theorem, openness could benefit them only if the gains from trade were redistributed massively in their favor; and such an action was not even coherently proposed, much less seriously considered.[144]

The consequences have been all but inevitable. Labor, and the more labor-intensive economic sectors, have turned sharply protectionist as trade's share of GDP has expanded dramatically since 1973–1974.[145] At the same time, however, the gains of ever-expanding trade have flowed to those factors in which the United States is abundantly endowed, namely capital and (despite agriculture's much publicized travails) land, and to enterprises that use either factor intensively; labor, the scarce factor, has lost ground.[146] Even within the United States, the more land-abundant re-

[140] Ferguson 1984, esp. 62 and 90–92.

[141] In 1947, 36 percent of world exports originated in North America; the comparable figure for 1937 had been 17 percent, for 1926 21 percent. Woytinsky and Woytinsky 1955, 45.

[142] Admittedly, union leaders endorsed Roosevelt's very modest measures of trade liberalization even in the 1930s (see the discussion at n. 29 of chapter 3), but they did so only as part of a "package" in which pro-union legislation was the obvious bait (Ferguson 1984, 89). After World War II, they became persuaded, or so their literature steadily announced, that free trade directly served American labor's interests.

[143] Labor's endorsement of free trade for a period of some thirty years, in an extremely labor-scarce economy with few redistributive mechanisms (see immediately below), cannot be reconciled with the Stolper-Samuelson theorem or with the derivative theory advanced here. The mystery is compounded by U.S. policies toward taxation and investment that virtually guaranteed the export of jobs (Kojima 1977, cited in Schmiegelow 1985, 278).

[144] One obvious route would have been to finance a major expansion of welfare benefits out of a new value-added tax.

[145] On U.S. labor, see for example Zysman 1983, 277–78. On average between 1960 and 1966, trade—the sum of exports and imports—constituted 9.5 percent of U.S. GDP; between 1967 and 1972, 10.8 percent. In 1973, this figure rose to 13.7 percent; in 1974, to 17.3 percent; and on average between 1975 and 1980, to 18.2 percent. Organization for Economic Co-operation and Development 1982, 62–63.

[146] Between 1973 and 1980, hourly nominal wages in manufacturing rose on average by 8.6 percent per year in the United States; over the same period, consumer prices rose by 9.2 percent per year. Over the total period, then, wages fell in real terms by about 4 percent. During the same interval, real GDP per capita rose on average by 1.3 percent annually, or a total of 9.5 percent. Organization for Economic Co-operation and Development 1982, 77 and 84.

gions, the West and South, have gained at the expense of the more labor-abundant East and of the "rust belt" of the Upper Midwest.[147]

Political strength has, as expected, shifted in tandem with economic power. The unions and the Democratic party have grown continually weaker, and the political center of gravity has moved palpably to the right. It would be hard not to play the prophet in these circumstances: as far as one can now foresee, the Democrats, repudiating a tradition that dates back to their nineteenth-century defense of southern and western agriculture, will increasingly embrace protectionism and, much like Labour in Britain, will be reduced to a regional party of industrial decay.[148] In the burgeoning and export-oriented West and South the Republicans will achieve something close to one-party domination; and class tensions, often masquerading as racial conflict,[149] will become increasingly embittered.

In the Soviet Union, Hough (1986a and b) has argued cogently, the opening of the economy to foreign competition, and particularly the pursuit of exports (following the East German model),[150] has come to be seen as the sine qua non of efforts at economic reform. Inevitably, moves in this direction meet desperate opposition from entrenched rent seekers in management and in the party; but—and here is the profound contrast to labor-abundant eastern Europe—economic liberalization also threatens labor. Just as in the labor-scarce United States, openness in the labor-scarce economy of the USSR can only mean (barring, again, improbable redistributions of the gains from trade) a real decline in workers' incomes.

In eastern as in western Europe, trade tends to unite capital and labor; in the USSR, as in the United States, trade pits labor against capital. In eastern Europe, to be more precise, expanding world trade strengthens a reformist and free-trading coalition of labor and advanced management; only rent seekers and the dwindling landed sector embrace continued protection. In the USSR, growing world markets entice only the competitive managers of state industry and agriculture; not only rent seekers, but the great mass of workers, demand continued protection.[151] The Stalinist era of course reminds us that workers' opposition can be crushed in the USSR (see again chapter 3); but the alignment described here surely makes open-

---

[147] Norton 1986, 3, 16–17, and 25–27.
[148] This passage was written in the summer of 1987. I find little pleasure in rereading it, for final revision, less than four weeks before the 1988 U.S. presidential elections.
[149] The majority of blacks and Hispanics in the United States are still workers, and the working classes of many old industrial centers are disproportionately black or Hispanic.
[150] Hough 1986a, 500.
[151] "[Under Brezhnev] protectionism for the managers also meant protectionism for the workers, and this social policy was a key part of the Soviet formula of political stability." Hough 1986a, 496n.

ness and restructuring more problematic in the Soviet Union than they have been, or are likely to be, in eastern Europe.[152]

Similar conflicts, similar divisions, and a similar shift of power away from labor and toward capital and land can be observed in Australia, New Zealand, and Canada in the postwar period. In all three countries, expanding international markets have enticed the most capital-intensive and efficient domestic industries to join primary producers and retailers in questioning policies of high protection that had long seemed untouchable. In all three, workers and, more particularly, trade unions have allied with internationally uncompetitive producers to oppose almost every step toward greater openness. And in all three the resultant conflicts have shattered old alliances and led to dramatic reversals of traditional positions and loyalties. In Australia and New Zealand, the balance of political power has moved clearly to organized labor's disadvantage; in Canada the result remains more ambiguous. I propose to examine Australia as the paradigm case, treating the other two histories only in brief comparison.

The traditionally protectionist Australian Labor party,[153] which had held power since 1941, lost in 1949 to a slightly less protectionist coalition of the Liberal and Country[154] parties, representing respectively (and rather directly) capital and land. Labor, as few observers then foresaw,[155] would regain national power only after an absence of twenty-four years and would hold it in all for only five of the thirty-five years between 1949 and 1984.[156] (This is a point to which it will prove helpful to revert.)

Depending overwhelmingly on external markets, Australian agriculture had always been free-trading; so, as soon as their ores began to find lucrative outlets in Japanese mills, were the country's extractive industries.[157] By the 1960s, however, these groups found increasing sympathy among sectors of large-scale, capital-intensive Australian industry and from an Australian state that saw Japanese and American friendship as strategically desirable.[158] Demands for greater openness intensified when, in the world

[152] Poland, as the eastern European economy whose land-labor ratio most closely approximates that of the USSR (see Table 4.4), must illustrate graphically for the Soviet elite the risks that economic openness can bring (cf. Hough 1986a, 490); even as Hungary, with somewhat similar factor endowments, indicates the opportunities.

[153] See my discussion in chapter 2.

[154] More recently, the Country party, seeking a wider electorate, renamed itself first the National Country party, and then simply the National party. See the fuller discussion below.

[155] Alexander 1980, 183; Greenwood 1974c, 419.

[156] The period 1972–1975 and from 1983.

[157] Tsokhas 1984, 42–44 and 63.

[158] The Australian Industries Development Association (AIDA), which represented the larger firms and had traditionally been protectionist, began in this period to take a markedly less rigid view of tariffs than its traditional ally, the Associated Chambers of Manufactures of Australia; the latter was the voice of the smaller and less capital-intensive firms. The Metal

recession of the later 1960s, Australia began to manifest at least a mild case of the "Latin American disease" common to protectionist agricultural exporters: inflation, exchange-rate problems, and a declining balance on current account.[159] Only through lower costs for wages and machinery, primary-product exporters contended, could they meet international competition and regain lost markets; moreover, as both agriculture and export-oriented industry perceived, Australian protection might be traded away for reciprocal concessions from Japan and the newly industrializing countries (NICs) of Asia.[160] State action responded to these concerns: the nominally autonomous Tariff Board, with authority to set rates, began publicly to examine, and then to remedy, cases of "overprotection." Duties fell, if at first only modestly; and Liberal-Country cabinets deftly turned aside the outraged protests of the inefficient.[161]

The changing situation threw party politics askew. In startling reversals of form, the leader of the Country party emerged as an impassioned protectionist, and the leader of the Labor party as a strong advocate of greater openness.[162] Each, in the opinion of many observers, saw the chance of a breakthrough into new and more promising electorates: Country might finally gain an urban foothold, among import-threatened smaller businesses; Labor could hope to attract—and, on the evidence to date, did attract[163]—consumption-oriented possessors of human capital among the rapidly expanding professional and white-collar groups. To simplify drastically, Country pursued urban losers and Labor pursued urban professionals. (Country's change of name, to National, was of course a part of its strategy.)

In the event, the incumbents' moderate corrections did not avail. Labor regained power on a wave of economic discontent in late 1972 and, when hit almost immediately by the world oil crisis of 1973, adopted with a vengeance the measure that its leader, Whitlam, had advocated: a 25 percent "across the board" cut in existing tariffs.[164] The medicine proved too

---

Trades Industry Association also came to favor greater openness (Tsokhas 1984, 1 and 24). It should also be observed that industry as a whole was rapidly becoming more capital-intensive, not least because of the high level of Australian wages: Alexander 1980, 309. On the importance of the Japanese and U.S. connections, see Alexander 1980, 204–5 and 210.

[159] Alexander 1980, 265, 275–75, and 285; Jupp 1982, 54. More recently, the country's plight has been compared explicitly with that of Argentina: *New York Times*, 3 April 1985, sec. 1, p. 11, and 19 January 1987, p. D6.

[160] Tsokhas 1984, 19–20 and 42–43.

[161] For the history of this period, see the invaluable discussion of Tsokhas 1984, 18–25.

[162] Jupp 1982, 80; Tsokhas 1984, 18 and 25. Country leader McEwen's embrace of protection predictably provoked outrage among rural groups, including particularly the woolgrowers: Tsokhas 1984, 45.

[163] See for example Kemp 1985, and Aitken 1985, 212–15.

[164] Alexander 1980, 305.

strong: unemployment shot up dramatically, most notably in the long-coddled and hopelessly uncompetitive automobile industry (and, of course, in its ancillary suppliers);[165] and inflation, fueled both by Labor's already expansive fiscal policies and by outlays to succor the jobless, accelerated wildly.[166] The trade unions, Labor's traditional mainstay, denounced the tariff cuts and tempered their support of the cabinet.[167] In an atmosphere of unusual acrimony and constitutional crisis, Labor was driven from office in late 1975.[168]

The restored Liberal-Country coalition promptly braked inflation and sought to expand exports.[169] It moderated, but did not abandon, Labor's tariff reductions.[170] An expert commission, the Crawford Study Group, reporting in 1979, urged a further dismantling of protection, and the government largely pursued that policy, proceeding however with extreme caution where major losses of employment would ensue.[171] It could easily be foreseen, however, that more drastic action would be required if major losses to the economy as a whole were to be avoided.

That however would entail an even greater abridgment of labor's influence, which had already waned considerably under Liberal-Country hegemony. Even in the 1950s and 1960s, changes in Australian labor legislation and economic structure (the substitution of oil and gas for coal, the pronounced shift of employment to the tertiary sector and to white-collar jobs) and the displacement of Communists from positions of leadership had markedly tamed the once notoriously prickly and powerful trade unions.[172] That tendency accelerated under the Fraser government after 1975.[173] The vitiation of the unions in turn weakened the traditional Labor party base.[174]

---

[165] Tsokhas 1984, 25. Unemployment, officially at 2.25 percent in 1972, had reached 4.0 percent by 1976. (It of course rose still higher in the ensuing deflation.) Alexander 1980, 308. On the automobile industry, see the conclusions of the Crawford Study Group, summarized in Alexander 1980, 346.

[166] Alexander 1980, 289 and 318. From an average of 3.5 percent per year between 1950 and 1970, inflation had reached 6 percent in 1972–1973. Under Labor, it was 13 percent in 1973–1974, 17 percent in 1974–1975. Alexander 1980, 308.

[167] Tsokhas 1984, 26.

[168] In a startling and probably unconstitutional stroke, the governor-general dismissed the Labor ministry while it still had a majority in the House. In the ensuing elections, however, Labor was soundly beaten: its share of the popular vote fell from 49 to 43 percent; its share of House seats, from 52 to 28 percent. Archer and Maddox 1985; Jupp 1982, appendix.

[169] Alexander 1980, 309 and 346.

[170] Tsokhas 1984, 26.

[171] Alexander 1980, 346; Tsokhas 1984, 26.

[172] Alexander 1980, 216–20; Kemp 1985, 198–200.

[173] Tsokhas 1984, 147–49.

[174] On relations between the Labor party and the unions, see Jupp 1982, 103–5. A crucial factor in Labor's long exile from office was the secession, in 1955, of anticommunist and

Ultimately, the Labor party found that its only hope lay in a far-ranging abandonment of its traditional ideology and working-class base; that was mirrored not only in the daring move on protection but in the pursuit of white-collar votes, an amnesia about state ownership and "socialism," and efforts to curtail inflationary wage settlements.[175] Since Labor's resumption of office in 1983, these tendencies have expanded dramatically: protection of both goods and services has been significantly reduced, the currency devalued and then floated, and real wages reduced by some 5 percent.[176] Capital's response has been enthusiastic, but labor's rank and file have threatened revolt.[177] Nonetheless, the overall effect, even in circumstances of a world slump in commodity prices, has been more favorable for the government than conventional wisdom would have suggested.[178]

In New Zealand, similarly, a protectionist Labour party has traditionally captured most workers' votes; the urban middle and upper classes, and most farmers, have backed a National party that favored greater economic openness.[179] As in Australia, Labour lost power in 1949, rarely to hold it again: it governed in only six of the ensuing thirty years, 1957–1960 and 1972–1975.[180] In power, the National party removed controls on imports and foreign exchange and shifted investment away from industry and toward agriculture, which as late as 1977 still provided over three-quarters of New Zealand's export earnings.[181] It also succeeded in whittling away many of the legal guarantees of trade union power.[182] By the late 1970s, Labour had been compelled to offer firm guarantees about trade policy to the farming sector and to dilute its economic (if, to be sure, not its foreign-policy) socialism almost out of existence.[183] Since its resumption of office

---

largely Catholic sections to form what eventually became the Democratic Labor party. Alexander 1980, 190–93.

[175] Woodward 1985, 158–61; Jupp 1982, chap. 7 and p. 117; Alexander 1980, 305.

[176] *New York Times*, 7 January 1985, p. D10; 28 February 1985, p. D19; 3 April 1985, sec. 1, p. 11; 15 February 1987, sec. 4, p. 3.

[177] *New York Times*, 7 January 1985, p. D10, and 3 April 1985, sec. 1, p. 11. Farmers, battered by plummeting world commodity prices, have also demanded greater relief, including specifically greater pressure to open American and European markets: *New York Times*, 28 July 1986, sec. 4, p. 1, and 19 January 1987, p. D6.

[178] *New York Times*, 15 February 1987, sec. 4, p. 3.

[179] On the demographics of party support, see Levine 1979, 88–89, and Levine and Robinson 1976, chap. 11, esp. p. 139; on Labour's greater support of protection, Condliffe and Airey, 1953, 278–79.

[180] Election results are listed comprehensively in Levine 1979, appendix. Labour regained office in July 1984; see immediately below.

[181] Mitchell 1969, 107–8; Senghaas 1985, 116.

[182] Levine 1979, 72.

[183] Levine 1979, 73; Webber 1978. By "foreign-policy socialism" I mean the party's anti-nuclear and anti-ANZUS positions.

in 1984, Labour has swung sharply to the right in economic policy. Exactly as in Australia, the currency has been floated, import regulations and subsidies dismantled, and social benefits and real wages reduced.[184] Despite the resistance of many workers, these policies have proved surprisingly popular.

Canadian politics, notoriously, are crosscut by a myriad of ethnic, linguistic, regional, and religious cleavages that make interpretation exceedingly difficult.[185] Still, I will advance here the hypothesis, subject to detailed examination by specialists, that the recent "two-and-one-half" party system at the federal level—Liberals, Progressive Conservatives, and New Democrats—can be understood in its broadest outlines as a parallel to the Australian configuration. The Canadian Liberals, like the Australian party of the same name, represent essentially the interests of urban capital; the Progressive Conservatives are Canada's "Country" party, standing particularly for the primary producers of the prairies and the eastern seaboard; and the New Democrats are emerging as a genuine labor party, embodying the interests of urban workers and of labor-intensive farmers.[186]

From this perspective, the Conservatives' frenzied pursuit of grain exports, the country's long slide into the economic doldrums under its policy of industrial protection, the elites' recent and reluctant acceptance of greater economic openness, the emergence of the New Democrats as a substantial bloc, and the curtailment of trade union power can all be seen as parallels to the Australian experience and, at least in part, as effects of the global expansion of trade.[187] Particularly the recent turn to reciprocal free trade with the United States, advocated by a Royal Commission (under Donald Macdonald) appointed by the Liberals and pushed energetically by the Progressive Conservative government of Brian Mulroney, resembles (albeit under different auspices) the policy shifts of Australia and New Zealand.[188]

CONCLUSION

It must again be emphasized that shifting patterns of trade, even when they are so dramatic as the postwar world expansion, can explain only a fraction

[184] *New York Times*, 10 June 1985, p. D8.

[185] I have found no secondary literature so confusing, provincial, or uninformative as that on recent Canadian politics. See, for representative examples, Fox 1977, esp. chaps. 4, 8, and 10; Thorburn 1979; and Clarke, Jensen, le Duc, and Pammett 1984.

[186] For evidence on the regional and class distribution of the Canadian vote, see Thorburn 1979, appendix; Clarke et al. 1984, appendix; and Wilson 1976, esp. table 5.

[187] For general sketches of the postwar period, see Finlay and Sprague 1979, pt. 6, and Clarke et al. 1984, chaps. 1 and 7.

[188] A concise and useful account of the shift can be found, surprisingly, in the protectionist tract of Laxer 1986, esp. chap. 1. Also see the *New York Times*, 16 March 1987, p. 1.

of domestic politics. They are one current, albeit a powerful one, among many. Such purely internal factors as culture, institutions, and leadership play, and surely have played in the post-1945 world, an important role that the discussion here wholly neglects. (Who can doubt, for example, that postwar French history would have been entirely different in the absence either of a heritage of religious conflict or of the towering personality of de Gaulle?)

Still, the correlation between factor endowments and the general pattern of politics in these years seems impressively close to what the theory would lead us to expect. (I shall discuss further below what appear to be the major exceptions.) We may be justified in seeing trade's impact on factor endowments as a kind of constraint, within which other aspects produce lesser effects.

Only in labor-rich and capital- and land-poor Asia in this period, for example, do we observe major social revolutions backed indisputably by landless laborers and the poorer peasantry: first in China, then in Vietnam, Laos, and Cambodia, soon (one may predict) in the Philippines and South Korea. The attempts—earlier in the Philippines, in Indonesia, and in Malaysia—are also significant. Whether, within this category, a country avoids or suppresses revolutionary activity, or whether its revolution occurs bloodily or in relative peace, must depend on domestic or accidental factors; but the likelihood of greatly increased working-class power and assertiveness we can safely attribute to trade and endowments.

Similarly, it is only in land-rich and capital-poor Latin America that we see a reassertion of landed power, either in its traditional military form or in the coalition with foreign capital that underpins the "bureaucratic-authoritarian" regime; only here do we encounter a suppression of *both* labor and protectionist local capital. Again, such factors as military tradition, leftist strength, and even international experience of military and bureaucratic elites undoubtedly affect individual countries' relative vulnerability; but these work within the constraints (or so it appears) set by the region's factor endowments and its exposure to expanding international markets.

A far-reaching and durable reconciliation of labor and capital, with substantial concessions from each, appears almost exclusively in developed Europe and Japan—regions that are, not coincidentally, abundant in both those factors. And a renewed assertiveness of capital—a willingness to risk, and often an ability to win, major conflicts with labor—is to be found principally in the world's few capital-rich and labor-poor economies, including the United States and the USSR. Both categories, however, exhibit seeming anomalies, which should be frankly addressed.

1. Until about 1970, the labor-scarce developed economies of the West—the United States, Australia, New Zealand, and Canada—appeared to parallel western Europe's forms of class accommodation. Even today,

the predicted assault on labor is fully evident only in the case of the United States. My tentative answer to this apparent anomaly is to point to the effective insulation from world markets that, through various means—the exercise of hegemonic power and seigniorage by the United States, overt protectionism in the other cases—all of these labor-scarce advanced economies maintained until the late 1960s. To continue their isolation now would cost more in forgone gains of trade than, probably, any of these societies is willing to bear; and the predictions of increasing class conflict and diminishing labor influence can be taken as future tests of the theory's accuracy.

2. The United Kingdom under Margaret Thatcher *does* exhibit the kind of class polarization and evisceration of labor that are predicted to arise in labor-scarce, rather than labor-abundant, advanced economies. The obvious parallel, frequently drawn in the popular press and by the principals, is between Britain and the United States rather than between Britain and Europe; even Thatcher's degree of working-class support resembles Ronald Reagan's.

There is of course one crucial parallel between Britain and the United States, which is not addressed by the theory advanced here: in both, segments of organized labor had been able, through domestic monopoly and international hegemony, to extract large rents.[189] In both, the beneficiaries of those arrangements naturally objected when exposure to larger markets—America's larger trade share of GDP after 1973, Britain's accession to the European Community—broke the monopolies. Nonetheless, an essential difference is predicted, and the prediction may serve as a future test of the theory: in Britain the protectionism will fade and labor will accommodate with capital on the continental model; in the United States, protection will find a mass base and will kindle a long and bitter struggle between labor and the rest of the society.

· · ·

As may be expected when one analyzes events that are still in flux, our results for the post-1945 period are somewhat more ambiguous and tentative than those of earlier chapters. Still, the overall conformity of events to the theory seems good enough to justify further elaboration and testing. I propose now to extend our examination, by way of contrast, to three much earlier episodes of changing exposure to trade: classical Greece, the declining Roman Empire, and sixteenth-century Europe.

[189] The wages of U.S. workers in the automobile and steel industries, or the featherbedding of British craft unions in many sectors, are obvious examples.

CHAPTER FIVE

Earlier Periods of Changing Trade: Classical Greece, the Declining Roman Empire, and Sixteenth-Century Europe

THE VARIATIONS in world trade over the past two centuries have exceeded, in volume and geographical extent, everything in previous human history. We should err, however, if we concluded that earlier fluctuations had been insignificant. Historians are well aware of the importance of international and interregional commerce, and of the collapse of such trade, in previous epochs; and, if the theory advanced in these pages is correct, it should illuminate important features of those earlier episodes as well. To test the broader historical applicability of this approach, I propose to examine three cases that antedate the industrial revolution. First I shall treat in some detail the rapid expansion of trade, and its political consequences, in ancient Greece; then, much more summarily, the collapse of commerce in the last centuries of the Roman Empire and its renewed expansion in the sixteenth-century West.

CLASSICAL GREECE

Changes in Trade and in Factor Endowments

By the sixth and fifth centuries B.C., the Greek states had developed an international trade of surprising extent and quantity. Athens derived much of its grain supply from what is now southern Russia and its tin (needed for the manufacture of bronze) from Britain; Greek metalwares and pottery regularly reached modern Switzerland and Bavaria and traveled singly almost to modern Paris and the suburbs of today's Stockholm;[1] Greek colonies (among them Marseilles and Odessa) were planted as far afield as the

---

[1] Boardman 1964, 223–29. Archaeological evidence and scholarly expertise have become essential for any reading of the primary sources from this period. (To take only the most startling example, it now appears more than likely that the famous fragment on the *Constitution of Athens* was not Aristotle's work but must be understood as a piece of prodemocratic propaganda from the last years of the Peloponnesian War: Hopper 1976, 189–91.) It is for this reason, and out of a sharp awareness of my own lack of the requisite expertise, that despite the ready availability of translated classical sources I rely principally on secondary works in this discussion.

east coast of Spain and the eastern shore of the Black Sea; and Greek trading posts extended to Spain's Atlantic coast and into Egypt.[2]

After an earlier expansion of trade under the "Minoan" civilization of
ancient Crete, which collapsed no later than 1300 B.C.,[3] Greece had fallen
into a Dark Age (roughly 1200 to 750) of local self-sufficiency and rule by
a landholding, warrior aristocracy: the society that we encounter in Hesiod
and Homer.[4] Even the art of writing disappeared; the Homeric epics were
transmitted orally for centuries, and the Minoan linear scripts were first
partially deciphered again in our own century. The Greeks achieved literacy again only in the middle of the eighth century, with an alphabet borrowed from the Phoenicians.

The renewed expansion commenced soon after 800 B.C., when some of
the Greek communities became severely overpopulated: they outgrew
what the land, under prevailing techniques of production (principally the
primitive cultivation of barley), could provide.[5] We can plausibly infer the
consequences of this demographic pressure from the experience of it in
Athens over a century later, where it was recorded in persuasive if sometimes tantalizingly incomplete detail by one major participant, Solon, and
by such later authorities as Aristotle and Plutarch: an increase in sharecropping and indebtedness among the lesser peasants and rural laborers,
the occasional sale into servitude of defaulters, and a strengthening of the
landed aristocracy into what Aristotle called "an oligarchy that was far too
absolute."[6] In its broad outlines this is only what elementary economics
would lead us to expect in an isolated society experiencing such a demographic change: real returns to the increasingly scarce factor, land, must
have grown; those to the (over)abundant factor, labor, must have declined.[7]

The principal options available to a society in these straits are: to turn to
more productive and labor-intensive cropping, for example, by irrigation;

[2] Forrest 1966, 72–73; Bury and Meiggs 1975, 84–87.

[3] The quotation marks are in order because, as A. R. Burn (1982, 26) has observed, "to
divide the [Cretan civilization of] the centuries before 1600 into Early and Middle Minoan
[is] like calling our own early and middle ages Early and Middle Victorian." For useful sum-
maries of the current state of research on this tantalizing culture, which seems to have enjoyed
both wealth and, to judge by the absence of arms or of depictions of combat in its tombs,
peace, see Bury and Meiggs 1975, 8–19, and particularly Burn 1982, 35–45.

[4] Because Hesiod wrote, and the Homeric epics were transcribed from the oral tradition,
after 800, when Archaic Greek civilization was already beginning to dissolve, neither provides
a fully reliable guide. On the period generally, and the sources of our knowledge of it, see
Bury and Meiggs 1975, 63 and 67; Forrest 1966, chap. 2; and Hopper 1976, chap. 4.

[5] Bury and Meiggs 1975, 3. Among others Sparta, Corinth, its neighbor Megara, Chalkis,
and Eretria are known to have felt these pressures. Hopper 1976, 165; Forrest 1966, 68.

[6] Hopper 1976, 189–95; Forrest 1966, 147–50; *Politics* 1273b–74a.

[7] Implicitly, I am rejecting here the suggestion of Hasebroek (1933, vii–viii) that ancient
man was not subject to the same economic motivations as his modern counterpart.

to seek out more land, whether by reclamation, conquest, or colonization; and to trade. Greece's mountainous and infertile terrain virtually foreclosed the first possiblity,[8] and reclamation could also achieve but little. The chief answers actually adopted were conquest, colonization, and trade.

Sparta, notably, resorted to conquest and dispossession of the neighboring Messenians in the late eighth century B.C., eventually reducing the surviving remnant to the helots that Strabo trenchantly described as "state slaves."[9] So fruitful was the Messenian plain, and so thorough the Spartans' conquest of it, that this stroke, which roughly doubled their arable, long guaranteed the militant state's self-sufficiency.[10] It seems also likely that the shadowy war in this same period between Chalkis and Eretria for the Lelantine Plain, one of the few extensive areas of good land on the island of Euboea that these two states shared, had a similar motive.[11] The incidence of war, with territory as its object, appears to have risen generally throughout the Aegean after 750 B.C.[12] The eighth century also marked the beginning, however, of a great burst of colonization. By 700 B.C., Greeks had settled over a dozen sites in Sicily and Italy, finding there in abundance the fertile soil that they lacked at home.[13] In the following century, they opened the even richer lands of the Black Sea shores and settled also in northern Africa, at Cyrene.[14]

Beginning tentatively about the same time, but reaching significant levels only after about 600 B.C., many of the Greek states turned to trade. A few states—notably Miletus, Corinth, Megara, Samos, and again the Euboean cities of Chalkis and Eretria—had involved themselves very early in a substantial carrying trade in luxury goods of the distant East and West.[15] These cities' colonies increasingly took the character of trading posts rather than agricultural settlements: examples include al-Mina, on the Syrian coast, and Pithecusae, in southern Italy, both established jointly by Chalkis

---

[8] The one significant innovation in cropping was the olive, whose oil became a mainstay of the Greek diet and—used for lighting and cleaning—of the Greek household. On its dispersion, see Forrest 1966, 154–56. Both the harvesting of the olive and its pressing into oil were labor intensive: see the well-known British Museum *amphora* that depicts the harvest (portrayed in Bury and Meiggs 1975, 122). The tree was also an important form of capital: Burn (1982, 124) observes that "the olive, which gives little return for thirty years, is a long-term investment." The olive, however, could not provide a complete diet and was best traded for other victuals.

[9] Jones 1967, 9; Hopper 1976, 165–67; Bury and Meiggs 1975, 93–95.

[10] Forrest 1966, 127.

[11] Hopper 1976, 120–23.

[12] Hopper 1976, 92.

[13] Graham 1982, 160–62; Hopper 1976, 86.

[14] Hopper 1976, 94–95; Bury and Meiggs 1975, 85–86. Even Sparta, before its conquest of Messenia, had founded a colony in Italy: Hopper 1976, 90.

[15] Forrest 1966, 68–69; Hopper 1976, 86ff.

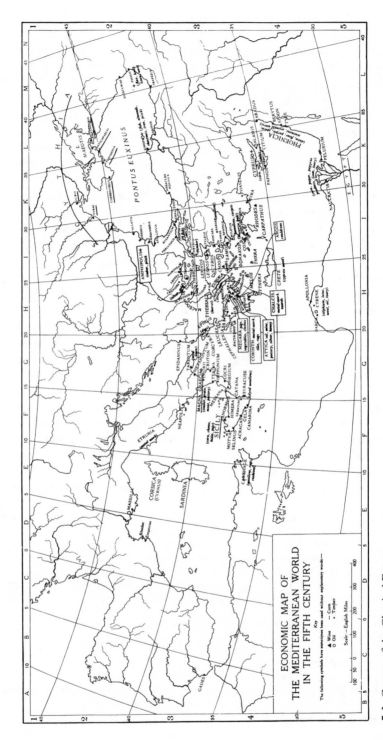

5.1 Greece of the Classical Era

and Eretria before 750 B.C.[16] From the former, the Greeks imported chiefly armor, jewelry, works of ivory, and semiprocessed metals;[17] from the West they drew also metals, above all tin.[18] What the Greeks exported is less certain: to the West, certainly pottery; to the East, perhaps slaves.[19]

Out of this primitive conveyance of luxuries, however, there quickly evolved a much more substantial trade in foodstuffs and manufactures of mass consumption. Eastern Miletus for example exported olive oil, salted fish, textiles, clothing, furniture, and pottery, largely to Black Sea ports and colonies, in exchange for raw wool and flax, fruits, hides, grain, timber, metals, and dyes.[20] The numerous agricultural colonies discovered that they could produce, on their fertile new lands, grain far beyond their own needs; and the grain of course found a ready market at excellent prices in the still-crowded Greek motherland.[21] With their profits, colonists bought those labor-intensive products that the home cities could more advantageously produce: olive oil, pottery, textiles, metalware, sculpture, and wine.[22] By the late seventh century B.C., Egypt too had been opened as a source of grain: in a major innovation, some dozen Greek cities jointly induced the Pharaohs of the Twenty-sixth Dynasty to grant them a shared trading post, which they named Naukratis ("sea queen").[23]

Athens, eventually the preeminent trading city of Greece, came late to the field; but it illustrates what in another context has been called "the advantages of backwardness."[24] Freed at first by a more favorable land-labor ratio from the demographic pressure that afflicted the other Greek states,[25] Athens was able to bypass the stage of colonization[26] and, beginning in earnest sometime in the seventh century, to move directly—and triumphantly—into trade.[27] By the middle of sixth century, Athenian pottery, already renowned for its artistry and workmanship for some two hundred years, had swept the markets of the known world, driving com-

[16] Bury and Meiggs 1975, 70; Hopper 1976, 89.

[17] Boardman 1964, 61–70 and 80–101.

[18] Boardman 1964, 177.

[19] Boardman 1964, 65 and 178–79. Recall that Solon, at a later but analogous period in Athenian history, claimed to have "brought back to Athens . . . many sold abroad into slavery" (quoted in Hopper 1976, 194).

[20] Dunham 1915, chap. 2.

[21] Forrest 1966, 68.

[22] Bury and Meiggs 1975, 81; Boardman 1964, 146 and 179; Hopper 1976, 95.

[23] Herodotus 2.178; Hopper 1976, 124; Boardman 1964, chap. 4.

[24] Gerschenkron 1962, chap. 1.

[25] Forrest 1966, 145 and 154.

[26] Athens established none before 600 B.C.; thereafter, four, all near the Hellespont and all for strategic reasons (of which more presently). Boardman 1964, 275–76.

[27] Some evidence suggests a tentative entry into trade in the early eighth century, followed by a retreat that was broken only in the period discussed here. Hopper 1976, 176–77.

peting Corinth out of production.[28] Beginning also in the seventh century, Athenian olive oil and wine, transported in mass-produced *amphorae*, began to be exchanged in quantity for Black Sea grain[29] and were traded also to Egypt, Syria, and Etruria.[30] By 600 B.C., Athens—and, we may assume from the increasing reliance on naval warfare and blockades, many other Greek states—had come to depend on trade, and particularly on imported grain, for its very survival.[31]

Two things followed in all of the cities that turned to trade. First, in a textbook example of the gains of specialization, they grew rich: not only manufacturing cities like Miletus, Corinth, Megara, and Athens, but such outposts of the grain trade as Syracuse and Sybaris (which became even to succeeding languages a byword for luxury), rapidly achieved enviable levels of wealth and civic splendor.[32] Nor were all these gains consumed: both in the periphery and at the center of the Greek trading world, much physical and human capital was accumulated: olive trees, tools and factories, artisanal skills, newly cleared land. Second, the affected states began to adopt conscious policies, of protectionism or of openness, toward external trade. The Spartans, at one extreme, pursued autarky at almost any cost, barring even the crucial innovations—above all silver coinage[33]—that facilitated trade.[34] Their isolation impoverished them and rendered their once-lively culture barren, but they continued it undeterred. At the opposite end of the spectrum, the Athenian state advanced trade by a great variety of measures: a coinage of unusual excellence,[35] standard and comprehensible weights and measures,[36] the easy admission of resident foreign merchants and craftsmen[37] and the offer to them of eventual citizenship,[38] rapid and

[28] Forrest 1966, 145; Boardman 1964, 29 and 33–34.

[29] Forrest 1966, 154–56.

[30] Boardman 1964, 72, 146, 152, and 212.

[31] Forrest 1966, 154.

[32] There is of course a contrary tradition in scholarship, which stems from Hasebroek (1933) and has been continued by Finley (1985), that holds trade to have remained peripheral to Greek life, and the Greek states' policies to have been directed chiefly by the needs of war and of wartime food supply. While in some respects this school has provided a valuable corrective to earlier excesses, its more sweeping theses seem to me to depend on an almost perverse reading of the evidence, especially of recent archaeology (see, e.g., the incisive critique of this tendency by Vinogradov 1981, 19–20); but this is too broad a question to address fully here.

[33] On the introduction of coinage (from Lydia) in Greece, and on its crucial importance for trade and investment, see Bury and Meiggs 1975, 83–84, and Hopper 1976, 141–42.

[34] The Spartans retained the antique form of iron bars, or spits, as their only legal tender: Bury and Meiggs 1975, 96; Hopper 1976, 110–14.

[35] Forrest 1966, 187.

[36] Forrest 1966, 177.

[37] Then still an unusual practice in Greece: Hasebroek 1933, 122.

[38] Bury and Meiggs 1975, 123.

fair adjudication of commercial disputes,[39] decrees encouraging export specialization in olives,[40] the early construction of a powerful navy that could protect trade routes from pirates and inimical states,[41] and—*after* the turn to trade—the acquisition of colonies and protectorates at strategic points along the crucial Black Sea route.[42]

These struggles over commercial and foreign policy were, as might be expected, part of a larger conflict among factors and classes that involved such grand issues as democracy, tyranny, and oligarchy. The Greeks themselves clearly saw trade as a cause of these divisions;[43] and it remains for us to sketch out its effects in detail and to examine the congruence between theoretical prediction and historical reality.

Categories and Expectations

In overpopulated central Greece at the beginning of the expansion of trade, labor was self-evidently abundant and land was scarce. Relative to most of the known world, human and physical capital—the skills of potters, artists, and sailors, the olive groves that took long years of care to bring to fruition, roads and harbor facilities—were probably also more abundant here. We should therefore expect expanding trade to have occasioned greater demands by, and eventually a shift of power to, labor and capital; and owners of these factors should in turn have embraced further dependence on trade. Owners of land in central Greece must have feared, and often experienced, a loss of power; and we expect that they will have pursued protection, autarky, and conquest.

In most of the periphery with which the Greeks dealt, the abundance of factors was exactly reversed: land was plentiful, capital and labor were both scarce. Here we expect, exactly as in the "frontier" societies of nineteenth-century America and Oceania, that landowners will have pursued free trade while workers and capitalists will have sought protection; certainly expanded trade should have strengthened land and weakened the urban groups.

In those few outlying areas whose wealth and crafts rivaled those of the metropole, however—Miletus is the most obvious example—both capital and land were abundant; and we should expect owners of those two factors

---

[39] Hasebroek 1933, 171–72; Finley 1985, 162.
[40] Bury and Meiggs 1975, 122; Burn 1982, 120.
[41] Burn 1982, 165–66.
[42] Boardman 1964, 275–77; Bury and Meiggs 1975, 129ff.
[43] For the Plato of the *Republic* (2.370–74), justice becomes problematic only when the *polis* trades and grows wealthy; similarly, Thucydides sees no need for further explanation when he states summarily (1.13) that "as Hellas became more powerful and as the importance of acquiring money became more and more evident, tyrannies were established in nearly all the cities."

to have united to maintain free trade and to suppress labor, which will have supported protection.

Evidence

I have already indicated that our knowledge of the politics and government of the immediate preclassical period is tenuous. Certainly rule was concentrated in a hereditary, landowning aristocracy often known as *eupatrid*, or "well-born." It appears that this dominant caste was obliged to seek the consent of the wider male citizenry for such major decisions as war and peace.[44] Certainly the *ecclesia*, or gathering of all males capable of bearing arms, was by historical times an institution with a long tradition in all the Greek states.[45] Popular influence was exercised also through a poorly understood structure of family, clan (phratry), and tribe.[46] Kings, probably powerful in the Mycenaean period, were weak or elective where they still existed at all; real power lay with a "senate" of leading aristocrats (at Athens, the Areopagus; at Sparta, the Gerousia) rather than with any strong executive. From (and, in practice, by) this senate, also, all of the chief officials of the state—executives, generals, judges—were chosen. The state was weak, and politics more consensual than conflictual.[47] These isolated polities, then, were republics, in fact if not in name, in which all men of substantial wealth[48] enjoyed influence and even poorer ones had at least the right to be consulted. Beyond this dim outline we cannot go: we simply lack detailed evidence of major political decisions, or of the patterns of political competition.

Typically, we know, change began in the societies of central Greece in the seventh century with growing unrest, among what may loosely be called the lower and middle classes, against the traditional landowning elite.[49] Among the chief demands were a cancellation of debts, a redistribution of land, and some more neutral system of justice, including both a written legal code and a relaxation of the eupatrids' judicial monopoly. The characteristic response to such discontent, when it could no longer be ignored, appears to have been the appointment of a "lawgiver": a regular magistrate, and therefore normally a patrician, appointed with extraordinary powers to propose or to promulgate reforms of the legal code, of

[44] Recall the assembly portrayed in the second book of the *Iliad*.

[45] Burn 1982, 68 and 120; Hopper 1976, 183.

[46] Forrest 1966, 50–58.

[47] Bury and Meiggs 1975, 63–64.

[48] Land being, here as in most densely populated premodern societies, the only significant form of wealth: cf. Forrest 1966, 46.

[49] Bury and Meiggs 1975, 87; Burn 1982, 97–98. At Athens, the first discontent can be fairly clearly located among the rising numbers of sharecroppers and bondsmen, and among newly wealthy traders and olive growers. Forrest 1966, 147–60.

property rights, and even of the system of governance. Athens knew two such episodes, those of Draco (ca. 621 B.C.) and Solon (594 B.C.), and Sparta could claim the almost certainly mythical Lycurgus; but Greece of the seventh century "is thick with lawgivers."[50]

In their chief features the Athenian reforms may be taken as typical: partial or total forgiveness of debts; codification of the law, greater popular control of the law courts (e.g., by permitting appeal from them to the *ecclesia*, or to a committee of it); a lowering of barriers to citizenship and to the franchise; substitution of property for birth as the requisite qualification for office (thus opening it to *nouveaux riches*); and creation of a representative body, or council, alongside the aristocratic senate that had formerly provided the only continuing leadership.[51]

Sometimes in place of, but more commonly after, these attempts at peaceful renovation, a *tyrant* might come to power. The first, apparently, was Cypselus of Corinth, probably around 650 B.C.;[52] his example was quickly imitated in nearby Megara and Sicyon.[53] Athens' turn came, parallel with its delayed economic development, later: Pisistratus seized power in 561 B.C., was twice overthrown but twice restored, and achieved lasting domination in 540; his sons succeeded him but the last of these was deposed in 510.

About these episodes two things should be borne in mind. First, the Greek tyrant is rarely the despot that the modern word connotes but rather a political "boss" more given to sharp practice and a contempt for the niceties than to outright violence: a Huey Long, rather than a Stalin or even a Pinochet.[54] Second, as Aristotle (*Politics* 1310b) observed, the tyrants were uniformly defenders of the people (*demos*) and the masses (*plethos*) against the notables; or, as modern historians have put it, the tyrants "all performed the same function of overthrowing aristocracies."[55]

The tyrants' methods were also of a piece: the most dangerous aristocrats were expelled and expropriated, some land (including that seized from the aristocracy) was redistributed to the poor, popular and employment-generating public works such as aqueducts,[56] canals, and temples were undertaken, and—by no means least—the tyrant carefully organized

---

[50] Forrest 1966, 143; cf. Bury and Meiggs 1975, 104, and Jones 1967, 7.

[51] For full discussions of the Draconian and Solonian reforms, and of the present-day controversy about their true nature, see Burn 1982, 120–22; Bury and Meiggs 1975, 123–24; Forrest 1966, 160–74; and Hopper 1976, 195–201.

[52] Forrest 1966, chap. 4; but cf. Hopper 1976, 133.

[53] Bury and Meiggs 1975, 106–13.

[54] See generally Burn 1982, 98; on Pisistratus, Bury and Meiggs 1975, 128.

[55] Bury and Meiggs 1975, 105.

[56] "This concern for the public water supply, which the aristocracies with their private wells had neglected, is a policy typical of tyrants [in this period]." Bury and Meiggs 1975, 132.

his mass following and, usually,[57] assembled a small "bodyguard" of enforcers.[58] Often the tyrant did not bother to change the existing constitution in any formal way. Pisistratus, for example, was almost as solicitous of the Solonian constitution as Augustus was later of the outward forms of Republican Rome[59]—but simply engineered the election of his followers to all important posts.[60]

Finally, after an interval ranging from a few years to (at Sicyon) a century, the tyrannies were supplanted by more regular forms of rule, usually a democracy or (as at Corinth) a "moderate oligarchy" (we would call it a representative democracy) with a property-based franchise. At Athens, the new constitution was proposed by Cleisthenes and was enacted, despite attempts at a conservative coup d'etat and a Spartan intervention, about 507 B.C.[61] It broadened the franchise to include all free men permanently domiciled in Attica[62] and replaced the Solonian Council with a new and much more powerful Council of 500, chosen annually by a mixture of election and lot.[63] This new body, or more normally its executive committee,[64] supervised the magistrates (whose election remained subject to property qualifications), controlled finance and foreign affairs, had substantial judicial powers, and prepared the agenda and recommended resolutions for the *ecclesia*. The powers of the still predominantly aristocratic Areopagus were reduced.[65]

From this point movement toward "radical" democracy—an abandonment of property qualifications, use of the lot instead of election for most offices, and payment of officers to permit the poor to participate—seemed inevitable. In the mid-fifth century B.C., the Athenian Areopagus was deprived of its remaining political functions, sortition replaced election for all offices except those of the ten generals of the armed forces (still annually elected), property requirements were further lowered, and pay was intro-

[57] Cypselus of Corinth "dispensed with a guard during the whole of his reign" (*Politics* 1315b); but Aristotle presumably mentions the fact because it was exceptional.

[58] Burn 1982, 98–99; Bury and Meiggs 1975, 106–13 and 128–32.

[59] Bury and Meiggs 1975, 128.

[60] Forrest 1966, 182.

[61] See, on the Cleisthenic constitution generally, Bury and Meiggs 1975, 136–38; Burn 1982, 155–57; Forrest 1966, chap. 8; on the Areopagus, Bury and Meiggs 1975, 215, and the partially dissenting view of Forrest 1966, 209–12.

[62] Burn 1982, 153; but cf. Jones 1957, 10.

[63] Burn 1982, 156–57; Bury and Meiggs 1975, 137–38.

[64] Called the committee of "presidents," chosen essentially by lot from the larger Council.

[65] After the reforms of Solon, the only route of entry into the Areopagus was honorable retirement (as certified by the Assembly) from the office of archon—the supreme magistracy, similar to the consulate at Rome. Solon had of course removed from this office the prerequisite of aristocratic birth, but he had substituted a very high property requirement, which in practice only aristocrats could easily meet. Bury and Meiggs 1975, 123; Burn 1982, 121.

duced for the magistrates and for jury service.[66] At the same time, and surprisingly against earlier practice, requirements for citizenship were tightened: in future, only the legitimate child of two citizen-parents would be automatically enrolled; naturalization required a specific act of the Assembly.[67]

Nonetheless, the general trend in Athens and throughout central Greece was democratic: effective power moved away from the landowning aristocracy and toward the new commercial groups and the masses. In interpreting this statement, it is important to dispel the myth, cultivated assiduously by Hasebroek and still widely accepted, that the Greek citizenries consisted wholly of *rentier* aristocracies, who depended for their subsistence on the labor and commerce of slaves and metics—or, at Athens, on imperial tribute.[68] The best estimates suggest that Athens of the early fifth century B.C. had some thirty thousand adult male citizens and six thousand adult male metics; of the citizens, half to two-thirds were likely *thetes*, members of the class too poor to serve as *hoplites*.[69] Slaves, whose total numbers we cannot reliably infer but who may have constituted a quarter of the population,[70] can have been owned only by a quarter or a third of the citizens;[71] and they appear to have predominated only in one sector, mining. There is ample evidence that Athenian citizens in large numbers were manual laborers, that they found nothing dishonorable in hard work, and that the great majority pursued some kind of remunerative trade.[72] That even the poorest of them could have lived satisfactorily off public office is hardly possible: both the pay and the odds of selection were too low.[73] In short, Greek democratization was what it appeared to be: a loss of power by old elites, including particularly landowners; a dramatic gain of power by merchants, manufacturers, and laborers. What remains to be seen is the extent to which the whole process was associated with expanding exposure to trade.

It should first be observed that the emergence both of lawgivers and of tyrants seems to have been closely correlated with rising dependence on trade. The great lawgivers and reformers of the period—the unknown author of the code of Gortyn on Crete, Charondas at Catane, Pheidon at Argos, Draco, Solon, and Cleisthenes in Athens—arise in trading cities,

---

[66] Forrest 1966, chap. 9; Bury and Meiggs 1975, 163–65 and 215–17.
[67] Bury and Meiggs 1975, 217.
[68] Hasebroek 1933, 22–43. A more moderate statement of the view is Finley 1982, chap. 6.
[69] Jones 1957, 8.
[70] Starr 1958, 21–22, cited by Finley 1982, 102.
[71] Jones 1957, 16.
[72] Jones 1957, 12–17.
[73] Jones 1957, 17–18; Burn 1982, 242–43.

and during periods of expanding trade; they are unknown in those backward and isolated states, such as Thessaly and Macedonia, that remained outside the general current of expanding trade.[74] Similarly, the earliest well-documented tyrannies arise between 650 and 600 B.C. in Corinth, Megara, Sicyon, Miletus, and Mytilene; and all of these except Sicyon[75] were early and intense traders.[76] Certainly such isolated areas as Arcadia, Elis, Thessaly, and Boeotia, which remained more self-sufficient, knew little of tyranny;[77] and regions that, like Athens, came only belatedly to rely on trade also experienced tyranny later than other states.[78]

In Athens, the crisis that occasioned Solon's reforms directly involved trade-related cleavages. The two contending parties of the period were those of the Plain, consisting of aristocratic grain growers, and of the Shore (*Paraloi*), who, on the most plausible explanation, were principally export-oriented growers of olives.[79] It is in this light that Solon's specifically trade-oriented legislation—a prohibition on the export of all agricultural products save olives and their oil, as noted previously—must be understood: on the one hand it was a sop to the masses, who would no longer see grain exported in times of dearth;[80] on the other, it acted as a primitive subsidy to the export of oil and impelled grain growers to cultivate olives, thus altering their long-term interests.[81]

If we examine more closely the class basis and the economic policies of the tyrannies, we find an even clearer connection. The tyrants' public works, including notably the aqueducts, favored the urban middle and lower classes; their redistributions of land, the rural laborers and sharecroppers; and the new rulers uniformly favored trade and opposed protection. At Corinth, Cypselus gave a strong new impetus to Adriatic colonization and trade,[82] and his son Periander cultivated good relations with Miletus (then the major participant in the Black Sea trade) and Egypt; archaeology confirms an upsurge of Corinthian pottery and coinage in

[74] Bury and Meiggs 1975, 104.
[75] Sicyon was not notably overpopulated, had sent out no colonies, and has left no evidence of substantial trading activity. On ancient testimony, its tyranny may have arisen more out of ethnic than economic conflict: Bury and Meiggs 1975, 110; Hopper 1976, 145 and 210.
[76] Bury and Meiggs 1975, 105–13; Burn 1982, 97–100.
[77] Hopper 1976, 145; Westlake 1935, 29.
[78] Bury and Meiggs 1975, 120; Hopper 1976, 184–86. There were however earlier attempts in Athens that had failed: Forrest 1966, 145–46.
[79] Bury and Meiggs 1975, 125–26; Hopper 1976, 202.
[80] Burn 1982, 120.
[81] Hopper 1976, 200; but cf. Bury and Meiggs 1975, 122. Suppose, by way of analogy, that some nineteenth-century German lawgiver had, instead of protecting rye, forbidden the export of all agricultural products save vegetable and animal fats. Would such a measure not have dramatically encouraged the kind of readjustment that Gerschenkron (1943) retrospectively advocated?
[82] Graham 1982, 131.

both areas during his rule.[83] Periander also cut a paved road, doubtless at great expense, across the Corinthian isthmus to simplify the transhipment of cargoes; portions of it survive to the present day.[84] Thrasybulus, the contemporaneous tyrant of Miletus, exchanged friendship and advice with Periander and—perhaps with his reciprocal assistance for favors granted by Miletus in the Black Sea—established exceedingly close relations with Syracuse, in the West.[85] To judge by the archaeological evidence, Thrasybulus also undertook a new wave of colonization: some six foundings,[86] including the crucial one of Odessus (modern Odessa) can be dated to the years of his rule.[87] Evidence on Pheidon, tyrant of Argos, is weak; but he appears to have intervened in favor of the Cypselids at Corinth[88] and was anciently reputed to have standardized weights, measures, and perhaps coinage, to facilitate commerce.[89]

As usual, the evidence is clearest with respect to Athens. We can establish with some confidence the sources of support and opposition to Pisistratus and the main lines of his policy. The tyrant himself led a new party, called that of the Hill (or the Heights; the group was labeled variously *hyperakrioi* and *diakrioi*), which almost certainly consisted chiefly of crofters and urban laborers and embraced "extreme democracy."[90] For some period of time, Pisistratus was allied with Megakles, leader of the olive-growing and export-oriented party of the Shore. He was consistently opposed by the land-owning aristocracy of the Plain.[91]

Thus Pisistratus's seizure of power must be interpreted as a defeat of the traditional landowners, a victory of the landless, and an outcome that the commercial and export-oriented sectors could at least accept. In power, Pisistratus redistributed the land of aristocratic émigrés to his neediest followers and encouraged mass participation in politics, expanding the influence and prestige of such Solonian bodies as the juries and the representa-

[83] Bury and Meiggs 1975, 106–7; Hopper 1976, 135–36; Boardman 1964, 72 and 146; cf. Forrest 1966, 118–19.
[84] Bury and Meiggs 1975, 108.
[85] Bury and Meiggs 1975, 107.
[86] Apollonia Pontica, Cepi, Hermonassa, Nymphaeum, Odessus, and Panticapaeum.
[87] Graham 1982, 160–62.
[88] Some solidarity among tyrants is evident. A curious footnote is the role of the Oracle at Delphi, which—having long favored, and served as a clearing house of information for, colonization and trade (Graham 1982, 144–46; Hopper 1976, 88)—now began to offer advice and legitimation to tyrants (e.g., its prophecy of Cypselus's rise to power in Corinth). Perhaps, some experts have suggested, this was a way of breaking aristocratic opposition to trade: Bury and Meiggs 1975, 106 and 113; Hopper 1976, 212; Forrest 1966, 111 and 143.
[89] Forrest 1966, 116–18; Bury and Meiggs 1975, 101; Hopper 1976, 111–12, is more skeptical.
[90] Burn 1982, 123; Bury and Meiggs 1975, 127; Hopper 1976, 202.
[91] Bury and Meiggs 1975, 128.

tive Council.[92] Even in the realm of ideology and symbolism, Pisistratus favored the plebeian cult of Dionysus and the historical legend of Theseus, plausibly an earlier "man of the Hill."[93]

Pisistatrus also consistently expanded Athens' reliance on trade. Like Periander at Corinth, he allied himself with eastern Miletus to win access to the grain and raw materials of southern Russia and the Black Sea. To secure the route, he firmly established Athenian control of the crucial outpost of Sigeum on the Hellespont, emphasizing its importance by installing his natural son as governor.[94] Under his auspices, another Athenian colony was planted on the opposite Thracian peninsula.[95] In general, however, Pisistratid foreign policy—in sharp contrast to that of earlier, more aristocratic rule—was remarkably pacific:[96] war, after all, endangered trade; it was to be undertaken only when vital sources or markets were at stake.

At home, the tyranny established a new Athenian coinage, the "Owl," whose fineness soon made it the standard of Mediterranean commerce;[97] made Athens more livable (not least for the regime's mass following) by the construction of aqueducts and public spaces;[98] attracted foreign traders and craftsmen with even easier grants of citizenship than the Solonian laws allowed;[99] and strongly encouraged the planting of olives and the export of oil and pottery, not least by redistribution of confiscated estates and by state credits to those who would work marginal land.[100] Archaeology dates to the years of Pisistratid rule a great expansion of Athenian pottery exports, the introduction (about 530 B.C.) of the advanced red-figure technique of vase decoration, and the triumph of Athenian wares over the previously dominant Corinthian competition.[101] The era was remembered by later Athenians as a "golden age" of prosperity and growth.[102]

Even so, tyranny eventually lost support in every state. It appears to have been a transitional form of rule, representing—to borrow Marx's phrase from the *Eighteenth Brumaire*—classes that could not yet represent themselves. The increasingly prosperous and numerous laborers and manufacturers outgrew their tutelage—at Athens, in no small part because of the education that Pisistratid governance had given them—and sought to

[92] Forrest 1966, 180; Bury and Meiggs 1975, 129.
[93] Bury and Meiggs 1975, 129; Forrest 1966, 182–83.
[94] Bury and Meiggs 1975, 131–32.
[95] Graham 1982, 121.
[96] Bury and Meiggs 1975, 129–30.
[97] Bury and Meiggs 1975, 129; Forrest 1966, 180 and 187.
[98] Bury and Meiggs 1975, 131–32.
[99] Burn 1982, 153.
[100] Bury and Meiggs 1975, 129; Burn 1982, 124.
[101] Burn 1982, 124; Boardman 1964, 29–30.
[102] Forrest 1966, 181–82.

transform apparent into real participation. Typically these efforts led the threatened tyrants to become more oppressive; their eventual overthrow usually occurred only through assassination or foreign intervention. Occasionally, as at Miletus (see my subsequent discussion) and Megara, the tyranny was followed by prolonged and violent conflict;[103] more commonly, and especially where the tyrants had held power long enough to finish off aristocratic power, the groups that benefited from trade were able to establish a stable hegemony.

The Athenian tyranny was toppled by Cleisthenes, son of that Megakles who had led the old party of the Shore into alliance with Pisistratus. Cleisthenes required Spartan support, but there is little doubt that the Pisistratids had forfeited their popularity by increasingly brutal rule. Almost immediately pushed aside by the old elites of the Plain, Cleisthenes saw his only chance of power in leadership of the masses; and this he won by sponsorship of the reforms outlined earlier. It is plausible to see in his victory a revival of the old alliance of capital and labor—of the Coast and the Plain—with, this time, labor in an equal if not dominant position.[104] Certainly the further development of the democracy, with its reliance on sortition and its pay for public service, signified the extinction of landowners' prerogatives and the triumph of the "little men" who, though they might own small farms or businesses, had chiefly their labor to sell.[105]

The policies of the democratic regime fostered trade as vigorously as had those of the tyranny. The democracy spent large sums to build and fortify new deep-water harbors on the Piraeus and to improve facilities for merchants.[106] To liberate the Greek cities of the eastern Mediterranean from a Persian control that increasingly threatened vital trade routes, Athens risked, and then with the other Greek states fought, a devastating war that twice saw the Acropolis occupied by Xerxes' troops.[107] Even after the Persian invasion had been decisively repelled at the battles of Salamis (480) and Plataea (479), the Athenians insisted, against Spartan opposition, on continuing the war until the trade routes to the Black Sea were again secured—a goal achieved by the capture of Sestos in 478.[108] Less spectacularly, but in the long run perhaps more significantly, it was the mature democracy which devised and instituted the emporial courts that, by guar-

[103] Burn 1982, 128; Bury and Meiggs 1975, 113.
[104] Bury and Meiggs 1975, 136–37; Burn 1982, 152–55; but cf. Forrest 1966, 199–200, esp. 197.
[105] As a contemporary, if hardly disinterested, observer described the mature Athenian democracy, "in every way they give preferential treatment to the base, the poor, the men of the people, rather than the decent classes." The "Old Oligarch," cited by Burn 1982, 244.
[106] Herodotus 9.107; Bury and Meiggs 1975, 165 and 235–37.
[107] Bury and Meiggs 1975, chaps. 6 and 7; Burn 1982, chaps. 7 and 8.
[108] Bury and Meiggs 1975, 185.

anteeing swift and fair adjudication of trade disputes, made Athens even more attractive to merchants.

We are less well informed about the specific program that the landowners advocated at Athens, in part because they were defeated so thoroughly; but we can infer its lineaments from their philosophical positions,[109] from the policies of the Spartan state that they all so openly admired,[110] and from the results of conservative victory in the similarly situated commercial city of Megara. The conservative philosophers were all but unanimous in seeking to minimize trade;[111] and Sparta, we have already seen, pursued autarky with singular diligence. This alone may well have accounted, as conservatives believed, for much of Sparta's vaunted political stability.

Megara, just to the west of Attica, was an early trading and colonizing city in which social revolution failed:[112] a brief tyranny under Theagenes was followed by much instability and, in the early sixth century, by a conservative restoration. The results included growing economic isolation, alliance with Sparta, and a rapid decline into insignificance. The popularity among Athenian conservatives of the reactionary poems of the Megarian aristocrat Theognis, rather like the rage for French royalist laments among European high society after 1793, suggests a spiritual kinship of complaint and of remedy.

Within labor- and capital-rich central Greece, then, labor and capital allied, and usually prevailed, against land, winning both democracy and open markets. In such newly colonized areas as Magna Graecia and the Black Sea basin, by contrast, where land was abundant but labor and capital were scarce, we expect to find—as noted earlier—similar fronts but opposite positions and results: landowners should gain from free trade and should advocate it against the opposition of workers and of most capitalists.

[109] We can infer much from the almost unparalleled flowering of philosophical and political debate in Athens in these years, which was expressed not only in dialogues but in such dramas as the *Eumenides* of Aeschylus and the *Oedipus Rex* and *Antigone* of Sophocles. (See the use of such evidence by Burn 1982, 246–55; Bury and Meiggs 1975, 216; and Forrest 1966, 9–14 and 214–15.) The issues raised by these works were often inspired directly by contemporary political conflicts (Forrest 1966, 98–103).

[110] Aristotle, although he did not share the view wholeheartedly, admitted that the Spartan constitution was widely admired: *Politics* 1265b, 1333b; cf. Plato, *Republic* 544. Cimon, longtime leader of the conservative forces at Athens, went so far as to live in the Lacedaemonian style and to name one of his sons Lacedaemonios. (For a present-day parallel, we should have to imagine that George McGovern had affected Russian dress and named a daughter Sovieta.) Neither extreme seems to have diminished Cimon's conservative following. Bury and Meiggs 1975, 212; Burn 1982, 210.

[111] Hasebroek 1933, 175–82; Hopper 1976, 163–64. Recall that Plato (*Laws* 847), while opposing tariffs, urged a total ban both on "imports . . . for inessential purposes" and on "the export [of] anything that it is essential to keep in the state." The application of these rather vague desiderata was to be left to the Guardians.

[112] Bury and Meiggs 1975, 112–13; Burn 1982, 113.

While the evidence that I have been able to find is too sparse to justify more than continued investigation of the hypothesis, it is evident that landowner power fared considerably better in these distant regions than it did at home. In Syracuse and Acragas, the principal cities of Sicily, tyrants—respectively, Gelon and Theron—seized power in the early fifth century B.C. Unlike their counterparts in the Greek homeland, however, these rulers appear to have been military dictators who defended the landowning interest against popular discontent.[113] Similarly in such Black Sea colonies as Apollonia, Histria, Olbia, and the shores of the Cimmerian Bosporus, narrow oligarchies, most likely of leading landowners, seem to have prevailed.[114] Even in more industrial and commercial Miletus, where both land and capital were presumably abundant, fierce post-tyranny struggles between parties baldly labeled the Rich and the Workers led to foreign intervention and, according to a plausible interpretation of the ancient sources, to rule by the most prosperous landowners.[115]

Conclusion

The connection between expanding trade and political change in classical Greece, observed by the ancients themselves, has been confirmed by most recent historians. In the states of central Greece, the change involved a new assertiveness by, and usually a shift of power to, the locally abundant factors of labor and capital. Except in Sparta, which by conquest and dispossession achieved a new abundance of land, traditional landowning elites lost influence.

The outcome in the periphery of the Greek trading world is less clear. Although some evidence points to the predicted result of an attack on popular power and a new assertiveness by landowners, it is impossible to state this as a general consequence of increased trade. In those regions, the approach suggested here can only serve as a guide (or, perhaps, a target) for future research.

THE DECLINING ROMAN EMPIRE

Changes in Trade

Under the Principate, and particularly in the first and early second centuries A.D., most historians have concluded,[116] the Roman Empire achieved

---

[113] Bury and Meiggs 1975, 188–89.

[114] Vinogradov 1981, 23–26.

[115] Burn 1982, 126–28; cf. Dunham 1915, 129–31.

[116] A minority continues, here as in the case of Classical Greece, to deny the importance of Roman trade and to downplay all archaeological evidence of its extent. The most important dissident is A.H.M. Jones (see, e.g., Jones 1966, chap. 23); but consult also Pounds 1974, 27–32. A summation of the mainstream position is Previté-Orton 1952, 21.

an intensity and range of trade that surpassed what the Greeks had known and that were not to be regained until the eighteenth century of the modern era.[117] Rome, swollen to a population of perhaps three-quarters of a million, drew much of its grain supply from Egypt and North Africa;[118] Spanish olive oil was retailed in Syria and Roman manufactures in Britain; the wines and pottery of Gaul were carried into Africa and Russia; and products of India and China appeared in Roman markets.[119] Although this extensive commerce was still chiefly waterborne, in ships that now often carried over a hundred tons, merchants increasingly made use (for a fee) of the brilliant system of Roman military roads.[120]

The policies of Augustus and his immediate successors favored and furthered long-range trade. Roman troops suppressed brigandage; Roman law, uniform in its main features throughout the provinces, provided secure property rights and reduced transaction costs; Roman mails, lighthouses, roads, and harbors facilitated communication and travel; Roman currency permitted easy and reliable exchange.[121] Tariffs, kept stable and moderate—2.5 percent on almost all interprovincial trade, ranging up to a maximum of 25 percent on luxuries imported from outside the Empire— yielded the treasury more than any other source save the tribute of conquered provinces, yet scarcely impeded commerce.[122] Perhaps most importantly, Rome refused to grant monopolies; competition remained lively and efficient in almost every sector.[123] It is little wonder that, according to an anciently recorded incident, Augustus was hailed by passing merchant shippers near the end of his life as the source of their lives, liberty, and prosperity.[124]

The resultant trade, as Rostovtzeff concluded, embraced not chiefly luxuries but "articles of prime necessity": grain, wine, oil, metals, lumber, clothes and textiles, and pottery.[125] Moreover, its extent was such as to make trade the principal source of new wealth in this period.[126] Conducted

[117] The comparison to the eighteenth century is drawn by Lot 1931, 62.

[118] As late as the sixth century A.D., Byzantium imported 175,000 tons of wheat each year from Egypt—enough, reckoning that this yielded half its weight in flour, to supply nearly half a million persons with a pound of bread a day. Brown 1971, 12.

[119] For good general sketches, see Grant 1960, 79–84; Maier 1968, 77ff.; and above all Rostovtzeff 1926, 145–50.

[120] Vogt 1967, 23; on ship capacity, Jones 1966, 313.

[121] See generally on trade policy Grant 1960, 81–84, and Rostovtzeff 1926, 150; on Roman law, Scullard 1961, 369–73. Doyle 1986, 97–98, reaches similar conclusions about the effects of Roman rule on trade.

[122] Vogt 1967, 24.

[123] Rostovtzeff 1926, 159–60.

[124] Suetonius, *Augustus* 98, cited in Grant 1960, 81–82.

[125] Rostovtzeff 1926, 148.

[126] Rostovtzeff 1926, 145.

on this scale, the exchange of goods engendered an interprovincial division and specialization of labor that vastly increased the imperial economy's productivity:[127] Italy concentrated on wine, craftwares, banking, and insurance; Gaul, on wine and pottery; Spain, on grain and oil; Egypt, on grain, jewelry, and perfumes; North Africa, Sicily, and southern Russia, on grain; Syria, on glassware and textiles.[128] Productivity grew, inevitably, at the cost of increased interdependence: every major city of the empire relied on imported food, and all but the remotest villages drew their essential manufactures from other, and often quite distant, regions.[129]

In the late second and the third centuries A.D., almost all students agree, this vigorous interprovincial trade began to yield to a pattern of increasing local autarky.[130] Given the enormous gains that the preceding exchange had afforded, this turn to self-sufficiency can by itself account for much of the empire's manifest economic decline and depopulation in these years.[131] But what suddenly constricted trade? Rostovtzeff's hypothesis, that a simple dispersal of technology was responsible, will not do;[132] nor will the many efforts to attribute the growing autarky to the "exorbitant" costs of land transport.[133] Dispersal of technology does not override the laws of comparative advantage (indeed, in the present economic expansion trade has grown most rapidly among the most advanced economies);[134] and, had the costs of transport been too high, trade would never have arisen (only *increasing* costs of transport could account for a decline in trade).

---

[127] Maier 1968, 77.

[128] Rostovtzeff 1926, 148; on Italy as an exporter of financial services, Marsh 1963, 5. Greece does not appear in this list; exposed to wider competition, it appears to have found no productive niche (if one disregards its steady export of scholars and teachers) and to have become a kind of Roman Appalachia in these years: Rostovtzeff 1926, 161.

[129] Rostovtzeff 1926, 137–39, 158, and 167. Rostovtzeff's observation (167), based on copious archaeological analysis, that of the artifacts in second-century graves "throughout the Empire" and in excavations of the remotest villages of Egypt "hardly a single piece . . . was produced at home," may be contrasted with Pounds's assertion (1974, 32) that "the vast majority of peasants never possessed or used any artifact that was not made in their own neighborhood."

[130] See, among many examples: Rostovtzeff 1926, 163–67; Grant 1960, 84; Vogt 1967, 24–25; Alföldy 1985, 186; Previté-Orton 1952, 21. Even Pounds 1974, 32–33, who denies that trade ever mattered, observes that it diminished in the third century.

[131] In a remote sense, the famous thesis of Pirenne (1939) is thus borne out so far as it regards the *consequences* of an interruption of trade; but current scholarship dates the contraction to so early a point that Pirenne's putative cause—the Islamic conquest of much of the Mediterranean rim—cannot hold. I shall venture to suggest that Pirenne may, in fact, have reversed the order: Islam may have been a consequence, rather than a cause, of diminished Mediterranean trade.

[132] Rostovtzeff 1926, 168.

[133] Anderson 1974, 19, stresses that transport was "exorbitantly expensive." Cf. Brown 1971, 12–13, and (again) Rostovtzeff 1926, 167.

[134] See chapter 4.

The classical Marxist explanation, ably reformulated in recent years by Perry Anderson (1974), is more plausible: an economy that rested fundamentally on the agrarian exploitation of cheap slave labor could not survive once Roman expansion—and, with it, the abundant supply of new slaves—ceased. On this view, diminishing trade and rising autarky were consequences, rather than causes, of a more basic economic decline occasioned by rising wages in an obsolete structure of property rights. Again, however, a fundamental economic objection obtrudes: taken alone, the demonstrably rising price of slaves in this period should have shifted and stimulated, rather than inhibited, trade. Slaves had long been bought as well as captured (the chief Greek source, for example, was not conquest but purchase from the tribes of Scythia and Thrace),[135] and a rising price should merely have intensified the search for new suppliers—if, that is, slavery was as essential to the imperial economy as Anderson believes (see, *per contra*, the impressively documented view of Rostovtzeff).[136] Additionally, as Vogt has observed, a mere shortage of labor should have led to its replacement by capital (which, to judge by prevailing interest rates, remained freely available); it should not, by any known economic logic, have occasioned so catastrophic a decline.[137]

The likelier explanation is the straightforward one offered by Rémondon, Maier, Vogt, and others: that the barbarian incursions and the renewed civil wars from the late second century onward so overburdened both the transport system—frequently requisitioned for emergency movement of troops or supplies[138]—and the public fisc as to lead to brigandage, arbitrary exactions, inflation, and eventually a ruinous taxation (which, to circumvent the inflation, was increasingly levied in kind);[139] that these changes in turn rendered commerce so risky and costly as to inhibit it substantially (largely reconfining it, by the early fourth century, to the exchange of luxury goods[140]); and that the wider economic decline can be attributed mostly to the resultant collapse of trade and of specialization.[141]

[135] Bury and Meiggs 1975, 87.

[136] Rostovtzeff 1926, 191.

[137] Vogt 1967, 24–25.

[138] In the crisis of the third century, writes Rémondon (1964, 110), "Private means of transportation are evidently sacrificed. . . . The circulation of products is practically interrupted. Commercial routes wither. Lacking supply, the towns experience famine. Their artisanal and commercial activity is paralyzed."

[139] Grant 1960, 84–86; Brown 1971, 24ff.; Maier 1968, 77–78; Rostovtzeff 1926, 326–27, 342, 363, 399, and 417; Anderson 1974, 82–84; Vogt 1967, 26 and 75ff.

[140] Previté-Orton 1952, 21; Rémondon 1964, 311; Rostovtzeff 1926, 425 and 471. Rostovtzeff (421) further asserts that, during the third century, trade with India ceased altogether.

[141] Maier (1968, 77) emphasizes the devastating effects of the collapse of trade on Gaul, "which was one of the richest and most productive provinces of the West, but, with its export

Factor Endowments and Theoretical Expectations

Whatever the exact reasons, trade in the western empire declined precipitously.[142] Not only towns but, as early as the late second century, individual rural estates pursued self-sufficiency.[143] In these circumstances, we should expect conflict between owners of scarce and owners of abundant factors, with the former likely to gain at the expense of the latter. What factors, however, were scarce, and which were abundant, in each region? The answer is not obvious. While it is generally agreed that western Europe was less densely populated than Asia Minor or Egypt,[144] *fertile*—and, especially, irrigated—land was abundant in Egypt and North Africa.[145] Given that Egypt, North Africa, and Sicily exported huge quantities of grain, by far the most land-intensive of agricultural products, we must surmise, following the theorem of Heckscher and Ohlin,[146] that in these regions fertile land was more abundantly available than elsewhere; conversely, the export of labor-intensive wine, olive oil, and manufactured goods from Italy, Gaul, Spain, Asia Minor, and Syria suggests a relative abundance of labor in those areas.[147] Finally, we may associate the cultivation of olives and of the vine, in Rome no less than in Greece, with a relative abundance of capital.

If we can correctly infer that many areas of western Europe were, within the context of the larger empire, scarce in fertile land but abundant in capital and labor, then the extreme contraction of trade within this region (and, a fortiori, between it and other regions) should in theory have given rise to an urban-rural conflict in which the advantage shifted to the rural side. If, conversely, we can assume that such grain-producing regions as

---

of wine and pottery to regions as distant as Africa and Syria, also among the provinces most vulnerable to crises." See also Rémondon 1964, 110, quoted earlier. On the other hand Jones (1966, 367) stoutly denies—in conformity with his conclusion that trade was unimportant in the imperial economy—that the contraction of trade can have contributed to the general decline of the Empire.

[142] Trade in the eastern empire continued at a much more vigorous level. Anderson 1974, 97–98; Rémondon 1964, 311; Maier 1968, 83–84.

[143] Alföldy 1985, 187; cf. Rémondon 1964, 307.

[144] Lopez 1967, 20–21; Lot 1931, 66–70; and Rostovtzeff 1926, 194ff.

[145] For one thing, land in Egypt and North Africa was cropped every year; in Italy and most of Europe, only every second year. An excellent account of ancient agriculture is Jones 1966, chap. 22.

[146] According to this theorem, regions export products that use intensively their abundant factors and import ones that use intensively their scarce factors; cf. Leamer 1984, chap. 1.

[147] Paradoxically, Roman landlords appear to have extended labor-intensive Mediterranean techniques of agriculture into more land-rich Gaul. They thus farmed *as if* land were scarce even where it was not. Lopez 1967, 20–21. Only with the introduction of the heavy plow in the eighth century, as Fox (1971, 43–44) observes, were the heavy soils of northern Europe brought fully into production.

Egypt and North Africa were rich in fertile land but poor in capital and—relative to their other endowments—in labor, we should expect that the loss of their European markets would have assisted the cities and harmed the countryside. (At the same time, the total effect should be less, since trade persisted within these regions and between them and the East.) And if, finally, the exports of Syria and Asia Minor—textiles and luxury goods—permit us to conclude that this area enjoyed an abundance chiefly of labor, with relatively lesser endowments of land and capital, then we should expect to find here class conflict: an alliance of powerful urban and rural elites against the masses of both sectors.

Evidence

Rostovtzeff (1926), in an interpretation that remains highly controversial, viewed the final centuries of the western empire as a period of unremitting conflict between the cities and the countryside—a conflict that, needless to say, the cities ultimately lost. The controversy, however, chiefly surrounds Rostovtzeff's claim that, at the latest from the reigns of Marcus Aurelius and Commodus, the Roman state—or, more precisely, the peasant-based Roman army—sided decisively with the great landowners and mercilessly squeezed the cities.[148] If we leave to one side the *intent* of the Roman leadership, there is little doubt that the *consequence* of their policies was in fact what Maier has called "a gradual displacement of economic influence from the cities to the large landowners."[149] Although in the first barbarian incursions the empire's traditional concern for its urban centers[150] inspired a flight from rural insecurity into the relative safety of city walls,[151] the third and subsequent centuries indeed saw the strange reversal that we now recognize as incipient feudalism: an accelerating autarky of the rural estates, marked by the attraction into them of urban artisans;[152] a growing political independence of the manors, including evasions both of the ever-expanding burden of taxes and of imperial justice;[153] the rise of private armed retainers in the service of the major estate owners;[154] and, finally, the

[148] Rostovtzeff 1926, esp. pp. 331–43 and chaps. 9–12.

[149] Maier 1968, 85.

[150] On Roman civilization—and, indeed, ancient civilization in general—as city based, see particularly Anderson 1974, 19ff., and Brown 1971, 13–17. Recall also Hadrian's numerous foundings of new cities in the provinces, intended to cement Roman rule there: Rostovtzeff 1926, 318.

[151] Rémondon 1964, 85; but cf. Jones 1966, 308.

[152] Alföldy 1985, 187; Rémondon 1964, 307; Maier 1968, 86.

[153] Alföldy 1985, 215; Previté-Orton 1952, 22; Maier 1968, 79 and 89ff.

[154] Alföldy 1985, 215; Maier 1968, 90.

spread of the *patrocinium*, ancestor of the medieval commendation, by which smaller independent farmers, seeking security, made themselves clients and eventually vassals of the estate owners, who alone could shield them from banditry and imperial taxation.[155]

To be sure, the proximate cause of the economy's ruralization is likely to be found in the increasingly ruinous and arbitrary taxation that the beleaguered empire levied, and that fell with particular force on allegedly more accessible urban and commercial wealth. Yet Rostovtzeff is surely right in observing that earlier Roman governments had found it in their power to squeeze the peasantry and, in the bloody proscriptions of Sulla, the Second Triumvirate, and Tiberius, to expropriate even powerful fractions of the Senatorial and Equestrian landowning orders.[156] Why, then, should later imperial governments have found it more opportune to bleed the vital cities and shield the rural estates?

Rostovtzeff's answer to this central question—that the later imperial governments relied increasingly on the naked power of a largely peasant army, and had therefore to accede ever more to rural demands—raises doubts: the Roman army was, even in its later days, something less than a participatory democracy; and in any event peasants would hardly have favored the further aggrandizement of those same patricians who, since Second Punic War and the failed reforms of the Gracchi, had been ruthlessly devouring peasant holdings.

If, on the other hand, trade had so declined as to deprive much of the empire in western Europe of its ready access to the cheap food of Africa and Egypt, then it is easy to see why governments should have become more solicitous toward agriculture at home and why landowners could become more assertive: the relative price—in money, power, and status—of the locally scarce factor would simply have risen in circumstances of contracting trade. That, from the second century on, the relative price of grain rose in Italy and ever more land there was planted to it (rather than to such export crops as grapes and olives) tend to support this hypothesis.[157]

The counterpoise to the ruralization of Europe was, I conjecture, the flowering of urban civilization in North Africa and the Near East that we associate with the triumph of Islam. Even as the severing of trade routes must have placed a premium in Europe on the formerly imported good (grain) and on the factor required for its production (land), so in the for-

[155] Brown 1971, 37; Maier 1968, 82; Alföldy 1985, 215–16; Lot 1931, 131–32.
[156] See, on the proscriptions of Sulla and the Second Triumvirate, Marsh 1963, 118–22 and 278–79; on those of Tiberius, Grant 1960, 33.
[157] "Now that corn had become ever scarcer in Italy, corn-growing was at least as profitable as the production of wine, and it was less risky and required less personal attention alike from the landowners and from the tenants." Rostovtzeff 1926, 191.

mer grain-exporting regions the interruption will have raised the relative price of manufactures and of the factors (labor and capital) they require, and thus will have increased the importance of cities.

From this standpoint it is suggestive to observe that, despite Islam's undoubted first appeal to nomadic Bedouins, its Prophet was a wealthy merchant, that trade received "honour . . . in Moslem ethics," and that in the mature Caliphate (from the mid-eighth century—precisely at the point when Europe was at its most rural and benighted) the former granaries of Rome developed an urban life in which "learning, literature, art and civilization flourished in gorgeous profusion."[158] In further examining the hypothesis that, in contrast to what Pirenne believed, the decline of trade with Europe was cause rather than consequence of Islam's rise, we expect to find that the urban revival in these regions considerably antedated, rather than followed, the acceptance of the new faith.

Finally, we observe principally in the former regions of labor-intensive exports—where, we may infer, both land and capital were scarce—that peculiar and static alliance of landowners and capitalists that, according to some authorities, underlay the long-enduring Byzantine Empire.[159] The correlation of course is not exact, nor in light of military pressures should we expect it to be; yet the old craft-exporting regions of Asia Minor continued to form the core of Byzantine rule.[160]

Conclusion

Overall, the evidence for this period is at best suggestive—perhaps inevitably, given the intricate controversies that permeate the secondary literature. The approach developed here may best be regarded as yet another perspective from which to view the confused events of the later Roman and early Medieval eras. Still, if trade was as important to Rome as most historians still believe it to have been, then its steady decline after A.D. 200 must have had important regional effects of the kind that the Stolper-Samuelson theorem permits us to predict. Whether these effects constitute major elements of this period's history, or were overshadowed by the aspects

---

[158] See the sketches in Maier 1968, chap. 4, sec. ii, and Previté-Orton 1952, chap. 10; the quoted passages are from Previté-Orton 1952, 243. Of course, the revival of trade under the Caliphate contributed greatly to this urban explosion (Maier 1968, 286); but this trade took place largely *within* the Islamic empire; primitive and insecure Europe remained outside its ambit.

[159] Alföldy 1985, 219; cf. Brown 1971, 43–44.

[160] Like the areas that embraced Islam, the Byzantine lands continued a far more active trade than did western Europe (Brown 1971, 43); yet this commerce, by excluding Europe and all but the exchange of preciosities with the Caliphate (Maier 1968, 286), remained highly limited in comparison to the Roman period.

of military insecurity and general economic contraction, remains to be established.

THE "LONG" SIXTEENTH CENTURY, 1450–1650

Changes in Trade

After the ravages of the Black Death in the middle years of the fourteenth century, Europe's population began to expand again rapidly in the last decades before 1500. This time, in contrast to the fourteenth century, not Malthusian constraints but an expansion like that of ancient Greece prevailed: Europe turned to exploration, colonization, and trade. Navigation and shipping within Europe improved dramatically, opening major routes of commerce between the grain-growing Baltic and the capital-intensive factories and agricultures of England and the Netherlands.[161] The Portuguese and Spanish, followed rapidly by the English and Dutch, penetrated the Americas and the Orient to bring home bullion, spices, sugar, and silks. As the mines and plantations of the new world expanded, African slaves were added to the cargoes.[162]

By the last decades of the sixteenth century, this trade had achieved a volume that, for a still preindustrial age, was enormous: on average some 40,000 *Last*, or 6.5 million bushels, of grain passed through the Sound each year on its way from the Baltic.[163] As early as the 1560s, Poland was exporting 12 percent of its net rye and 6 percent of its net grain production; Baltic imports covered perhaps 14 percent of the Netherlands' total consumption of grain.[164] Counting traffic in both directions, by the 1590s over five thousand ships passed annually through the Sound.[165] In addition, Europe imported by this decade some 2,700 tons of Asian preciosities (chiefly spices) annually and just under 300 tons of American bullion, plus some 50,000 tons of other American goods.[166] The total volume of seaborne trade considerably exceeded these quantities: in 1570, Amster-

---

[161] The major intra-European trade routes of the later sixteenth century are usefully mapped in Wilson 1976, 40–41.

[162] A more inclusive recital of principal exports and imports is provided by Minchinton 1974, 92–93.

[163] Kriedte 1983, 29. The *Last* was a measure of volume, equivalent to 2 "register tons" or 200 cubic feet: Mitchell 1978, xviii; *Webster's New Collegiate Dictionary*, 2d ed., s.v. "ton." Rye normally weighs out at 56 pounds per bushel. Hence if most of the grain was rye, this total was equivalent to some 180,000 tons. It may be worth observing that this works out to about 12 pounds of imported grain per year for each of western Europe's then approximately 30 million inhabitants: see population figures in Kriedte 1983, 3, and Mols 1974, 38.

[164] Kriedte 1983, 26 and 28.

[165] Kriedte 1983, 40.

[166] Kriedte 1983, 40–41.

dam's commercial fleet had a carrying capacity of 232,000 tons; that of the Hansa, a capacity of 110,000 tons.[167] Beyond this, peasants with small boats plied an extensive coastal trade[168] and, as Braudel has reminded us, transport by land carried a greater volume, despite its many inconveniences, than transport by water.[169]

Exactly as in the ancient world, wider exchange and regional specialization brought large gains. Cities, able to nourish themselves from afar for the first time since the collapse of Rome, grew to encompass—despite their lamentable hygiene and endemic violence—populations of hundreds of thousands.[170] Throughout the sixteenth century, Europe's population grew: by about a quarter overall between 1500 and 1600, but by over half in the Low Countries, Britain, and Scandinavia.[171] Moreover, there is little doubt that the security, if not the average standard,[172] of living among this growing population steadily improved: diets grew richer and more varied, and regional famines yielded to improved transportation;[173] perhaps most conclusively, the plague, which battened always on the chronically malnourished, disappeared from Europe after 1665.[174]

Factor Endowments

As the pattern of imports and exports suggests, eastern Europe in this period (and, even more, the newly opened Americas) was abundant in land;

[167] Kriedte 1983, 45.

[168] Braudel 1982, 362.

[169] Braudel 1982, 350 and 357.

[170] In the early sixteenth century, only five European cities—Constantinople, Paris, Naples, Venice, and Milan—comprised more than 100,000 souls; none could boast of over 200,000. By the early seventeenth century, nine cities (London, Milan, Venice, Rome, Seville, Amsterdam, Lisbon, Palermo, and Antwerp) had populations of between 100,000 and 200,000; and Constantinople, Naples, and Paris counted over 200,000. Mols 1974, 42–43.

[171] Kriedte 1983, 3; the estimates of Mols 1974, 38, are similar except for Russia, where Mols projects a far more rapid rate of increase. The growth of the later fifteenth century may have been even swifter: perhaps 55 per cent for Europe as a whole between 1450 and 1500: Kriedte 1983, 18.

[172] Most authorities agree that the average real European wage, and presumably also the average standard of living, declined (except, probably, in the Netherlands) during the sixteenth century; at the same time, health appears to have improved (note the disappearance of the plague) and mortality to have receded. It appears that the *variance* of real wages diminished, not least through the reduction of local famine. See principally Braudel and Spooner 1967, esp. 425–30 and 482–83; Minchinton 1974, 94–100 and 115–17; Helleiner 1967, 24; Kriedte 1983, 51–54; and Wallerstein 1974, 77–85.

[173] Minchinton 1974, 116; Wilson 1976, 26. The strongest evidence is the rapid diminution of price differentials among regions in Europe: from ratios as high as 7:1 in 1500, they declined to about 4:1 by 1600. Wallerstein 1974, 70; Braudel and Spooner 1967, 396–99 and 472–73.

[174] Mols 1974, 18–19; cf. North 1981, 134 and 147.

western Europe's ratio of labor to productive land was far higher. Around 1600, the most densely populated regions of Italy had perhaps 120 inhabitants per square kilometer;[175] most of northern Italy, much of France, the Rhineland, and south central Germany, and all of northwest Europe (the Low Countries, southeast England, and even much of Ireland) registered considerably over 40; and virtually all of Europe east of the Elbe, Iberia, and the Ottoman Empire fell below that figure (see Map 5.2). Of the Americas, one leading student of the early colonizations has written that, "land was dangerously plentiful, labor almost non-existent."[176] As late as 1750, South and Central America had fewer than 1 inhabitant per square kilometer, North America fewer than 1 for each *ten* square kilometers.[177] Slavery and serfdom must be seen as ways, albeit desperate and horrible ones, of assuring even a minimal labor supply in these almost deserted regions.[178]

With almost equal clarity, we can see that capital was abundant only in northwestern Europe—above all in the Netherlands, but increasingly in London and southeast England—and, to a lesser and declining extent, in northern Italy. Venice, and after it Florence and Genoa, had been the centers of capital-intensive manufacture, principally in textiles and shipbuilding, in the fourteenth and fifteenth centuries.[179] Now Antwerp, Amsterdam, and London—and, even more, the "new draperies" of the countryside around them—surpassed these older leaders;[180] with the capital-intensive agriculture that made the Netherlands a cornucopia of dairy and vegetable production[181] they established northwestern Europe as the "core" of the new world economy, the region in which capital was most abundant and most rapidly accumulated. [182] Precisely why capital flowed so generously to these northern regions is an intriguing subject of scholarly dispute, which need not detain us here.[183] What matters is only the fact that capital did abound in these "core" regions, and only in them.

[175] Mols 1974, 39.

[176] Rich 1967, 307.

[177] Rostow 1978, 2, estimates the population of North America in 1750 at 2 million; that of South and Central America, at 16 million. North America has an area of 21.5 million square kilometers, South and Central America together an area of 20.5 million square kilometers (United Nations 1961, 41).

[178] Rich 1967. Cf. Wallerstein 1974, 99, on the chronic shortage of labor in the periphery.

[179] See generally Braudel 1984, chap. 2.

[180] Kriedte 1983, 31–40; Braudel 1984, 138–57 and 177–205; and Sella 1974, esp. 413ff.

[181] Kriedte 1983, 22–23 and 26–27; Maddalena 1974, esp. 312–22; Braudel 1984, 177–80. Comparative yield ratios—i.e., of harvest to seed—clearly demonstrate the superiority of Dutch and English agriculture: Wilson 1976, 17; Maddalena 1974, appendix.

[182] Wallerstein 1974, esp. chaps. 2 and 5.

[183] Most famously, Max Weber argued that the ethical system of Calvinism had made possible the accumulation of capital in these regions—a hypothesis that, as Wilson (1976, 99ff.) cogently argues, is hard to reconcile with the evidence that has subsequently emerged. Wall-

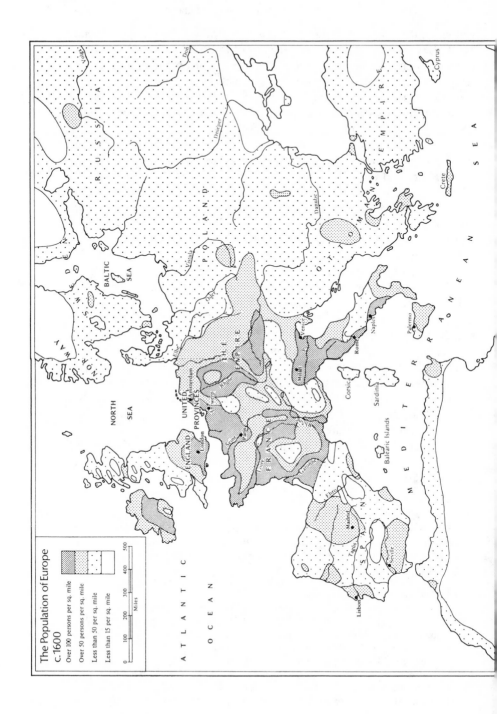

The Population of Europe
c.1600

Over 100 persons per sq. mile

Over 50 persons per sq. mile

Less than 50 per sq. mile

Less than 15 per sq. mile

0 100 200 300 400 500

Miles

Categories and Expectations

We see, then, three regions in this widening system of exchange: northwestern Europe and northern Italy, abundant in both capital and labor but poor in land; the remainder of Europe west of the Elbe (excepting northern England, Scotland, and Iberia), abundant in labor but poor in capital and land; and the broad reaches of eastern Europe, Russia, southwest Asia, Spain, northern Britain, and the New World, abundant in land but poor in capital and labor. The first region exports manufactured goods and imports the agricultural ones that use land intensively (chiefly grain);[184] its domestic agriculture is Europe's most capital intensive (involving dikes, drainage, dung, and double-cropping). The second engages in labor-intensive agriculture and some labor-intensive manufactures (printing, watch-making),[185] importing the more capital-intensive manufactures of the northwestern "core." The third region, the "periphery," exports land-intensive primary products such as grain, ores, and sugar and imports virtually all manufactures.[186]

A persistent puzzle in much of the best scholarship on this period has been why the same cause, namely expanding trade, should have had almost opposite social and political effects in eastern as against northwestern Europe—contributing in the latter to urban supremacy, an intensified transition to cash rents, and a freeing of the peasantry; in the former, to urban decline, an expansion of labor dues, and the "second serfdom."[187] From the perspective adopted here, there is little mystery. Expanding trade must, in northwestern Europe, have strengthened the locally abundant factors of labor and capital (i.e., the urban sectors) and have weakened owners of land; in eastern Europe, where land was plentiful (and, indeed, in Spain,

---

erstein (1974, 98ff.) developed the argument that "a slight [and, presumably, fortuitous] edge" at a critical juncture might permit one region to plunder others and thereby to achieve greatly superior endowments of capital. And North and Thomas (1973) contended that superior property rights explained the Dutch and English advance. These are only a few of the efforts at explanation; a related, broader, and useful survey is Holton 1985.

[184] Given the great disparity in land-labor ratios, it seems idle to speculate (as Wallerstein 1974, 99, does) that western Europe might well have become the "breadbasket" of eastern Europe, rather than vice-versa.

[185] See the discussion of these trades in Sella 1974, 379–84.

[186] In this period and for two centuries more, shipping remained too expensive to permit the Americas to send grain profitably to Europe. Once they could do so, eastern Europe faced a fateful economic challenge. See again chapter 2.

[187] See the classic discussions of, among others, Dobb 1946, 37–70; Moore 1967, chaps. 7–9; Wallerstein 1974, chap. 2; Brenner 1977; and Braudel 1982, 249–97. It should be remarked that Dobb's analysis (1946, 55–57) rightly emphasizes the importance of differing land-labor ratios between East and West; cf. Holton 1985, 84. On the other hand Brenner's effort to attribute the different outcomes to varying patterns of class organization and strength (Brenner 1976; cf. Brenner 1982) is rightly questioned by Postan and Hatcher (1978).

Portugal, and the Americas), it will have strengthened that factor and weakened the locally scarce ones of labor and capital. I shall offer further evidence momentarily to show that this is what actually happened.

In the second region, where only labor abounded—a region that, so far as I can see, is identical to Immanuel Wallerstein's (and Fernand Braudel's) "semiperiphery"[188]—we expect quite a different pattern to emerge: not urban-rural conflict, but a coalition of rural and urban elites (landowners and capitalists), against labor, in which *class conflict* is occasioned by a rising and assertive body of workers.

Evidence

The case is plainest with respect to the periphery, where the expansion of landowning power and the subjugation of both capital and labor can be measured by the growth of the demesne, the reassertion of labor dues, and the displacement of local merchants and manufacturers. In central and eastern Europe, the tale merely generalizes Carsten's (1954) portrait of the Prussian experience. In Poland, the average seigneurial holding grew by about 40 percent in the course of the sixteenth century and doubled in all between 1500 and 1650; in 1500 peasants had held over twice as much land as lords, but by 1600 they held only 90 percent as much.[189] (The average size of a manor in 1600 was 320 acres, or one-half a square mile; of this the demesne comprised just under half.)[190] Labor dues, which in many cases had become extinct or had fallen to a few days a year, grew to one day a week by 1520, to three by 1550, and to six—which, thereafter, was the norm throughout eastern Europe—by 1600.[191] Almost identical expansions of the demesne and of labor dues occurred in Hungary, Rumania, western Russia, and the European parts of the Ottoman Empire.[192] At the same time, in Poland as in the Prussian cases so carefully chronicled by Carsten, growing reliance on imports, shrinking demand among enserfed peasants, the intensification of direct links between lords and foreigners, and the drive to foreclose a route of escape for serfs combined to extinguish a once vigorous urban life.[193]

In the even more lightly populated American periphery, similar patterns early became deeply entrenched. On sugar and indigo plantations, in mines, and on the *encomiendas* of Spanish America, African slaves or Native

---

[188] Wallerstein 1974, 105, observes that the greater abundance of labor in the semiperiphery helps explain why sharecropping, rather than the serfdom or slavery of the periphery, was adopted there. Cf. Braudel 1984, 39–40.

[189] Kriedte 1983, 28.

[190] Maddalena 1974, 309.

[191] Braudel 1982, 267.

[192] See the general discussion in Maddalena 1974, 287–91.

[193] Kriedte 1983, 29; Wilson 1976, 19–20.

American serfs did the landowners' bidding.[194] (One may speculate that, had these crops been naturally suited to smaller-scale production, expanding trade might have benefited smallholding farmers, as it did in nineteenth-century Africa and North America.)[195] Cities, except as ports and administrative centers, were absent; almost no local artisans or manufacturers, and few local merchants, appeared.[196]

In the regions of the economic "core," quite to the contrary, the landholders yielded. In England, Tudor rule displaced the church, decimated the magnates through attainders, outlawed private armies, and, by augmenting the parliamentary representation of the boroughs, shifted power toward the urban sector. When Elizabeth's Stuart successors undertook to turn the clock back, they harvested revolution and the Commonwealth that sealed the fate of the old aristocracy.[197] The Dutch landed elite had always been weak in comparison to the urban patriciate.[198] In the wars of independence, weakened by many members' ties to the hated Spanish and to Catholicism, the aristocracy was eclipsed by the wealthier and more sagacious leadership of the Province of Holland and the Estates General.[199] With the achievement of self-rule in 1609, the northern Netherlands also passed irretrievably under urban control.[200]

Within this privileged region, and in contrast to others as we shall shortly see, there is little evidence of class conflict. Neither peasants nor urban workers revolt in the economically progressive sections of England until the rising of the Levellers in the Revolution of the 1640s;[201] nor, with the exception of some half-hearted strikes during the seventeenth century in Leyden, do we find manifestations of conflict between labor and capital in the Netherlands.[202] Part of the secret of this surprising docility will have been, as Braudel observes, the existence of "an enormous subproletariat" in most of the cities, eager and able to replace any who struck.[203] But a larger part, I suspect—particularly when one draws the contrast to the re-

[194] See the penetrating and sapient discussion by Wallerstein 1974, 87–94.

[195] Hopkins 1973, 125; cf. Watkins 1963.

[196] Braudel 1984, 40.

[197] See the general discussion of Lockyer 1964. On parliamentary representation, see Elton 1968, esp. 243; on the specific position of the aristocracy, Stone 1965; on developments under the Stuarts, Wilson 1976, chap. 12.

[198] "In the states of [the province of] Holland the nobility had only one vote, against eighteen votes for the cities; in Zeeland, too, the towns had all the votes but one." Daalder 1966, 196.

[199] Wilson 1976, chaps. 8–10; Daalder 1966, 190–94.

[200] North 1981, 153–54; see however the more qualified view of Braudel 1984, 193–97.

[201] Even C.G.A. Clay, who emphasizes the importance of peasant resistance to enclosures, concedes that "neither the scale nor the frequency of . . . [English] disturbances in any way compared to the widespread and often ferocious peasant risings on the Continent." Clay 1984, 78.

[202] Braudel 1982, 496–504.

[203] Braudel 1982, 506ff.

mainder of Europe—must lie in the natural alliance of this abundant labor with the abundant capital of the "core" regions.

In much of the rest of western Europe, however, and, as several students have observed, particularly in its most abundantly populated and most rapidly reproducing regions, revolt was extensive, bitter, and endemic. (This, again, forms a sharp contrast to the dumb submission, under far more outrageous exactions, of the eastern European masses.)[204] The *Bauernkrieg* that exploded across southern Germany in 1525 was only the most powerful and visible of a series of "innumerable revolts" that characterized the less advanced parts of Europe in the sixteenth century;[205] but its very prominence affords us a better and closer perspective on what may have been general characteristics of mass rebellion.

Three aspects of the *Bauernkrieg* (and of its immediate predecessors, the *Bundschuh* and "Poor Conrad" movements) attract our particular attention. First, despite its historical title the *Bauernkrieg* was not merely a peasant revolt; rather it united landless and land-poor peasants with miners and urban workers.[206] In some areas, indeed, it principally involved the lesser craftsmen of the towns.[207] It was, as its own manifestos proclaimed and its enemies conceded, a revolt of "the poor common man in town and countryside."[208] Second, and despite early sympathy among some urban (in particular, Reformation) elites, it soon aroused the united opposition of the urban patriciate and the landowning gentry.[209] Clearly indicative of the shift was Luther's abandonment of the revolutionary implications of his earlier writings and the appearance of his infamous tract "Against the Robbing and Murdering Hordes of Peasants." There is little to suggest a rural-urban cleavage in the events of 1525; rather, the evidence indicates an alliance of rural *and* urban masses against rural *and* urban elites—that is, class conflict.[210]

Finally, the most significant social correlates of the revolt appear to be increasing prosperity, or at the least increasing agricultural prices; rising

---

[204] As Moore (1967, 463) observes, only one revolt of any importance is known to have occurred in the East Elbian regions, at Königsberg in 1525.

[205] Braudel 1982, 493–95.

[206] Brady and Midelfort 1981, xi, xii, and xx; Blickle 1981, chap. 7. Sabean, however, has suggested that the rebellion may have originated as a movement of village elites *against* the growing numbers of day-laborers (cf. the critical discussion of this view by Blickle 1981, 14–15). Obviously, if Sabean's hypothesis is right, the interpretation advanced here cannot be correct.

[207] This was true chiefly of the Rhineland and Westphalia: Brady and Midelfort 1981, xx.

[208] Blickle 1981, 122–23.

[209] Blickle 1981, chap. 7, esp. pp. 117–19; cf. the earlier success of the aristocracy of Württemberg in "splitting the rebels by redressing urban grievances" (Brady and Midelfort 1981, xiii).

[210] Moore's (1967, 464) interpretation, based on older secondary sources, is more reserved, contending that "at different times and places [the peasants] were in opposition to nearly every conceivable group and in alliance with some other."

demographic pressure; and expanding access to markets.[211] All of this conforms well with our theoretical expectations: labor becomes most restive where it (and no other factor) is most abundant, where markets expand most rapidly, and where, consequently, it is best positioned to gain economically—but where it is held back by antiquated political institutions and property relations.

The immediate outcome was, of course, a clear defeat for the rebels: tens of thousands were executed, the leaders with particular cruelty; and, despite the efforts of the Imperial Diet to mediate the grievances at Speyer in 1526, in most regions the old order was at first restored in all its severity.[212] Events quickly revealed, however, that "the feudal ruling class simply could not ruthlessly restore the pre-1525 forms of domination."[213] The growing wealth of the lower orders, coupled with a stubborn passive resistance, soon compelled many lords to negotiate explicit contracts, which often granted nearly all of what the rebels had originally demanded.[214]

Here as in other cases, these observations are best regarded as tentatively supported hypotheses that deserve, and require, further investigation. It appears, however, that in its regionally diverse impact the extension and intensification of world trade in the sixteenth century further demonstrates the usefulness of the theory developed earlier. In both the "core" and the "periphery" of the new system, urban-rural conflict ensued: in the core, however, the urban coalition of capital and labor won the upper hand, whereas in the periphery landowners defeated both groups and all but eliminated urban life. In the "semiperiphery," characterized by a scarcity of land and capital and an abundance of labor, class conflict erupted, with urban and rural workers—lesser craftsmen and land-poor peasants—rising against a united elite of landowners and urban patricians. Defeated in open combat, the "common man" in these regions nonetheless gained from the inexorable progress of the market. Baden, Württemberg, Bavaria, and the Rhineland remained beacons of peasant liberty and, in later centuries, of liberalism against the unrelieved Junker power of the East Elbian spaces.

CONCLUSION

The plausibility of the Stolper-Samuelson hypotheses as I have applied them to these three quite separate cases suggests the theory's broader util-

---

[211] The aspect of increasing prosperity is emphasized particularly by Moore 1967, 465, but qualified by Blickle 1981, 51; demographic pressure is stressed both by Blickle 1981, e.g., 50–51 and 76–78, and Sabean 1969 and 1972. Blickle 1981, 71–72, points to peasants' orientation toward expanding markets, which had induced them to concentrate on such labor-intensive commodities as garden crops, cattle, and wine.

[212] Blickle 1981, chap. 10.

[213] Blickle 1981, 172.

[214] Blickle 1981, chaps. 11 and 12; Maddalena 1974, 292.

ity as a tool of historical analysis. In each instance, I am all too aware, I have been able to offer only a partial and derivative account. Students who know these epochs and areas more intimately will have to pronounce on the interpretations that I have advanced.

Still, the parallels between the historical and the more recent cases, and the order that the present theory invites us to see beneath confused and often contentious historical episodes, speak strongly for its value. If the "frontier" societies of the ancient Greek world, in Thrace and Magna Graecia, responded with cleavages like those of the Americas and Oceania in the nineteenth century, while the democratization of Athens and Corinth resembled that of nineteenth-century northwestern Europe; if, as Barrington Moore, Jr., once suggested,[215] there are clear parallels of political and cultural sentiment between the declining Roman landed elite and the rurally based fascism of our own century; and if the vicious class conflicts of the European semiperiphery in the sixteenth century prefigure those of backward nineteenth-century Europe and twentieth-century Asia, then the present theory suggests reasons, both for the similarities and for their historical timing.

Even more sharply, this perspective helps to explain why, and when, Athens evolved differently from Sparta or Thessaly; why at the decline of Rome western Europe moved toward feudalism, North Africa and the Levant toward Islam, and southeast Europe and Asia Minor toward Caesaro-Papism; and why the revival of the "long" sixteenth century expanded freedom in western Europe but brought a "second serfdom" to eastern Europe and slavery to the Americas. It helps also to clarify ongoing scholarly controversies, suggesting for example why Postan and Le Roy Ladurie are likely to be right, and Brenner is likely to be wrong, about the importance of demographic factors in the economic and political evolution of European regions.[216]

Neither trade nor—as its leading student has observed[217]—the "trading state" is a product only of the last two centuries. Both prevailed in earlier epochs; and both, I contend, have had at all times similar traits and consequences.

[215] Moore 1967, 491–96.
[216] Postan and Hatcher 1978; Le Roy Ladurie 1978; Brenner 1976 and 1982.
[217] Rosecrance 1986.

CHAPTER SIX

Some Implications for Other Theories and Conjectures in the Social Sciences

ONE IMPORTANT TEST of a theory is its empirical accuracy: its ability to explain persuasively and, in the ideal case, to predict events. To do that has been the chief aim of the preceding chapters. A second test however matters almost as much. That is the theory's power to illuminate and subsume previous accounts of the same events. To the extent that a new hypothesis can resolve old confusions, make sense of seeming riddles, and regulate long-standing controversies, it strikes us as more persuasive.

The previous chapters have often indicated, if only peripherally, some points at which this perspective might serve such a purpose—for example, with respect to the land-capital alliance that Moore stressed, the old Pirenne controversy, or the "Brenner debate" among present-day historians. In this brief chapter, I shall suggest more directly a few of the ways in which an account based on the Stolper-Samuelson theorem may help us better to understand some of the discipline's more stubborn mysteries and controversies.

MUST INDUSTRIAL "LATECOMERS" DEVELOP STRONG STATES?

In an essay that first appeared in 1952,[1] Alexander Gerschenkron advanced the brilliant, powerful, and soon highly influential hypothesis that "latecomers" to economic development required, if they were to succeed, strong states—stronger, indeed, the later the commencement of their developmental effort. The reason, to abbreviate a subtle argument drastically, was the need to contend with ever more vigorous and capital-intensive competition. Britain had faced no rivals and had made its crucial breakthrough in textiles, the least capital-intensive of industries. By the time France reached the threshold, railroads—demanding far greater outlays of capital—were an essential prerequisite; France had to (and did) build a better system of railroads than Britain then possessed. When Germany began to industrialize, others already dominated the more capital-intensive production of iron; hence Germany succeeded only by "leapfrogging" into the yet more capital- and knowledge-intensive sectors of steel and chemi-

---

[1] Gerschenkron 1962, chap. 1. The essay first appeared as a chapter in Hoselitz 1952.

cals. And as Russia commenced its effort, first under Witte and Stolpyin and later under Stalin,[2] foreign competition could be met only by yet more massive and capital-intensive enterprises.

In each case, Gerschenkron argued, the need for more capital and bigger enterprises could only be met by the wider involvement of a more powerful state.[3] Whereas Britain had raised capital almost wholly by private means, relying on the state only to reform property rights and provide right-of-way (Enclosure and Railway Acts), France had already needed the *Crédit Mobilier* and state-favored investment banks.[4] Germany had required a powerful and authoritarian state, closely allied with bankers and industrialists and itself deeply enmeshed in such enterprises as mines and railroads. Russia, of course, had ultimately relied on totalitarian methods to "catch up" quickly.

The argument was convincingly framed; but Albert Hirschman (1968) challenged it, observing that the even later industrializers of Latin America had defied Gerschenkron's hypothetical pattern.[5] These nations had focused on consumer goods, had leapfrogged no one, and had developed nothing like the powerful state apparatus of a Germany or a Russia.

Although other explanations of this disparity between Gerschenkron and Hirschman, or between the European and the Latin American experience, can surely be plausibly advanced, the present theory suggests the centrality of the fact that the European latecomers were *labor rich*, the Latin American ones *labor poor*. It may be that Gerschenkron's hypotheses apply only to the former. By definition (as outlined in chapter 1), an economically backward society is scarce in capital. If, at the same time, it is abundant in labor, as Europe was, expanding trade of the kind Gerschenkron presupposes must induce conflict between labor and capital: labor will seek freer trade and greater political power; capital will demand protection (usually in concert with landowners) and will attempt to repress labor. The faster trade expands, the more intense these conflicts will be; and they will explode particularly over efforts to accumulate capital rapidly, through forced savings from the masses. Even the introduction of capital-intensive modes of production is likely to arouse opposition by its displacement of abundant labor. The combination of abundant labor, a backward econ-

---

[2] See also chapters 2 and 3.

[3] For Gerschenkron, foreign borrowing offered no alternative route to capital abundance: Russia, after all, had pioneered in what subsequent students have called "indebted industrialization" (see chapter 2).

[4] Industrialization in the United States, it should be recalled, depended almost as much on the state as it did in France: land grants to railroads, subsidized banks, an extensive system of technical education, and protective tariffs were crucial elements of the rapid postbellum expansion.

[5] A helpful further discussion of these points is Kurth 1979a.

omy, and rapidly expanding external trade, then, conduces to intense class conflict, which only a stern and (if capital is to be accumulated) undemocratic state can resolve.

In *labor-scarce* underdeveloped economies—of which most of Latin America, as we have repeatedly seen, is a chief exemplar—the situation is reversed. Because both labor and capital are scarce, they are natural allies on the key issue of trade: both are threatened by an expansion of markets, and both endorse protection. This crucial area of agreement diminishes direct class conflict (even though urban-rural disagreements may well be intense) and makes arbitration by a powerful state less urgent. Moreover, capital accumulation is less controversial, since the protective tariffs that both labor and capital support have that effect; and highly capital-intensive modes of production are readily accepted, since labor is in any event scarce (and, ordinarily, well remunerated). In light of all these considerations, it seems less surprising that Latin America—or, for that matter, the Americas generally—has failed to conform to Gerschenkron's "orderly system of graduated deviations" from the model of Britain's first industrialization.[6]

Even for the set of labor-abundant economies, moreover, we can see that Gerschenkron's original hypothesis must be amended: what matters is not only how "late" a country arrives at the threshold of industrialization, but whether its economic development *precedes* or *follows* a significant increase in exposure to trade. If, as in Britain's case, the economy is relatively advanced when the great burst of trading activity commences (in the nineteenth century), then both capital and labor are abundant and can unite. If, as it has in almost all other labor-abundant societies, trade expands before industry, capital, being scarce, must oppose labor—the more bitterly the scarcer capital is, which is to say the more backward the economy; and, the more bitter the opposition of these two crucial factors, the likelier is the need for a powerful and controlling state to accumulate capital.

WHY IS THERE NO SOCIALISM IN THE UNITED STATES?

Scholars have proposed many answers to Sombart's famous question: America's social mobility, ethnic diversity, non-feudal past, open frontier, or early achievement of mass suffrage supposedly accounts for the weakness of its socialist tendencies. The considerations advanced in this volume suggest the importance of a rather different factor, namely the enduring *scarcity of labor* in the United States. Historically, earlier chapters have indicated, militant movements of the working class[7] have arisen most readily where labor has benefited from expanding trade and capital has not—

[6] Gerschenkron 1962, 44.
[7] I exclude from this category the milder and more reformist socialisms of Australia and New Zealand.

where labor is abundant and capital is scarce. In those circumstances, labor is progressive and capital is reactionary—the tale of nineteenth-century Europe and twentieth-century Asia—and class conflict is correspondingly intense.

Where labor is scarce, however, it can never gain from rising trade but achieves the resources for militancy only during sharp contractions of the international market (the New Deal in the United States, populism in Latin America); and even then it opposes capital only where that factor is abundant, that is in advanced economies. American labor's dependence on *isolation* from international competition has made it, in an era of generally expanding trade, peculiarly tentative and imperialist.

Powerful and radical socialist movements, if the present theory is right, are confined to backward and labor-rich economies under conditions of expanding trade; and Sombart's question is perhaps better phrased as: Why is there so little militant socialism in labor-scarce economies?[8]

WHY DID AMERICAN ABOLITIONISTS FAVOR PROTECTION?

In a masterful and provocative chapter of *Social Origins of Dictatorship and Democracy* (1967, chap. 3), Barrington Moore, Jr., not only sought to portray the U.S. Civil War as "the last bourgeois revolution" but raised the question of why American Free-Soilers and abolitionists (notably in the early Republican party) had so strongly favored protection, and why their combined platform had gained the support of so broad a coalition, including northern capitalists and workers and western farmers. More than a puzzle in the historiography of the nineteenth-century United States was involved here. That workers, especially ones locked in a mortal struggle for human freedom, should embrace protection seemed odd; and so, even more, did increasingly export-dependent farmers' adherence to the cause.

Moore offered, very tentatively, three answers: a shift in domestic trade relations (western farmers began to find more lucrative markets in the northeastern cities than, as before, in the South; and Southerners shipped their cotton to England); a deep fear of slave competition among smallholding Western farmers; and a classic logroll, in which capitalists got their tariff and farmers and workers got a Homestead Act.

The present perspective offers a somewhat simpler answer. First, the common interest of workers and capitalists in protection now seems self-evident: where labor and capital are both scarce, both are harmed by expanding trade. But opponents of slavery must also have supported tariffs. Expanding trade, in the labor-scarce Americas, could only have depressed

---

[8] If, as I have argued (chapter 3), Sweden and Norway were also characterized by a relative scarcity of labor in the interwar years, their socialisms' lack of militancy after 1920 may be more easily understood.

wages;[9] and such a development would in turn have *intensified and pro-longed slavery*. Slaves, after all, already received a lower wage than they would voluntarily have accepted (else why coerce them?); and any trade-induced lowering of the overall wage rate would presumably have further depressed their real wage and would have expanded the number of pursuits in which only slave labor could offer a profitable return. (Consider the parallel effect of expanding trade in the periphery of the sixteenth-century world economy, as described in chapter 5.)

To slaveowners, conversely, protection was inimical in two ways. As land-intensive producers in a country where land was abundant, slaveown-ers would lose directly from any constriction of trade (again, a simple re-statement of the Stolper-Samuelson result). Less immediately apparent, but made vivid by the rapidly expanding efforts of the Underground Rail-way, every rise in free-sector wage rates, by increasing incentives to flee, raised slaveowners' costs of supervision and control.[10] Protection in the labor-scarce U.S. economy would inevitably bring a considerable net in-crease in the prevailing real wage rate, over and above what other trends might already imply. Such a change must further undermine the whole slave system. Hence protection was the enemy, not only of the planters' markets, but of their method of labor control and of their slave assets.

The mystery, as Moore also emphasized,[11] remains the support that this protectionist coalition achieved among western farmers. They, as land-in-tensive producers, might have been expected to join the southern planters in support of free trade. Two factors, I think, enter in. First, the small farms, while surely more land intensive than urban enterprises, also used capital and labor—the American economy's scarce factors—far more inten-sively than the southern plantations. The greater labor intensity of the small family farm is legendary; and it was in the West that such capital investments as McCormick's reaper, the steel-shared plow, and even the sewing machine found their natural market.[12]

Second, and likely of greater importance, western farmers' opposition to slavery must have outweighed all doubts about protection. Despite slav-ery's high (and, as we have seen, growing) costs of supervision, and despite

---

[9] Or, at least, would have retarded their advance. Other trends—a growing skill-level, more capital-intensive production—were raising wages independent of protection's effects.

[10] It also raised the price of slaves dramatically (Moore 1967, 120)—just as a rise in free-market rentals augments the real price (in search costs, bribes, etc.) of rent-controlled apart-ments.

[11] Moore 1967, 127ff.

[12] Ironically, midwestern farms were less land-intensive in part because Congress's long delay of a Homestead Act (Moore 1967, 129–30) restricted the availability of new land. In this sense, the early passage of such an act by the Republicans may, by making western farmers more land-intensive, have sown the seeds of later populism: see again chapter 2.

its unsuitability to skilled pursuits, its lower labor costs[13] maintained it as a formidable competitor to free agriculture. In Arkansas and Texas—and, for all anyone knew, in Missouri, Kansas, or even Nebraska—slave competition might drive out, or at a minimum might drive down the returns to, free farmers.[14] The world could be made safe for the small farmer, it seemed, only if slavery were weakened or confined; and protection, as the slaveowners themselves incessantly averred, would weaken slavery.

Protection, then, directly benefited both workers and capitalists; by raising overall wage levels it weakened slavery; and by weakening slavery it removed a possibly mortal threat to western farmers. It no longer seems quite so mysterious that the tariff enjoyed so central a position in Republican ideology; or that workers, capitalists, abolitionists, and farmers allied in support of it.

PROTECTIONISM, FREE TRADE, AND THE THEORY OF HEGEMONIC STABILITY

The years between 1815 and about 1875 were, despite some exceptions, a period of increasingly freer trade: Britain lowered duties and then repealed the Corn Laws; Latin America's newly independent republics embraced liberalism and free trade; Prussia, first in the *Zollverein* and then in the North German Confederation and early empire, moved Germany toward lower duties; and France, under the Cobden-Chevalier Treaty of 1860, drastically lowered its tariffs.[15] After 1875, restrictions were again increased in many states, albeit only moderately. The interwar period, by contrast, and particularly the 1930s, was characterized by tariff wars and by boundless protectionism. The years since 1945 have witnessed spectacular new reductions in tariffs; but some have seen since the mid-1970s harbingers of a "new mercantilism" that may again interrupt world trade.[16]

In attempting to explain these secular fluctuations of tariff policy, an important school of analysts that includes prominently such figures as Charles Kindleberger (1973), Robert Gilpin (1975), Stephen Krasner (1976), and Robert Keohane (1980) has elaborated the well-known theory of "hegemonic stability": when a single power dominates the world,

---

[13] With Rostow (1978, 781–82), I regard the cliometric efforts of Fogel and Engerman 1974 as largely irrelevant to these considerations. If it be seriously argued that the real wage rate of slaves exceeded that of free workers in the antebellum United States, one must ask why free workers did not sell themselves in droves into so enviable an estate; or why owners spent so much to prevent slaves from fleeing a condition that only fools would leave.

[14] Cf. Moore 1967, 119–20.

[15] A useful survey of tariff policies in the nineteenth and twentieth centuries is Kenwood and Lougheed 1971, chaps. 4, 13, and 18.

[16] See the immediately succeeding section.

or a substantial portion of it, free trade is likelier.[17] The dominant state, drawing disproportionate benefit from the collective good of free trade, is likelier to guarantee and supply it, both by safeguarding routes and markets and by exerting suasion against would-be protectionist powers; absent such a trusted guarantor, a "prisoners' dilemma" of protectionism is likely[18] to prevail. Thus it is no accidental connection that the mid-nineteenth century was a period of uncontested British hegemony, that this hegemony waned after 1875 and was destroyed in World War I, and that U.S. hegemony only came to be fully asserted after 1945—and, according to many accounts, has declined since the early 1970s.[19]

The theory of hegemonic stability has of course met vigorous criticism on a variety of grounds:[20] it does not explain why the hegemonic power should always find free trade in its interest, why some states that possessed the means to pursue hegemony—the United States in the interwar period—have failed to do so, or by what precise means a hegemon "guarantees" free trade; in addition, the theory's empirical support, which on closer inspection is fragile,[21] is confined to two cases, the hegemonies of modern Britain and the United States.

Some earlier cases examined in the previous chapter—those of Athens and of early Imperial Rome—suggest strongly the wider applicability of the theory of hegemonic stability; and the perspective advanced here helps also to clarify the model's underlying logic. The theory, I contend, is rightly understood as one not of *political*, but of *economic*, hegemony.

Since at the latest the early seventeenth century,[22] political hegemony has always been associated with a gap in capital endowments: the leading power has far more physical capital, and pursues more capital-intensive manufactures, than do others. Being abundant in capital and, in all but the rarest circumstances, in at least one other major factor (in Athens, Rome, the Netherlands, and Britain labor; in the United States, land), the hege-

[17] The summary that follows is an amalgam of these several theorists' points; it characterizes no one of them perfectly.

[18] But not certain: Keohane 1984. The view of free trade as a public good, likely to give rise to a prisoners' dilemma, is widespread. See, e.g., Lake 1988, 35ff.

[19] For a dissenting view, see Russett 1985.

[20] One of the most powerful critiques, which addresses the game-theoretic deficiencies of the underlying model, is Snidal 1985.

[21] The usual account, it has been asserted, considerably overstates the extent to which freedom of trade was actually achieved in the nineteenth century. See principally Stein 1984.

[22] In earlier epochs, as McNeill (1954) first observed, advanced economies were frequently dominated or conquered by more primitive states. The last known example of an economically retarded international hegemon, however, was sixteenth-century Spain, and its course demonstrates the improbability of a sequel: it was decisively defeated by two territorially minuscule, weakly governed, but economically flourishing powers: England and the Netherlands.

mon's capitalists will seek, and usually will achieve, a policy of free trade. At the same time, other powers' relative *scarcity* of capital, coupled with their naturally weak endowment of at least one other factor (in the Americas and Africa, labor; in most of the rest of the world, land) inclines them to embrace protection. When the protectionists approach victory, the hegemonic power can attain its goal of free trade only by extensive side payments[23] or by political means: the use of suasion or coercion to open the markets of less developed lands. *Political* hegemony, then, appears as a consequence of *economic* supremacy and, as I shall argue, loss of political domination equally follows loss of economic preeminence.

We can predict, moreover, the domestic groups that will ally most eagerly with the hegemon, namely the owners and intensive users of the only factor in which the given backward economy happens to abound. Thus in the Americas, large landowners and land-intensive farmers were the natural allies of British—and, later, of U.S.—hegemony;[24] but in Europe (and, one suspects, in Asia) workers and labor-intensive manufacturers sympathized more with British policies and institutions. The more powerful these "natural allies" of the hegemon are in the given society, the easier it is for that leading economy to penetrate and shape domestic politics.[25]

A second point, however, is almost as significant: to the hegemon, the desirability of such penetration depends on how well the backward economy's endowments complement its own. Britain, scarce in land, found it particularly urgent to keep open the economies of Latin America (and, to a lesser extent, of Africa) that could supply its needs for food and fiber and would import its own more labor-intensive products. U.S. priorities, as Latin American students of dependency have long observed,[26] are exactly the reverse: Latin America is if anything a rival exporter of agricultural goods, and the labor-abundant but capital-poor regions of Asia are more desirable trading partners.

What, however, if clear-cut economic hegemony is lacking or if, having once been achieved, it falters? If several states enjoy roughly equal levels of capital abundance, all are likely to support open markets. In each such state, a coalition of capital and the other locally abundant factor—in the United States and the USSR at the present day, land; in Europe and Japan, labor—will seek to sacrifice (or, more sensibly, to compensate: see my subsequent discussion) the locally scarce factor and to pursue the considerable

---

[23] Cf. Stein 1984.

[24] Cf. James and Lake 1989.

[25] Because ownership of land often confers political power in backward societies, free trade is most easily achieved where land is the abundant factor of a less-developed economy (as in Latin America) and will be most opposed where land is scarce (as in nineteenth-century continental Europe).

[26] See, e.g., Sunkel with Paz 1973, 436ff.

gains of trade.[27] On one level, trade then obviously becomes easier: at a minimum, these advanced economies can trade easily with each other. At the same time, however, it becomes harder to induce less advanced states— which, as the present approach emphasizes, incline more to protection— to keep their economies open. Which power, in particular, is to bear the burden of bribing or coercing open the protectionist periphery? Here the problem of "collective goods" arises even more sharply than the received theory of hegemonic stability has portrayed it.

The several leading economies may well devise collaborative means of financial and moral suasion, such as the present-day International Monetary Fund; but direct coercion, which is still invoked where access to vital raw materials is at issue,[28] presents thornier problems. No single power— a waning hegemon, for example—will willingly foot forever the considerable costs of such operations, when others benefit at least as much; nor will the others necessarily trust it to safeguard their national interests.[29] In the worst case, as in the rivalry between Britain and Germany at the end of the nineteenth and the beginning of the twentieth century, each leading state begins to assemble its own means of force; and these, even if intended only to safeguard trade,[30] are easily perceived as direct threats to other major powers. As perhaps a next-worse outcome, the several economically advanced powers may carve the less developed world into spheres of influence, if not outright empires, over which each claims exclusive right of intervention.[31]

This discussion, obviously, does not resolve the many controversies that surround the theory of hegemonic stability. It does, however, suggest reasons why economic hegemony requires, and is the precondition for, political hegemony; why specific hegemons attend to specific countries and elites; and why weak or shared hegemony necessarily makes international trade more problematic.

THE "NEW" PROTECTIONISM AND ITS ANTIDOTES

As trade has expanded in the postwar era, and particularly since the petroleum crises of the 1970s increased the need for foreign exchange, pressure

[27] Again, there are crucial exceptions. Even though Germany had achieved capital abundance by the early twentieth century, powerful owners of locally scarce resources—above all, of land—propelled it repeatedly toward the pursuit of autarky and conquest.

[28] Krasner 1978, chap. 8.

[29] The recent Persian Gulf war, and the longer-term issue of how to deal with a petroleum cartel, casts these issues in bold relief.

[30] Ekkart Kehr's (1973) pioneering researches (originally published in 1930) demonstrated in detail that Germany's commercial elites had principally advocated the construction of a large fleet and that concern for the security of markets had animated them. David Calleo (1978) has amplified these points in the light of more recent research.

[31] Cf. Doyle 1986, chap. 10.

for restrictions has intensified in many countries:[32] American automobile workers, European and Japanese farmers, German and French electronics firms, textile manufacturers in many countries, have sought and, in not a few cases, have received some shelter from the competition of imports. Some analysts have even expressed fears of a "new mercantilism" and a collapse of the international trading order that would mirror that of the 1930s.[33] But why should international trade be most resisted now, exactly when it has most significantly multiplied collective welfare? And by what means, if any, can this resistance be allayed and the perils of a new trade war avoided?

The resistance to trade is only partially explained by the present theory. To be sure, each unanticipated expansion of trade (such as the one that occurred in the 1970s) threatens anew the owners and intensive users of locally scarce factors: farmers in Japan, workers in the United States, capitalists (including, very significantly, managers of state enterprises) in the Third World. Absent mechanisms of the kind I shall outline momentarily, these groups can be expected to resist, desperately and justifiably, their unhappy economic fate.

At the same time, and separately from the focus of this volume,[34] growing trade and broader competition threaten extractors of *rents*[35] in each society. American automobile workers, French farmers, British stockbrokers and coalminers, African city dwellers, the Soviet party and managerial elite—all have used their monopoly power or political "clout" to obtain real returns far above their costs of production. The more they are exposed to foreign competition, the more their local monopoly is undermined and the dearer it becomes for their societies or governments to continue to subsidize them.[36] We may therefore expect great resistance to trade where monopoly and privilege have most pervaded economic life, for example, in some of the "socialist" societies.[37]

On the first point—the inevitable threat that expanding trade poses to locally scarce factors—it is helpful to recall the concluding sentences of Stolper and Samuelson's original essay:

[32] As will quickly become evident, I mean by the phrase "new protectionism" efforts to return to protection by whatever means. In a different usage, Greenaway 1983, distinguishes a "new" protectionism of nontariff interventions from the "old" one of quotas and imposts.

[33] For a fair, if highly skeptical, summary of these arguments, see Strange 1985.

[34] I hope to cover issues of rent seeking, trade, and war in a future volume.

[35] In the economic sense, a rent is "any income received by a factor over the amount necessary to keep that factor in its present employment." Hanson 1977, 395.

[36] It is a commonplace of economic analysis that cartels can survive only if they are protected from foreign competition; or, as populists once put it more polemically in this country, that "the tariff is mother of the trust."

[37] See again Hough 1986.

Our argument provides no political ammunition for the protectionist. . . . the harm which free trade inflicts upon one factor of production is necessarily less than the gain to the other. Hence, it is always possible to bribe the suffering factor by subsidy or other redistributive devices so as to leave all factors better off as a result of trade.[38]

The gains from trade necessarily outweigh the summed losses to owners and users of scarce factors; the victims can be fully compensated without removing all of the winners' gains. Moreover, as one trenchant student of these issues has observed, the need for civil peace and the costs of repression often dictate that the victims *should* be compensated.[39] As expansions of international trade become more frequent and more sweeping, the question of compensation will grow more acute.

One way of blunting protectionism, then, is to provide credible guarantees of compensation; and this, according to a variety of students,[40] is what the elaborate social insurance systems and the extensive social welfare expenditures of the most trade-dependent states do. By making compensation automatic and universal, they reduce fears of adjustment. Almost as important, they remove issues of compensation from the arena of partisan and pressure-group politics.

That is crucial, because the second problem in avoiding protectionism is to minimize the level of rent extraction and rent seeking in the given society. A monopolistic sector or union is already an obstacle to openness; a mechanism that encourages overcompensation of genuinely injured factors presents steadily rising impediments to free trade. Hence the importance of making compensation automatic and universalistic rather than ad hoc and particularistic; and hence, too, the need to channel and centralize affected interests' access to the loci of real political power.[41]

At one extreme we may set a system like that of the United States: decentralized institutions, weak parties, a powerful legislature, and direct election of representatives from 435 districts and 50 states mean that even trivially small interests—dairy or sugar farmers, a motorcycle or department-store firm, textile or lumber workers—can, by promises of votes or campaign funds, reasonably hope to affect legislation and policy. The opposite model can be represented by the Netherlands, where the state is unitary, the entire country forms a single parliamentary constituency, and members are elected by list proportional representation. Parties are pow-

[38] Stolper and Samuelson 1941, 73.
[39] Strange 1985, 236. For a more technical summary of the chief arguments for compensation, see Greenaway 1983, chap. 10.
[40] The most comprehensive statement of the position is that of Katzenstein 1985, esp. chap. 2; see also Tillotson 1986 and Cameron 1978.
[41] The argument that follows is laid out more fully in Rogowski 1986.

erful and disciplined (because the list system means that leaders alone decide who is renominated), rank-and-file parliamentarians can defy local pressures, and interest-group leaders must deal directly with national party leaders—who, of course, are disinclined to deal with any but large and disciplined organizations. At ill-defined points between these two extremes lie such cases as modern Britain (with centralized parties but a decentralized method of election) and the USSR (with, obviously, a centralized and dictatorial party but many domains of entrenched interest-group influence *within* that party).[42]

A system like that of the United States—or, given its far greater reliance on nonmarket allocation, the USSR—practically guarantees resistance, rent seeking, and excessive compensation under conditions of rapidly expanding trade. A regime like that of the Netherlands—whose pattern, as I have shown elsewhere,[43] is approached by other industrial states in almost direct proportion to their reliance on trade—is far better suited to adapt successfully, and without protectionism, to such an external shock.[44]

To minimize protectionist, scarce-factor resistance to sharp expansions of trade, then, governments are well-advised to have in place extensive and universalistic schemes of social insurance and to insulate their chief political institutions from the local pressures that conduce to rent seeking. Not surprisingly, these are the methods that the most successful trading states have already adopted.

CONCLUSION

The ability of a new theory to subsume, or at a minimum to reinterpret and enrich, older approaches has long been taken as a crucial test of its worth. I hope to have suggested here a few of the ways in which a Stolper-Samuelson perspective on trade and cleavages can make that kind of contribution. I suspect, but cannot here adequately argue, that the approach will also have implications for such other issues as: class and sectoral solidarity across national boundaries; demands for the enlargement or fragmentation of states; and coalitions and conflicts among states.

[42] In part, it appears, the policy of *glasnost* is intended to help penetrate and tame these preserves.

[43] Rogowski 1986, 214.

[44] See the similar argument of Katzenstein 1985, 150–56.

CHAPTER SEVEN

Conclusion

LET US SUPPOSE that further analysis and testing of the theory advanced throughout this volume support it as a reliable guide to interpretation and action and lead us to believe that it is substantially true. What difference will such a finding make, for scholarship and for everyday affairs; and what direction will it give to future research?

Most obviously, historians and political scientists would gain from such a conclusion a different and more complete understanding of political cleavages and realignments. In studying any "realigning" election or event—the 1640s in England, 1879 in Germany, 1896 and 1932 in the United States, the 1930s and the 1980s in the Soviet Union, 1966 in West Germany, 1981 in France—scholars will have to assess how much changing exposure to trade contributed to the shift of political allegiance and to the pattern of conflict. Analysts may also see more clearly how issues of trade have restricted the possibilities of realignment: how remote, for example, was the chance that workers and farmers could coalesce in the United States or in modern Germany; that workers could find common ground with any kind of capitalist in any of the less developed regions of nineteenth-century Europe; or that capitalists and farmers could unite in modern Latin America.

To practicing politicians and incumbent leaders, the points adumbrated here should suggest both the risks and the coalitional opportunities that rapid shifts in trade afford. To European and Japanese leaders today, for example, continued expansion of trade carries only slight domestic risks: further alienation of a dwindling agricultural sector, and perhaps (see later discussion) of less skilled labor; but a cementing of the productive postwar alliance between organized capital and organized labor, the two factors that these economies hold in abundance. Even in a downturn, agriculture in these countries, as in Britain or the Netherlands in the 1930s, is by now so weak as to present little danger.

In the United States, Canada, Australia, and the USSR, abundant in both land and capital, expansion of trade carries a larger but probably still manageable danger: protest from (but a simultaneous weakening of) workers and rent-dependent groups, opposed by a twentieth-century coalition of "iron and rye"—that is, of agriculture and the most advanced industrial sectors. Any new collapse of trade like that of the 1930s, however, would sorely challenge these societies' stability: workers would be strengthened, albeit (given their reduced share of the population) less dramatically than in the New Deal; and owners of land and capital might resort to authoritarian measures to fend them off.

Most of Latin America and Africa, we have seen, is abundant in land but scarce in capital and labor. In these regions expanding trade tends to strengthen farmers and to exacerbate urban-rural conflict; but in most places the protectionist alliance of business, urban politicians, and workers is deeply entrenched. Landowners are a danger, particularly when they can attract allies among the military and among foreign investors; but their threat is only slightly greater than that presented by workers in the advanced land-rich economies. Downturns in trade of course weaken the landowners even more. Hence the great danger to these economies is not deep conflict but the stagnation and immiseration that their protectionist policies necessarily impose.

In Asia, the Caribbean, much of Central America, and the few densely populated areas of Africa (e.g., Liberia and Kenya: see Table 4.4), expanding world trade, today as in China and Vietnam after World War II, will strengthen and radicalize labor. Serious class conflict between that abundant factor and the two scarce ones of land and capital can hardly be ruled out, whether one speaks of the pitifully stagnant Philippine or Liberian economies or the vibrant South Korean one. Any collapse of world commerce, however, would have an even worse consequence: a new edition of the fascist, military, and often imperialist alliance of agriculture and industry that pervaded Asia in the 1930s. Both American and Soviet leaders would do well, even if they discount the domestic costs, to consider the extreme instability that fluctuations in world trade will inevitably visit on this numerous class of economies.

In each of these cases, it is important to recall, the gains of trade will always outweigh the sum of individual losses. Hence reliable mechanisms of compensation (as previously discussed), and political institutions that further and sustain them,[1] become everywhere more important for domestic stability as exposure to international trade expands. The debility and corruption of many less-developed states, however, shatter all hope of such mechanisms and institutions.

Within states, representatives of groups and factions may understand more clearly where their natural interests and allies reside during rapid expansions or contractions of international trade. In both the advanced, labor-scarce economies—chiefly the United States and the USSR—and the backward, labor-abundant ones of Asia and the Caribbean, working-class leaders find their best hope of support in the *least capital-intensive* sectors.

[1] Katzenstein 1985, esp. chaps. 1, 4, and 5; Rogowski 1987.

Where, conversely, labor and capital are both abundant (as in Europe and Japan) or both scarce (as in Latin America and Africa), workers find their natural allies in the *most capital-intensive* manufactures and industries, and among owners of capital.

Capitalists, it should already be clear, find their readiest partners among *landowners and land-intensive enterprises* (i.e., in agriculture) in both the advanced land-abundant and the backward land-poor economies: again, the present-day United States, USSR, and Oceania on the one hand; and Asia, the Caribbean, and Central America on the other. In Europe, Japan, Latin America, and Africa, however—where labor is as abundant, or as scarce, as capital—owners of capital coalesce easily with workers, especially with skilled workers, and with the enterprises that employ them intensively. (In the advanced, labor-rich economies, skilled workers are the most plentiful; in the backward, labor-poor regions, skilled workers are the scarcest.)

Landowners, finally, share interests with capital, and with the most capital-intensive sectors, in both the advanced land-rich and the backward land-poor economies (the United States, Canada, Australia; Asia and the Caribbean). Both in Europe (where capital is even more abundant than labor) and in Africa (where capital is even scarcer than labor), landowners can seek allies most profitably in the *least capital-intensive* branches. In Japan (even richer in labor than in capital) and in Latin America (with a greater scarcity of labor than of capital), landowners can best hope for support, or least acquiescence, from the *least labor-intensive* enterprises.[2] I suspect that we see signs of this perception already in the ties between farmers and uncompetitive industries in Europe, and between agriculture and large-scale industry in Japan and Latin America.

What, last of all, does this approach suggest as the most profitable directions of future research; or, to put the issue more pointedly, what changes in the approach itself might improve its utility? I shall confine myself to three conjectures.

First, the importance of capital in agriculture appears to have reached a point that virtually obviates consideration of land's abundance or quality: if Saudi Arabia can profitably export wheat, almost anything is possible. At the same time, as Japan's postwar development indicates,[3] quality of labor—the distinction between highly skilled and semi- or unskilled labor, and investment in human capital—has assumed a growing and perhaps

---

[2] In neither case will industry really support agriculture's demands. In Europe and Africa, however, the least capital-intensive sectors can most easily afford to accommodate agriculture on the issue of trade; in Japan and Latin America, the least labor-intensive branches can surrender with least pain.

[3] Zysman 1983, 238–51.

decisive importance. Taken together, these points suggest that a more useful threefold categorization of factors for future analysis may be, not that of land, labor, and capital employed throughout this book, but one of skilled labor, unskilled labor, and capital; or, almost equivalently, of labor, human capital, and physical capital.[4] Although I cannot begin here to trace through the implications of such a revised model, it shows some promise of helping to unravel some of the complexities of recent domestic conflicts in the most advanced economies.

Second, in any more complete application of the framework developed here, it will almost certainly be necessary to attack in detail a thorny issue that I have studiously played down, namely that of ownership and control of factors. Suppose, for example, that in some region land, being abundant, increases in value with an expansion of trade. What tells us that this gain will be captured by the current owners, rather than by some other group that forcibly expropriates them? Capital, too, may often be seized, by private parties or by the state; and even labor can be enslaved. For the most part, I have tacitly assumed that control remained with the previous holders, and for the most part I have doubtless been correct: the challenge of wholesale expropriation, and the resistance it promises to excite, has normally unnerved even the greediest souls. But it has not always done so; and the exceptions, by proving that the contrary outcome is possible, require us eventually to investigate what renders particular owners more (or less) vulnerable.

Third, we must also consider the possibility that this entire perspective on domestic politics is of principally historical utility; it may already have outlived its usefulness. As factors move with ever greater ease across national boundaries, a principal assumption of the Stolper-Samuelson theorem is violated. The crucial prediction of different effects on abundant and scarce factors falls away, and with it the underpinnings of all that has been said here. I doubt, at least on the evidence to date, any conclusion this radical. Even capital does not yet move freely, least of all across the borders of most Third World and communist countries; and the impediments to the migration of labor are even greater. We remain close enough to the assumptions of the Stolper-Samuelson theorem to retain the utility of a political analysis grounded in it.

．　．　．

The ancients held that the god of commerce (Hermes, or Mercury), who guaranteed the increase of herds, was god also of trickery and theft—able,

---

[4] I owe this suggestion, or at least the germ of it, to my colleague Richard Rosecrance.

out of impish whim, to make wealth vanish and so to stir up discord among his fellow gods.[5] Perhaps I have added to this insight only the mundane observation that men are as fallible as any gods; but I venture to think that we may have begun to understand better the source and flow of some of Hermes' pranks.

[5] Graves 1960, sec. 17.

Appendix

Table A.1
Pig Iron Output, 1850 (kilograms per capita)

United Kingdom	83.0
Belgium	32.8
France	13.4
Germany	6.3
Austria	4.3
Russia	3.4

Source: Mitchell 1978, 3–8 and 215–16.

Table A.2
Total Steam Power Production, 1850 (horsepower per thousand of population)

United Kingdom	46.9
Belgium	15.8
France	10.4
Germany	7.8
Netherlands	3.3
Austria	2.8

Source: Banks 1971, segment 1.

Table A.3
Cotton Spindles, 1852 (per thousand of population)

United Kingdom	762.1
Switzerland	376.1
France	126.1
Belgium	90.4
Austria	38.5
Germany	26.9

Source: Mitchell 1978, 3–8 and 258.

TABLE A.4
Aggregate Manufactures Per Capita, 1895 (in pounds sterling) (Mulhall Estimates)

United States	28
United Kingdom	22
Belgium	19
France	15
Switzerland	14
Germany	13
Netherlands	11
Sweden-Norway	9
Austria	8
Spain	7
All others	< 7

Source: Mulhall 1896, 386.

Bibliography

ARTICLES, CHAPTERS, AND UNPUBLISHED WORKS

Aitken, Don. 1985. "The New Electorate." Chap. 17 in Woodward, Parkin, and Summers 1985.

Ajayi, J. F. Ade, and J. B. Webster. 1966. "The Emergence of a New Elite in Africa." Chap. 9 in Anene and Brown 1966.

Alavi, Hamza. 1979. "Peasants and Revolution." Chap. 3 in Desai 1979. Originally published 1965.

Archer, Jeffrey, and Graham Maddox. 1985. "The 1975 Constitutional Crisis in Australia." Chap. 4 in Woodward, Parkin, and Summers 1985.

Arrighi, G. 1970. "Labour Supplies in Historical Perspective: A Study of the Proletarianization of the African Peasantry in Rhodesia." *Journal of Development Studies* 6: 197–234.

Ayandele, E. A. 1966. "External Influence on African Society." Chap. 8 in Anene and Brown 1966.

Baack, Bennett D., and Edward John Ray. 1983. "The Political Economy of Tariff Policy: A Case Study of the United States." *Explorations in Economic History* 20: 73–93.

———. 1985. "The Political Economy of the Origin and Development of the Federal Income Tax." *Research in Economic History* supplement 4: 121–38.

Bairoch, Paul. 1982. "International Industrialization Levels from 1750 to 1980." *Journal of European Economic History* 11: 269–333.

Baldwin, Robert E. 1971. "Determinants of the Commodity Structure of U.S. Trade." *American Economic Review* 61: 126–46.

Bates, Robert H. 1987. "The Agrarian Origins of Mau Mau." Chap. of forthcoming book.

Becker, Gary S. 1983. "A Theory of Competition among Pressure Groups for Political Influence." *Quarterly Journal of Economics* 98: 371–400.

Bovykin, Valery Ivanovich, and Juri Ilyich Kiryanov. 1977. "Der Klassenkampf in Russland am Vorabend und während der ersten russischen Revolution 1895 bis 1907." Pp. 203–37 in Buganov, Hoffmann, Pašuto, and Voigt 1977.

Brady, Thomas A., Jr., and H. C. Erik Midelfort. 1981. "Translators' Introduction." Pp. xi–xxvi in Blickle 1981.

Braudel, Fernand, and Frank Spooner. 1967. "Prices in Europe from 1450 to 1750." Chap. 7 in Rich and Wilson 1967.

Brenner, Robert. 1976. "Agrarian Class Structure and Economic Development in Pre-Feudal Europe." *Past and Present* 70: 30–75.

———. 1977. "The Origins of Capitalist Development: A Critique of Neo-Smithian Marxism." *New Left Review* 104: 25–92.

———. 1982. "Agrarian Class Structure and Economic Development in Pre-Industrial Europe: The Agrarian Roots of European Capitalism." *Past and Present* 97: 16–113.

Brown, Courtney. 1982. "The Nazi Vote: A National Ecological Study." *American Political Science Review* 76: 285–302.

Cameron, David R. 1978. "The Expansion of the Public Economy: A Comparative Analysis." *American Political Science Review* 72: 1243–61.

Chaudhuri, Binay Bhushan. 1979. "Agrarian Movements in Bengal and Bihar: 1919–39." Chap. 18 in Desai 1979. Originally published 1972.

Coase, A. H. 1960. "The Problem of Social Cost." *Journal of Law and Economics* 3: 1–44.

Colson, Elizabeth. 1969. "African Society at the Time of the Scramble." Chap. 1 in Gann and Duignan 1969.

Comisso, Ellen. 1986. "State Structures, Political Processes, and Collective Choice in CMEA States." *International Organization* 40: 195–238.

Comisso, Ellen, and Paul Marer. 1986. "The Economics and Politics of Reform in Hungary." *International Organization* 40: 421–54.

Copans, Jean. 1980. "From Senegambia to Senegal: The Evolution of Peasantries." Chap. 2 in Klein 1980.

Coquery-Vidrovitch, Catherine. 1986. "French Black Africa." Chap. 7 in Roberts 1986b.

Cotler, Julio. 1979. "State and Regime: Comparative Notes on the Southern Cone and the 'Enclave' Societies." Chap. 6 in Collier 1979.

Cotter, Richard. 1967. "War, Boom and Depression." Chap. 8 in Griffin 1967.

Crowther, William. 1986. "Philippine Authoritarianism and the International Economy." *Comparative Politics* 18: 339–56.

Daalder, Hans. 1966. "The Netherlands: Opposition in a Segmented Society." Chap. 6 in Dahl 1966.

Elliott, C. M. 1969. "Agriculture and Economic Development in Africa: Theory and Experience, 1880–1914." Chap. 5 in Jones and Woolf 1969.

Ethier, Wilfred J. 1984. "Higher Dimensional Issues in Trade Theory." Chap. 3 in Jones and Kenen 1984.

Ferguson, Thomas. 1984. "From Normalcy to New Deal: Industrial Structure, Party Competition, and American Public Policy in the Great Depression." *International Organization* 38: 41–94.

Gerschenkron, Alexander. 1960. "Problems and Patterns of Russian Economic Development." Pp. 42–72 in Black 1960.

Gies, Horst 1968. "Die nationalsozialistische Machtergreifung auf dem agrarpolitischen Sector." *Zeitschrift für Agrargeschichte und Agrarsoziologie* 16: 210–32.

———. 1972. "The NSDAP and Agrarian Organizations in the Final Phase of the Weimar Republic." Pp. 45–88 in Turner 1972.

Gollan, R. A. 1974. "Nationalism, the Labour Movement and the Commonwealth, 1880–1900." Chap. 4 in Greenwood 1974a.

Gough, Kathleen. 1979. "Indian Peasant Uprisings." Chap. 6 in Desai 1979. Originally published 1974.

Gourevitch, Peter Alexis. 1977. "International Trade, Domestic Coalitions and Liberty: Comparative Responses to the Crisis of 1873–1896." *Journal of Interdisciplinary History* 8: 281–313.

Graham, A. J. 1982. "The Colonial Expansion of Greece." Pp. 83–162 in Boardman and Hammond 1982.

Greenwood, Gordon. 1974b. "National Development and Social Experimentation, 1901–14." Chap. 5 in Greenwood 1974a.

———. 1974c. "Since World War II." Chap. 9 in Greenwood 1974a.

Hanisch, Tore. 1978. "The Economic Crisis in Norway in the 1930s: A Tentative Analysis of Its Causes." *Scandinavian Economic History Review* 26: 145–55.

Hansen, Erik. 1981. "Depression Decade Crisis: Social Democracy and Planisme in Belgium and the Netherlands, 1929–1939." *Journal of Contemporary History* 16: 293–322.

Helleiner, Karl F. 1967. "The Population of Europe from the Black Death to the Eve of the Vital Revolution." Chap. 1 in Rich and Wilson 1967.

Hibbs, Douglas A., Jr. 1978. "On the Political Economy of Long-Run Trends in Strike Activity." *British Journal of Political Science* 8: 153–75.

Hirschmann, Albert O. 1968. "The Political Economy of Import-Substituting Industrialization in Latin America." *Quarterly Journal of Economics* 82: 2–32. Chap. 3 in Hirschman 1971.

———. 1979. "The Turn to Authoritarianism in Latin America and the Search for Its Economic Determinants." Chap. 3 in Collier 1979.

Hody, Cynthia 1986. "From Protectionism to Liberalism: Institutional Changes and the Politics of American Trade Policy." Ph.D. dissertation, University of California, Los Angeles.

Hough, Jerry F. 1986a. "Attack on Protectionism in the Soviet Union? A Comment." *International Organization* 40: 489–503.

Iriye, Akira 1974. "The Failure of Economic Expansionism: 1918–1931." Chap. 9 in Silberman and Harootunian 1974.

James, Scott, and David A. Lake. 1989. "The Second Face of Hegemony: Britain's Repeal of the Corn Laws and the American Walker Tariff of 1846." *International Organization* 43: 1–29.

Jewsiewicki, B. 1986. "Belgian Africa." Chap. 9 in Roberts 1986b.

Kato, Shuichi. 1974. "Taishō Democracy as the Pre-Stage for Japanese Militarism." Chap. 8 in Silberman and Harootunian 1974.

Kaufman, Robert R. 1979. "Industrial Change and Authoritarian Rule in Latin America: A Concrete Review of the Bureaucratic-Authoritarian Model." Chap. 5 in Collier 1979.

Kemp, D. A. 1985. "Social Change and Political Cleavages in Australia." Chap. 16 in Woodward, Parkin, and Summers 1985.

Keohane, Robert. 1980. "The Theory of Hegemonic Stability and Changes in International Economic Regimes, 1967–1977." Pp. 131–62 in Holsti, Siverson, and George 1980.

Kindleberger, Charles P. 1951. "Group Behavior and International Trade." *Journal of Political Economy* 59: 30–46.

Kirchheimer, Otto. 1957. "The Waning of Opposition in Parliamentary Regimes." *Social Research* 24: 127–56.

———. 1966. "Germany: The Vanishing Opposition." Chap. 7 in Dahl 1966.

Kōshiro, Kazutoshi. 1983. "Japan's Labor Unions: The Meeting of White and Blue Collar." Chap. 8 in Murakami and Hirschmeier 1983.

Krasner, Stephen D. 1976. "State Power and the Structure of International Trade." *World Politics* 28: 317–47.

Krueger, Anne O. 1974. "The Political Economy of the Rent-seeking Society." *American Economic Review* 64: 291–303.

Kurth, James R. 1979a. "Industrial Change and Political Change: A European Perspective." Chap. 8 in Collier 1979.

———. 1979b. "The Political Consequences of the Product Cycle: Industrial History and Political Outcomes." *International Organization* 33: 1–34.

Leamer, Edward E. 1980. "The Leontieff Paradox, Reconsidered." *Journal of Political Economy* 88: 495–503.

Leontieff, Wassily. 1953. "Domestic Production and Foreign Trade: The American Capital Position Re-Examined." *Proceedings of the American Philosophical Society* 97: 332–49.

———. 1956. "Factor Proportions and the Structure of American Trade: Further Theoretical and Empirical Analysis." *Review of Economic Statistics* 38: 386–407.

Le Roy Ladurie, Emmanuel. 1978. "A Reply to Professor Brenner." *Past and Present* 79: 55–59.

Lewis, Arthur. 1954. "Economic Development with Unlimited Supplies of Labour." *Manchester School of Economic and Social Studies* 22: 139–91.

Linden, Ronald H. 1986. "Socialist Patrimonialism and the Global Economy: The Case of Romania." *International Organization* 40: 347–80.

Lipset, Seymour Martin. 1970. "Political Cleavages in 'Developed' and 'Emerging' Polities." Chap. 1 in Allardt and Rokkan 1970.

———. 1983. "Radicalism or Reformism: The Sources of Working-Class Politics." *American Political Science Review* 77: 1–18.

Lorwin, Val R. 1966. "Belgium: Religion, Class, and Language in National Politics." Chap. 5 in Dahl 1966.

McNaughtan, I. D. 1974. "Colonial Liberalism." Chap. 3 in Greenwood 1974a.

Maddalena, Aldo de. 1974. "Rural Europe 1500–1750." Translated by Muriel Grindrod. Chap. 4 in Cipolla 1974.

Maddison, Angus. 1962. "Growth and Fluctuation in the World Economy 1870–1960." *Banca Nazionale del Lavoro Quarterly Review* 61: 127–95.

Magee, Stephen P. 1978. "Three Simple Tests of the Stolper-Samuelson Theorem." Chap. 8 in Oppenheimer 1978.

Mehta, Uday. 1979. "Peasant Movement in India." Chap. 37 in Desai 1979. Originally published 1965.

Minchinton, Walter. 1974. "Patterns and Structure of Demand, 1500–1700." Chapter 2 in Cipolla 1974.

Mols, Roger. 1974. "Population in Europe, 1500–1700." Chap. 1 in Cipolla 1974.

Moran, Theodore H. 1970. "The 'Development' of Argentina and Australia: The Radical Party of Argentina and the Labor Party in Australia in the Process of Economic and Political Development." *Comparative Politics* 3: 71–92.

Mundell, Robert A. 1957. "International Trade and Factor Mobility." *American Economic Review* 47: 321–35.

Mussa, Michael. 1974. "Tariffs and the Distribution of Income: The Importance of Factor Specificity, Substitutability, and Intensity in the Short and Long Run." *Journal of Political Economy* 82: 1191–203.

Myint, Hla. 1958. "The 'Classical Theory' of International Trade and the Underdeveloped Countries." *Economic Journal* 68: 317–37.

Newbury, Colin W. 1969. "Trade and Authority in West Africa from 1850 to 1880." Chap. 2 in Gann and Duignan 1966.

Norton, R. D. 1986. "Industrial Policy and American Renewal." *Journal of Economic Literature* 24: 1–40.

Perrie, Maureen. 1972. "The Russian Peasant Movement of 1905–1907: Its Social Composition and Revolutionary Significance." *Past and Present* 57: 123–55.

Postan, M. M., and John Hatcher. 1978. "Population and Class Relations in Feudal Society." *Past and Present* 78: 24–37.

Pratt, Samuel. 1948. "The Social Basis of Nazism and Communism in Urban Germany." M.A. thesis, Department of Sociology, Michigan State University.

Ranga, N. G., and Sami Sahajanand Saraswathi. 1979. "Agrarian Revolts." Chap. 4 in Desai 1979.

Rich, E. E. 1967. "Colonial Settlement and Its Labour Problems." Chap. 6 in Rich and Wilson 1967.

Roberts, Andrew. 1986a. "East Africa." Chap. 13 in Roberts 1986b.

Rogowski, Ronald. 1982. "Iron, Rye and the Authoritarian Coalition in Germany after 1879." Paper presented at the Annual Meeting of the American Political Science Association.

———. 1986. "Trade and the Variety of Democratic Institutions." *International Organization* 41: 203–23.

———. 1987. "Political Cleavages and Changing Exposure to Trade." *American Political Science Review* 81: 1121–37.

Rokkan, Stein. 1966. "Norway: Numerical Democracy and Corporate Pluralism." Chap. 3 in Dahl 1966.

———. 1981. "Territories, Nations, Parties: Toward a Geoeconomic-Geopolitical Model for the Explanation of Changes within Western Europe." Pp. 70–95 in Merritt and Russett 1981.

Rosenberg, Hans. 1943. "Political and Social Consequences of the Great Depression in Europe, 1873–1896." *Economic History Review* 13: 58–73.

Russett, Bruce. 1985. "The Mysterious Case of Vanishing Hegemony; or, Is Mark Twain Really Dead?" *International Organization* 39: 207–31.

Sabean, David Warren. 1969. "The Social Background to the Peasants' War of 1525 in Southern Upper Swabia." Ph.D. dissertation, University of Wisconsin.

Schmiegelow, Michèle. 1985. "Cutting across Doctrines: Positive Adjustment in Japan." *International Organization* 39: 261–96.

Schmitter, Philippe C. 1973. "The 'Portugalization' of Brazil?" Chap. 6 in Stepan 1973.

Sella, Domenico. 1974. "European Industries 1500–1700." Chap. 5 in Cipolla 1974.

Sengupta, Kalyan Kumar 1979. "Peasant Struggle in Pabna, 1873: Its Legalistic Character." Chap. 12 in Desai 1979. Originally published 1973.

Serra, José. 1979. "Three Mistaken Theses Regarding the Connection Between Industrialization and Authoritarian Regimes." Chap. 4 in Collier 1979.

Sinclair, W. A. 1970. "Capital Formation." Chap. 1 in Forster 1970.

Skinner, G. William. 1964–1965. "Marketing and Social Structure in Rural China." *Journal of Asian Studies* 24: 3–43, 195–228, and 363–99.

Snidal, Duncan. 1985. "The Limits of Hegemonic Stability Theory." *International Organization* 39: 579–614.

Stein, Arthur A. 1984. "The Hegemon's Dilemma: Great Britain, the United States, and the International Economic Order." *International Organization* 38: 355–86.

Stolper, Wolfgang Friedrich, and Paul A. Samuelson. 1941. "Protection and Real Wages." *Review of Economic Studies* 9: 58–73.

Strange, Susan. 1985. "Protectionism and World Politics." *International Organization* 39: 233–59.

Tillotson, Amanda. 1986. "International Sources of Fiscal Policy in Western Europe, 1960–1980." Paper presented at the annual meeting of the American Political Science Association.

Volin, Lazar. 1960. "The Russian Peasant: From Emancipation to Kolkhoz." Pp. 292–311 in Black 1960.

Walshe, A. P. 1986. "Southern Africa." Chap. 11 in Roberts 1986b.

Watkins, Melville H. 1963. "A Staple Theory of Economic Growth." *Canadian Journal of Economics and Political Science* 29: 141–58.

Webber, Douglas C. 1978. "Trade Unions and the Labour Party: The Death of Working-Class Politics in New Zealand." Chap. 14 in Levine 1978.

Wilson, John. 1977. "The Canadian Political Cultures: Towards a Redefinition of the Nature of a Canadian Political System." Pp. 316–37 in Fox 1977. Originally published 1974.

Winkler, Heinrich August. 1972. "Extremismus der Mitte? Sozialgeschichtliche Aspekte der national-sozialistischen Machtergreifung." *Vierteljahrshefte für Zeitgeschichte* 20: 175–91.

Woodward, Dennis. 1985. "The Australian Labor Party." Chap. 12 in Woodward, Parkin, and Summers 1985.

Wrigley, C. C. 1986. "Aspects of Economic History." Chap. 2 in Roberts 1986b.

Yanagi, Susumu. 1983. "The Unsung Mainstays (2): Agriculture." Chap. 10 in Murakami and Hirschmeier 1983.

BOOKS

Abraham, David. 1981. *The Collapse of the Weimar Republic.* Princeton, N.J.: Princeton University Press.

Alexander, Fred. 1980. *Australia since Federation: A Narrative and Critical Analysis.* 4th ed. West Melbourne: Thomas Nelson.

Alföldy, Géza. 1985. *The Social History of Rome.* Translated by David Braund and Frank Pollock. London and Sydney: Croom Helm.

Alford, Robert R. 1963. *Party and Society: The Anglo-American Democracies*. Chicago: Rand McNally.

Allardt, Erik, and Stein Rokkan, eds. 1970. *Mass Politics: Studies in Political Sociology*. New York: Free Press.

Anderson, Perry. 1974. *Passages from Antiquity to Feudalism*. London: New Left Books.

Anene, Joseph C., and Godfrey N. Brown, eds. 1966. *Africa in the Nineteenth and Twentieth Centuries: A Handbook for Teachers and Students*. Ibadan: Ibadan University Press. London: Nelson.

Ardagh, John. 1982. *France in the 1980s*. Harmondsworth, Middlesex: Penguin Books, in association with Secker and Warburg.

Avakumovic, Ivan. 1978. *Socialism in Canada: A Study of the CCF-NDP in Federal and Provincial Politics*. Toronto: McClelland and Stewart.

Ayusawa, Iwao F. 1966. *A History of Labor in Modern Japan*. Honolulu: East-West Center Press.

Bain, George Sayers, and Robert Price. 1980. *Profiles of Union Growth: A Comparative Statistical Portrait of Eight Countries*. Oxford: Basil Blackwell.

Bakhash, Shaul. 1984. *The Reign of the Ayatollahs: Iran and the Islamic Revolution*. New York: Basic Books.

Banks, Arthur S. 1971. *Cross-Polity Time-Series Data*. Cambridge: MIT Press.

Barber, William J. 1961. *The Economy of British Central Africa: A Case Study of Economic Development in a Dualistic Society*. London: Oxford University Press.

Barnett, A. Doak. 1963. *China on the Eve of the Communist Takeover*. London: Thames and Hudson.

Bates, Robert H. 1981. *Markets and States in Tropical Africa: The Political Basis of Agricultural Policies*. Berkeley: University of California Press.

Becker, William H. 1982. *The Dynamics of Business-Government Relations: Industry and Exports, 1893–1921*. Chicago: University of Chicago Press.

Bell, Daniel. 1960. *The End of Ideology*. Glencoe, Ill.: Free Press.

Berger, Suzanne. 1972. *Peasants against Politics: Rural Organization in Brittany, 1911–1967*. Cambridge: Harvard University Press.

Berghahn, V. R. 1982. *Modern Germany: Society, Economy and Politics in the Twentieth Century*. Cambridge: Cambridge University Press.

Berry, Sara S. 1975. *Cocoa, Custom, and Socio-Economic Change in Rural Western Nigeria*. Oxford: Clarendon.

Bhagwati, Jagdish N., and Padma Desai. 1970. *India: Planning for Industrialization: Industrialization and Trade Policies since 1951*. London: Oxford University Press.

Bianco, Lucien. 1971. *Origins of the Chinese Revolution, 1915–1949*. Translated by Muriel Bell. Stanford, Calif.: Stanford University Press.

Binder, Leonard. 1980. *Revolution in Iran: Three Essays. Middle East Review*, Special Studies, no. 1. New Brunswick, NJ: Transaction Periodicals Consortium.

Binder, Leonard, James S. Coleman, Joseph La Palombara, Lucian W. Pye, Sidney Verba, and Myron Weiner. 1971. *Crises and Sequences in Political Development*. Princeton, N.J.: Princeton University Press.

Birmingham, David. 1981. *Central Africa to 1870: Zambesia, Zaf're, and the South Atlantic*. Chapters from the Cambridge History of Africa. Cambridge: Cambridge University Press.

Black, Cyril E., ed. 1960. *The Transformation of Russian Society: Aspects of Social Change since 1861*. Cambridge: Harvard University Press.

Blake, Robert. 1968. *Disraeli*. Garden City, N.Y.: Doubleday, Anchor Books.

Blickle, Peter. 1981. *The Revolution of 1525: The German Peasants' War from a New Perspective*. Translated by Thomas A. Brady, Jr. and H. C. Erik Midelfort. Baltimore: Johns Hopkins University Press.

Boardman, John. 1964. *The Greeks Overseas*. Baltimore: Penguin Books.

Boardman, John, and N.G.L. Hammond. 1982. *The Cambridge Ancient History*. 2d ed. Vol. 3, pt. 3: *The Expansion of the Greek World, Eighth to Sixth Centuries B.C.* Cambridge: Cambridge University Press.

Bonjour, E. 1948. *Die Gründung des schweizerischen Bundesstaates*. Basel: B. Schwabe.

Boussard, Isabel. 1980. *Vichy et la Corporation Paysanne*. Paris: Presses de la fondation nationale des sciences politiques.

Bowden, Witt, Michael Karpovich, and Abbott Payson Usher. 1937. *An Economic History of Europe since 1750*. New York: American Book Company.

Braudel, Fernand. 1982. *Civilization and Capitalism, 15th–18th Century*. Vol. 2: *The Wheels of Commerce*. Translated by Siân Reynolds. New York: Harper and Row.

————. 1984. *Civilization and Capitalism, 15th–18th Century*. Vol. 3: *The Perspective of the World*. Translated by Siân Reynolds. New York: Harper and Row.

Brogan, Dennis W. 1967. *The Development of Modern France, 1870–1939*. Rev. ed. London: Hamish Hamilton.

Brown, Peter. 1971. *The World of Late Antiquity: From Marcus Aurelius to Muhammad*. London: Thames and Hudson.

Buckley, Roger. 1985. *Japan Today*. Cambridge: Cambridge University Press.

Buganov, V. I., P. Hoffmann, V. T. Pašuto, and G. Voigt, eds. 1977. *Klassenkampf und Revolutionäre Bewegung in der Geschichte Russlands*. Berlin: Akademie-Verlag.

Burn, A. R. 1982. *A Pelican History of Greece*. Baltimore: Penguin.

Burnham, James. 1941. *The Managerial Revolution: What Is Happening in the World*. Westport, Conn: Greenwood Press.

Burnham, Walter Dean. 1970. *Critical Elections and the Mainsprings of American Politics*. New York: W. W. Norton.

Bury, J. B., and Russell Meiggs. 1975. *A History of Greece to the Death of Alexander the Great*. 4th ed. New York: St. Martin's Press.

Bury, J. B., S. A. Cook, and F. E. Adcock, eds. 1927. *The Cambridge Ancient History*, vol. 5: *Athens 478–401 B.C.* Cambridge: Cambridge University Press.

Butler, David, and Donald Stokes. 1971. *Political Change in Britain*. 2d ed. New York: St. Martin's Press.

Butlin, Noel G., A. Barnard, and J. J. Pincus. 1982. *Government and Capitalism: Public and Private Choice in Twentieth Century Australia*. Sydney: George Allen and Unwin.

Calleo, David P. 1978. *The German Problem Reconsidered: Germany and the World Order, 1870 to the Present.* Cambridge: Cambridge University Press.

Cardoso, Fernando Henrique, and Enzo Faletto. 1979. *Dependency and Development in Latin America.* Expanded and emended version of *Dependencia y desarrollo en América Latina.* Translated by Marjory Mattingly Urquidi. Berkeley and Los Angeles: University of California Press.

Carocci, Giampiero. 1975. *Italian Fascism.* Translated by Isabel Quigley. Harmondsworth, Middlesex: Penguin Books.

Caron, Francois. 1979. *An Economic History of Modern France.* Translated by Barbara Bray. New York: Columbia University Press.

Carr, Raymond. 1966. *Spain, 1808–1939.* Oxford: Clarendon.

Carsten, Frederick L. 1954. *The Origins of Prussia.* London: Oxford University Press.

———. *The Rise of Fascism.* 1967. Berkeley and Los Angeles: University of California Press.

Castellan, Georges. 1969. *L'Allemagne de Weimar, 1918–1933.* Paris: Armand Colin.

Ch'ên, Jerome. 1965. *Mao and the Chinese Revolution.* London: Oxford University Press.

Childers, Thomas. 1983. *The Nazi Voter: The Social Foundations of Fascism in Germany, 1919–1933.* Chapel Hill: University of North Carolina Press.

Childs, David. 1986. *Britain since 1945: A Political History.* 2d ed. London: Methuen.

Cipolla, Carlo M. 1965. *Guns, Sails and Empires: Technological Innovation and the Early Phases of European Expansion, 1400–1700.* New York: Pantheon Books.

———, ed. 1974. *The Fontana Economic History of Europe.* Vol. 2: *The Sixteenth and Seventeenth Centuries.* Glasgow: Collins/Fontana Books.

Clarke, Harold D., Jane Jensen, Lawrence le Duc, and Jon H. Pammett. 1984. *Absent Mandate: The Politics of Discontent in Canada.* Toronto: Gage.

Clay, C.G.A. 1984. *Economic Expansion and Social Change: England 1500–1700.* Cambridge: Cambridge University Press.

Clubb, O. Edmund. 1972. *Twentieth-Century China.* 2d ed. New York: Columbia University Press.

———. 1978. *Twentieth-Century China.* 3d ed. New York: Columbia University Press.

Cobban, Alfred. 1965. *A History of Modern France.* Vol. 3: *France of the Republics, 1871–1962.* Harmondsworth, Middlesex: Penguin Books.

Codding, George Arthur. 1961. *The Federal Government of Switzerland.* Boston: Houghton Mifflin.

Cohen, Robin. 1974. *Labour and Politics in Nigeria, 1945–71.* London: Heinemann.

Collier, David, ed. 1979. *The New Authoritarianism in Latin America.* Princeton, N.J.: Princeton University Press.

Condliffe, J. B., and W.T.G. Airey. 1953. *A Short History of New Zealand.* 7th ed. Christchurch: Whitcombe and Tombs.

Conference of Socialist Economists, London Working Group. 1980. *The Alterna-*

tive Economic Strategy: A Response by the Labour Movement to the Economic Crisis.
London: CSE Books.

Cook, Chris, and John Paxton. 1986. *European Political Facts, 1918–84.* Basingstoke and London: Macmillan.

Dahl, Robert, ed. 1966. *Political Oppositions in Western Democracies.* New Haven, Conn.: Yale University Press.

Dederke, Karlheinz. 1984. *Reich und Republik: Deutschland 1917–1933.* 5th ed. Stuttgart: Klett-Cotta.

D'Elía, Germán. 1982. *América Latina: De la crisis de 1929 a la Segunda Guerra Mundial.* Montevideo: Ediciones de la Banda Oriental.

De Gaulle, Charles. 1971. *Memoirs of Hope: Renewal and Endeavor.* Translated by Terence Kilmartin. New York: Simon and Schuster.

Denoon, Donald. 1983. *Settler Capitalism: The Dynamics of Dependent Development in the Southern Hemisphere.* Oxford: Clarendon Press.

Desai, A. R., ed. 1979. *Peasant Struggles in India.* Bombay: Oxford University Press.

Dobb, Maurice. 1946. *Studies in the Development of Capitalism.* London: George Routledge and Sons.

Doyle, Michael W. 1986. *Empires.* Ithaca: Cornell University Press.

Dozer, Donald Marquand. 1979. *Latin America: An Interpretive History.* Rev. ed. Tempe, Ariz.: Center for Latin American Studies, Arizona State University.

Dunham, Adelaide Glynn. 1915. *The History of Miletus, Down to the Anabasis of Alexander.* London: University of London Press.

Duverger, Maurice. 1959. *Political Parties: Their Organization and Activity in the Modern State.* 2d ed. Translated by Barbara and Robert North. New York: John Wiley and Sons.

Easterbrook, W. T., and Hugh G. J. Aitken. 1958. *Canadian Economic History.* Originally published 1956. Toronto: Macmillan.

Elton, Geoffrey R. 1968. *The Tudor Constitution.* Cambridge: Cambridge University Press.

Emerson, Barbara. 1979. *Leopold II of the Belgians: King of Colonialism.* London: Weidenfeld and Nicolson.

Engel, Arthur J. 1983. *From Clergyman to Don: The Rise of the Academic Profession in Nineteenth-Century Oxford.* Oxford: Clarendon.

Ensor, R.C.K. 1936. *England: 1870–1914.* Oxford: Clarendon.

Esping-Anderson, Gøsta. 1985. *Politics against Markets: The Social Democratic Road to Power.* Princeton, N.J.: Princeton University Press.

Feis, Herbert. 1965. *Europe, the World's Banker, 1870–1914: An Account of European Foreign Investment and the Connection of World Finance with Diplomacy before World War I.* New York: Norton.

Feld, Warner J. 1981. *West Germany and the European Community: Changing Interests and Competing Policy Objectives.* New York: Praeger.

Feldman, Gerald D. 1966. *Army, Industry, and Labor in Germany, 1914–1918.* Princeton, N.J.: Princeton University Press.

Feuerwerker, Albert. 1975. *Rebellion in Nineteenth-Century China.* Michigan Papers in Chinese Studies, No. 21. Ann Arbor, Mich.: Center for Chinese Studies, University of Michigan.

Finlay, John L., and Douglas N. Sprague. 1979. *The Structure of Canadian History.* Scarbourough, Ontario: Prentice-Hall.

Finley, M. I. 1982. *Economy and Society in Ancient Greece.* Edited with an introduction by Brent D. Shaw and Richard P. Saller. New York: Viking Press.

————. 1985. *The Ancient Economy.* 2d ed. Berkeley: University of California Press.

Fogel, Robert William, and Stanley L. Engerman, eds. 1974. *Time on the Cross: The Economics of American Negro Slavery.* Boston: Little Brown.

Forrest, W. G. 1966. *The Emergence of Greek Democracy: 800–400 B.C.* New York: McGraw-Hill.

Forster, Colin, ed. 1970. *Australian Economic Development in the Twentieth Century.* London: George Allen and Unwin.

Fox, Edward Whiting. 1971. *History in Geographical Perspective: The Other France.* New York: W. W. Norton.

Fox, Paul W. 1977. *Politics: Canada.* 4th ed. Toronto: McGraw Hill-Ryerson.

Frohlich, Norman, Joe A. Oppenheimer, and Oran Young. 1971. *Political Entrepreneurship and Collective Goods.* Princeton, N.J.: Princeton University Press.

Gann, L. H., and Peter Duignan, eds. 1969. *Colonialism in Africa, 1870–1960.* Vol. 1: *The History and Politics of Colonialism, 1870–1914.* Cambridge: At the University Press.

Geertz, Clifford. 1963. *Agricultural Involution: The Process of Ecological Change in Indonesia.* Monographs of the Association for Asian Studies, no. 11. Berkeley: University of California Press.

Gerschenkron, Alexander. 1943. *Bread and Democracy in Germany.* Berkeley and Los Angeles: University of California Press.

————. 1962. *Economic Backwardness in Historical Perspective: A Book of Essays.* Cambridge: Belknap Press of Harvard University Press.

Gessner, Dieter. 1977. *Agrardepression und Präsidialregierungen in Deutschland 1930 bis 1933: Probleme des Agrarprotektionismus am Ende der Weimarer Republik.* Düsseldorf: Droste Verlag.

Ghose, Sankar. 1971. *Socialism and Communism in India.* Bombay: Allied Publishers.

Gilbert, Felix. 1970. *The End of the European Era: 1890 to the Present.* New York: W. W. Norton.

Gilpin, Robert. 1975. *U.S. Power and the Multinational Corporation.* New York: Basic Books.

Gourevitch, Peter Alexis. 1986. *Politics in Hard Times: Comparative Responses to International Economic Crises.* Ithaca, N.Y.: Cornell University Press.

Grant, Michael. 1960. *The World of Rome.* New York: The New American Library.

Graves, Robert. 1960. *The Greek Myths.* Rev. ed. Harmondsworth, Middlesex: Penguin.

Greenaway, David. 1983. *Trade Policy and the New Protectionism.* New York: St. Martin's Press.

Greenwood, Gordon, ed. 1974a. *Australia: A Social and Political History.* Reprinted with an additional chapter; originally published 1955. London: Angus and Robertson.

Griffin, James, ed. 1967. *Essays in the Economic History of Australia, 1788–1939.* Brisbane: Jacaranda.

Grosser, Alfred. 1980. *Deutschlandbilanz: Geschichte Deutschlands seit 1945.* 7th ed. Translated from the French by Roberta Hall and Margaret Carroux. Munich: Carl Hanser.

Gutkind, Peter C. W. 1974. *The Emergent African Urban Proletariat.* Centre for Developing-Area Studies, Occasional Paper No. 8. Montreal: McGill University.

Gutkind, Peter, C. W., Robin Cohen, and Jean Copans, eds. 1978. *African Labor History.* Beverly Hills, Calif.: Sage Publications.

Hamerow, Theodore S. 1966. *Restoration, Revolution, Reaction: Economics and Politics in Germany, 1815–1871.* Princeton, N.J.: Princeton University Press.

Hamilton, Richard. 1982. *Who Voted for Hitler?* Princeton, N.J.: Princeton University Press.

Hancock, M. Donald. 1972. *Sweden: The Politics of Postindustrial Change.* Hinsdale, Ill.: The Dryden Press.

Hannell, Krister. 1934. *Megarische Studien.* Lund: Lindstedts univ.-bokhandel.

Hanson, John Lloyd. 1977. *A Dictionary of Economics and Commerce.* 5th ed. Plymouth: Macdonald and Evans.

Hardach, Karl W. 1967. *Die Bedeutung wirtschaftlicher Faktoren bei der Wiedereinführung der Eisen- und Getreidezölle in Deutschland 1879.* Berlin: Dunker und Humblot.

Hasebroek, Johannes. 1933. *Trade and Politics in Ancient Greece.* Translated by L. M. Fraser and D. C. MacGregor. London: G. Bell and Sons.

Havighurst, Alfred F., ed. 1958. *The Pirenne Thesis: Analysis, Criticism, and Revision.* Boston: D. C. Heath.

Heberle, Rudolph. 1963. *Landbevölkerung und Nationalsozialismus: Eine soziologische Untersuchung der politischen Willensbildung in Schleswig-Holstein 1918 bis 1932.* Rev. and expanded version of Heberle 1945/1970. Stuttgart: Deutsche Verlags-Anstalt.

———. 1970. *From Democracy to Nazism: A Regional Case Study on Political Parties in Germany.* Originally published 1945. New York: Grosset and Dunlap.

Heidenheimer, Arnold J., and Donald P. Kommers. 1975. *The Governments of Germany.* 4th ed. New York: Harper and Row (Thomas Y. Crowell).

Helleiner, Gerald K. 1966. *Peasant Agriculture, Government, and Economic Growth in Nigeria.* Homewood, Ill.: Richard D. Irwin.

Hempel, Carl G. 1965. *Aspects of Scientific Explanation and Other Essays in the Philosophy of Science.* New York: The Free Press.

Hicks, John D. 1961. *The Populist Revolt: A History of the Farmers' Alliance and the People's Party.* Originally published 1931. Lincoln: University of Nebraska Press.

Hill, Polly. 1970. *Studies in Rural Capitalism in West Africa.* Cambridge: At the University Press.

Hindley, Donald. 1964. *The Communist Party of Indonesia, 1951–1963.* Berkeley and Los Angeles: University of California Press.

Hinton, William. 1966. *Fanshen: A Documentary of Revolution in a Chinese Village.* New York: Random House, Vintage Books.

Hirschman, Albert O. 1971. *A Bias for Hope: Essays on Development and Latin America.* New Haven, Conn.: Yale University Press.

Hobsbawm, E. J. 1962. *The Age of Revolution, 1789–1848.* New York: New American Library.

———. 1979. *The Age of Capital, 1848–1875.* New York: New American Library. Originally published 1975.

Hofheinz, Roy, Jr. 1977. *The Broken Wave: The Chinese Communist Peasant Movement, 1922–28.* Cambridge: Harvard University Press.

Hofstadter, Richard, ed. 1958. *Great Issues in American History: A Documentary Record.* 2 vols. New York: Vintage Books.

Holsti, Ole, Randolph Siverson, and Alexander L. George, eds. 1980. *Change in the International System.* Boulder, Col.: Westview Press.

Holt, John Bradshaw. 1936. *German Agricultural Policy, 1918–1934: The Development of a National Policy toward Agriculture in Postwar Germany.* Chapel Hill: University of North Carolina Press.

Holton, R. J. 1985. *The Transition from Feudalism to Capitalism.* Houndmills and London: Macmillan.

Hopkins, Anthony G. 1973. *An Economic History of West Africa.* New York: Columbia University Press.

Hopper, Robert John. 1976. *The Early Greeks.* London: Weidenfeld and Nicolson.

Hoselitz, Berthold Frank, ed. 1952. *The Progress of the Underdeveloped Areas.* Chicago: University of Chicago Press.

Hough, Jerry F. 1986b. *The Struggle for the Third World: Soviet Debates and American Options.* Washington, D.C.: The Brookings Institution.

Huntington, Samuel P. 1968. *Political Order in Changing Societies.* New Haven, Conn.: Yale University Press.

Ingham, Kenneth. 1965. *A History of East Africa.* 3d ed. London: Longmans, Green and Co.

Johnson, Chalmers A. 1962. *Peasant Nationalism and Communist Power: The Emergence of Revolutionary China, 1937–1945.* Stanford, Calif.: Stanford University Press.

Jones, A. H. M. 1957. *Athenian Democracy.* Oxford: B. Blackwell.

———. 1966. *The Decline of the Ancient World.* London: Longmans.

———. 1967. *Sparta.* Oxford: Blackwell & Mott.

Jones, E. L., and S. J. Woolf, eds. 1969. *Agrarian Change and Economic Development: The Historical Problems.* London: Methuen.

Jones, Ronald W., and Peter B. Kenen, eds. 1984. *Handbook of International Economics.* Vol. 1. Amsterdam, N.Y.: Elsevier Science Publishing Co.

July, Robert William. 1970. *A History of the African People.* New York: Scribner.

Jupp, James. 1982. *Party Politics: Australia, 1966–1981.* Sydney: George Allen and Unwin.

Katouzian, Homa. 1981. *The Political Economy of Modern Iran: Despotism and Pseudo-Modernism, 1926–1979.* New York: New York University Press.

Katzenstein, Peter J. 1985. *Small States in World Markets: Industrial Policy in Europe*. Ithaca, N.Y.: Cornell University Press.

Keddie, Nikki R. 1981. *Roots of Revolution: An Interpretive History of Modern Iran*. With a section by Yann Richard. New Haven, Conn.: Yale University Press.

Kehr, Eckart. 1973. *Battleship Building and Party Politics in Germany, 1894–1901*. Originally published 1930. Translated by Pauline R. and Eugene N. Anderson. Chicago: University of Chicago Press.

Kenkel, Joseph F. 1983. *Progressives and Protection: The Search for a Tariff Policy, 1866–1936*. Lanham, Md.: University Press of America.

Kenwood, A. G., and A. L. Lougheed. 1971. *The Growth of the International Economy, 1820–1960: An Introductory Text*. London: George Allen and Unwin.

Keohane, Robert O. 1984. *After Hegemony: Cooperation and Discord in the World Political Economy*. Princeton, N.J.: Princeton University Press.

Kevenhörster, Paul. 1973. *Wirtschaft und Politik in Japan: Interessengruppen, politische Meinungsbildung und wirtschaftspolitische Entscheidungen*. Wiesbaden: Otto Harrassowitz.

Keynes, John Maynard. 1919. *The Economic Consequences of the Peace*. London: Macmillan.

———. 1933. *Essays in Persuasion*. London: Macmillan.

Kindleberger, Charles P. 1973. *The World in Depression, 1929–1939*. Berkeley: University of California Press.

Kingston-Mann, Esther. 1983. *Lenin and the Problem of Marxist Peasant Revolution*. Oxford: Oxford University Press.

Klein, Martin A., ed. 1980. *Peasants in Africa: Historical and Contemporary Perspectives*. Sage Series on African Modernization and Development, vol. 4. Beverly Hills, Calif.: Sage Publications.

Kochan, Lionel. 1966. *Russia in Revolution, 1890–1918*. London: Weidenfeld and Nicolson.

Kogan, Norman. 1983. *A Political History of Italy: The Postwar Years*. New York: Praeger Publishers.

Kossmann, Ernst Heinrich. 1978. *The Low Countries, 1780–1940*. Oxford: Clarendon.

Krasner, Stephen. 1978. *Defending the National Interest: Raw Materials Investments and U.S. Foreign Policy*. Princeton, N.J.: Princeton University Press.

Kriedte, Peter. 1983. *Peasants, Landlords and Merchant Capitalists: Europe and the World Economy, 1500–1800*. Translated by V. R. Berghahn. Cambridge: Cambridge University Press.

Kuisel, Richard F. 1983. *Capitalism and the State in Modern France: Renovation and Economic Management in the Twentieth Century*. Originally published 1981. Cambridge: Cambridge University Press.

Lake, David A. 1988. *Power, Protection, and Free Trade: International Sources of U.S. Commercial Strategy, 1887–1939*. Ithaca: Cornell University Press.

Lambi, Nikolai. 1963. *Free Trade and Protection in Germany, 1868–1879*. Beiheft 44, Vierteljahrschrift für Sozial- und Wirtschaftsgeschichte. Wiesbaden: Franz Steiner.

Landes, David S. 1969. *The Unbound Prometheus: Technological Change and the*

Industrial Revolution in Western Europe from 1750 to the Present. London: Cambridge University Press.

Laxer, James. 1986. *Leap of Faith: Free Trade and the Future of Canada*. Edmonton: Hurtig Publishers.

Leamer, Edward. 1984. *Sources of Comparative Advantage: Theory and Evidence*. Cambridge: MIT Press.

Levine, Stephen. 1979. *The New Zealand Political System: Politics in a Small Society*. Sydney: Allen and Unwin.

Levine, Stephen, ed. 1978. *Politics in New Zealand: A Reader*. Sydney: Allen and Unwin.

Levine, Stephen, and Allen Robinson. 1976. *The New Zealand Voter: A Survey of Public Opinion and Electoral Behavior*. Wellington: Price Milburn for New Zealand University Press.

Lipset, Seymour Martin. 1963. *Political Man*. Garden City, N.Y.: Doubleday, Anchor Books. Originally published 1960.

————. 1971. *Agrarian Socialism: The Cooperative Commonwealth Federation in Saskatchewan*. Berkeley: University of California Press.

Lipset, Seymour Martin, and Stein Rokkan. 1967. *Party Systems and Voter Alignments*. New York: Free Press.

Lockyer, Roger. 1964. *Tudor and Stuart Britain*. London: Longmans.

Lopez, Robert S. 1967. *The Birth of Europe*. New York: M. Evans.

Lot, Ferdinand. 1931. *The End of the Ancient World and the Beginnings of the Middle Ages*. Translated by Philip Leon and Mariette Leon. New York: Alfred A. Knopf.

McInnis, Edgar. 1959. *Canada: A Political and Social History*. Rev. and enl. ed. Toronto: Rinehart.

McNeill, William H. 1954. *Past and Future*. Chicago: University of Chicago Press.

Magnus, Philip. 1964. *Gladstone: A Biography*. New York: E. P. Dutton.

Maier, Charles S. 1975. *Recasting Bourgeois Europe: Stabilization in France, Germany and Italy in the Decade After World War I*. Princeton, N.J.: Princeton University Press.

Maier, Franz Georg. 1968. *Die Verwandlung der Mittelmeerwelt*. Fischer Weltgeschichte, vol. 9. Frankfurt am Main: Fischer Taschenbuch Verlag.

Markovitz, Irving Leonard. 1977. *Power and Class in Africa: An Introduction to Change and Conflict in African Politics*. Englewood Cliffs, N.J.: Prentice-Hall.

Marsh, Frank Burr. 1963. *A History of the Roman World: From 146 to 30 B.C.* 3d. ed. revised by H. H. Scullard. London: Methuen; New York: Barnes and Noble.

Marx, Karl, and Friedrich Engels. 1978. *The Marx-Engels Reader*. 2d ed. Edited by Robert C. Tucker. New York: Norton.

Mauro, Frederic. 1975. *L'Amérique espagnole et portugaise de 1920 à nos jours*. Paris: Presses Universitaires de France.

Merritt, Richard L., and Bruce M. Russett, eds. 1981. *From National Development to Global Community: Essays in Honor of Karl W. Deutsch*. London: Allen and Unwin.

Meyer, Henry Cord, ed. 1973. *The Long Generation: Germany from Empire to Ruin, 1913–1945*. New York: Harper and Row.

Mielke, Siegfried. 1976. *Der Hansa-Bund für Gewerbe, Handel, und Industrie, 1909–1914*. Göttingen: Vandenhoeck und Ruprecht.

Mink, Gwendolyn. 1986. *Old Labor and New Immigrants in American Political Development: Union, Party, and State, 1875–1920*. Ithaca, N.Y.: Cornell University Press.

Mitchell, Austin. 1969. *Politics and People in New Zealand*. Christchurch: Whitcombe and Tombs.

Mitchell, Brian R. 1978. *European Historical Statistics, 1750–1970*. Abridged ed. New York: Columbia University Press.

Mokyr, Joel. 1976. *Industrialization in the Low Countries, 1795–1850*. New Haven, Conn.: Yale University Press.

Moore, Barrington, Jr. 1967. *Social Origins of Dictatorship and Democracy: Lord and Peasant in the Making of the Modern World*. Boston: Beacon Press.

Morley, John Terence. 1984. *Secular Socialists: The CCF/NDP in Ontario, a Biography*. Kingston and Montreal: McGill-Queen's University Press.

Morton, Desmond. 1983. *A Short History of Canada*. Edmonton: Hurtig Publishers.

Mueller, Bernard. 1965. *A Statistical Handbook of the North Atlantic Area*. New York: Twentieth Century Fund.

Mulhall, Michael G. 1892. *The Dictionary of Statistics*. London: George Routledge and Sons.

———. 1896. *Industries and Wealth of Nations*. New York and London: Longmans, Green, and Co. Reprinted 1972 by Johnson Reprint Corp.

———. 1903. *The Dictionary of Statistics*. 4th ed., revised to November. 1898. London: George Routledge and Sons.

Munro, J. Forbes. 1976. *Africa and the International Economy, 1800–1960: An Introduction to the Modern Economic History of Africa South of the Sahara*. London: J. M. Dent and Sons; Totowa, N.J.: Roman and Littlefield.

———. 1984. *Britain in Tropical Africa, 1880–1960: Economic Relationships and Impact*. London: Macmillan.

Murakami, Hyoe, and Johannes Hirschmeier, eds. 1983. *Politics and Economics in Contemporary Japan*. Tokyo: Kodansha International.

Myint, Hla. 1980. *The Economics of the Developing Countries*. 5th ed. London: Hutchinson.

Nelson, Joan. 1979. *Access to Power: Politics and the Urban Poor in Developing Nations*. Princeton, N.J.: Princeton University Press.

Nordlinger, Eric A. 1967. *The Working Class Tories: Authority, Deference, and Stable Democracy*. Berkeley: University of California Press.

North, Douglass C. 1981. *Structure and Change in Economic History*. New York: W. W. Norton.

North, Douglass C., and Robert Paul Thomas. 1973. *The Rise of the Western World: A New Economic History*. Cambridge: Cambridge University Press.

Nove, Alec. 1972. *An Economic History of the U.S.S.R.* Harmondsworth, Middlesex: Penguin.

O'Donnell, Guillermo A. 1979. *Modernization and Bureaucratic-Authoritarianism:*

Studies in South American Politics. 2d ed. Berkeley: Institute of International Studies, University of California.

Olson, Mancur. 1968. *The Logic of Collective Action: Public Goods and the Theory of Groups*. New York: Schocken Books.

———. 1982. *The Rise and Decline of Nations: Economic Growth, Stagflation, and Social Rigidities*. New Haven, Conn.: Yale University Press.

Oppenheimer, Peter, ed. 1978. *Issues in International Economics*. London: Oriel Press.

Organization for Economic Co-operation and Development. 1982. *Historical Statistics 1960–1980*. Paris: Organization for Economic Co-operation and Development.

Passant, E. J. 1962. *A Short History of Germany, 1815–1945*. Cambridge: Cambridge University Press.

Paxton, Robert O. 1972. *Vichy France: Old Guard and New Order, 1940–1944*. New York: Alfred A. Knopf.

Payne, Stanley G. 1970. *The Spanish Revolution*. New York: W. W. Norton.

Pirenne, Henri. 1939. *Mohammed and Charlemagne*. London: Allen and Unwin.

Popkin, Samuel. 1979. *The Rational Peasant: The Political Economy of Rural Society in Vietnam*. Berkeley: University of California Press.

Pounds, N.J.G. 1974. *An Economic History of Medieval Europe*. London: Longman.

Preston, Paul. 1978. *The Coming of the Spanish Civil War: Reform, Reaction and Revolution in the Second Republic, 1931–1936*. New York: Barnes and Noble.

Previté-Orton, C. W. 1952. *The Shorter Cambridge Medieval History*. Vol. 1: *The Later Roman Empire to the Twelfth Century*. Cambridge: At the University Press.

Puhle, Hans-Juergen. 1975. *Politische Agrarbewegungen in kapitalistischen Industriegesellschaften: Deutschland, USA und Frankreich im 20. Jahrhundert*. Göttingen: Vandenhoeck & Ruprecht.

Punnett, Robert Malcolm. 1971. *British Government and Politics*. 2d ed. New York: Norton.

Radkey, Oliver H. 1958. *The Agrarian Foes of Bolshevism: Promise and Default of the Russian Socialist Revolutionaries, February to October 1917*. New York: Columbia University Press.

Randall, Laura. 1978. *An Economic History of Argentina in the Twentieth Century*. New York: Columbia University Press.

Rauch, Georg von. 1972. *A History of Soviet Russia*. 6th ed. Translated by Peter Jacobsohn and Annette Jacobsohn. New York: Praeger.

Rémondon, Roger. 1964. *La crise de l'Empire Romain: de Marc-Aurèle à Anastase*. L'Histoire et ses problèmes, no. 11. Paris: Presses Universitaires de France.

Reischauer, Edwin O. 1974. *Japan: The Story of a Nation*. New York: Alfred A. Knopf.

Reynolds, Edward. 1974. *Trade and Economic Change on the Gold Coast, 1807–1874*. Harlow, Essex: Longman.

Riasanovsky, Nicholas V. 1977. *A History of Russia*. 3d ed. New York: Oxford University Press.

Rich, E. E., and C. H. Wilson, eds. 1967. *The Cambridge Economic History of Eu-*

rope. Vol. 4: *The Economy of Expanding Europe in the Sixteenth and Seventeenth Centuries*. Cambridge: At the University Press.

Roberts, Andrew D., ed. 1986b. *The Cambridge History of Africa*. Vol. 7: *1905–1940*. Cambridge: Cambridge University Press.

Robinson, Geroid Tanquary. 1932. *Rural Russia under the Old Regime: A History of the Landlord-Peasant World and a Prologue to the Peasant Revolution of 1917*. Berkeley and Los Angeles: University of California Press.

Rock, David. 1987. *Argentina, 1516–1987: From Spanish Colonization to Alfonsin*. Berkeley and Los Angeles: University of California Press.

Rokkan, Stein. 1970. *Citizens, Elections, Parties*. Oslo: Universitetsforlaget.

Rosecrance, Richard. 1986. *The Rise of the Trading State: Commerce and Conquest in the Modern World*. New York: Basic Books.

Rosenberg, Hans. 1967. *Grosse Depression und Bismarckzeit: Wirtschaftsablauf, Gesellschaft und Politik in Mitteleuropa*. Berlin: Walter de Gruyter.

Rostovtzeff, M. 1926. *The Social and Economic History of the Roman Empire*. Oxford: Clarendon.

Rostow, W. W. 1978. *The World Economy: History and Prospect*. Austin: University of Texas Press.

Sabean, David. 1972. *Landbesitz und Gesellschaft am Vorabend des Bauernkriegs: Eine Studie der sozialen Verhältnisse im südlichen Oberschwaben in den Jahren vor 1525*. Stuttgart.

Sarti, Roland. 1971. *Fascism and the Industrial Leadership in Italy, 1919–1940: A Study in the Expansion of Private Power under Fascism*. Berkeley: University of California Press.

Scalapino, Robert A. 1953. *Democracy and the Party Movement in Prewar Japan: The Failure of the First Attempt*. Berkeley and Los Angeles: University of California Press.

Scalapino, Robert A., and George T. Yu. 1985. *Modern China and Its Revolutionary Process: Recurrent Challenges to the Traditional Order, 1850–1920*. Berkeley: University of California Press.

Scammell, W. M. 1983. *The International Economy since 1945*. 2d ed. London and Basingstoke: Macmillan.

Schattschneider, E. E. 1960. *The Semi-Sovereign People: A Realist's View of Democracy in America*. New York: Holt, Rinehart and Winston.

Schedvin, C. B. 1970. *Australia and the Great Depression: A Study of Economic Development and Policy in the 1920s and 1930s*. Syndey: Syndey University Press.

Schmitter, Philippe C. 1971. *Interest Conflict and Political Change in Brazil*. Stanford: Stanford University Press.

Schoenbaum, David. 1967. *Hitler's Social Revolution; Class and Status in Nazi Germany, 1933–1939*. Garden City, N.Y.: Doubleday, Anchor Books.

Scullard, Howard H. 1961. *A History of the Roman World from 753 to 146 B.C.* 3d ed. New York: Barnes and Noble.

Seal, Anil. 1968. *The Emergence of Indian Nationalism: Competition and Collaboration in the Later Nineteenth Century*. Cambridge: At the University Press.

Sen, Sunil. 1982. *Peasant Movements in India: Mid-nineteenth and Twentieth Centuries*. Calcutta and New Delhi: K. P. Bagchi.

Senghaas, Dieter. 1985. *The European Experience: A Historical Critique of Development Theory*. Translated by K. H. Kimmig. Dover, N.H.: Berg Publishers.

Seton-Watson, Hugh. 1967. *The Russian Empire, 1801–1917*. Oxford: Clarendon Press.

Sheehan, James J. 1978. *German Liberalism in the Nineteenth Century*. Chicago: University of Chicago Press.

Silberman, Bernard S., and H. D. Harootunian, eds. 1974. *Japan in Crisis: Essays on Taishō Democracy*. Princeton, N.J.: Princeton University Press.

Skidmore, Thomas E., and Peter H. Smith. 1984. *Modern Latin America*. New York: Oxford University Press.

Skocpol, Theda. 1979. *States and Social Revolutions: A Comparative Analysis of France, Russia, and China*. Cambridge: Cambridge University Press.

Smith, Michael Stephen. 1980. *Tariff Reform in France, 1860–1900: The Politics of Economic Interest*. Ithaca, N.Y.: Cornell University Press.

Solberg, Carl E. 1987. *The Prairies and the Pampas: Agrarian Policy in Canada and Argentina, 1880–1930*. Stanford, Calif.: Stanford University Press.

Spalding, Hobart A. 1977. *Organized Labor in Latin America: Historical Case Studies of Workers in Dependent Societies*. New York: New York University Press.

Stegmann, Dirk. 1970. *Die Erben Bismarcks: Parteien und Verbände in der Spätphase des Wilhelminisichen Deutschlands; Sammlungspolitik 1897–1918*. Cologne and Berlin: Kiepenheuer und Witsch.

Stein, Arthur A. 1980. *The Nation at War*. Baltimore: Johns Hopkins University Press.

Stepan, Alfred, ed. 1973. *Authoritarianism in Brazil*. New Haven, Conn.: Yale University Press.

Stockwin, J.A.A. 1982. *Japan: Divided Politics in a Growth Economy*. 2d ed. New York: W. W. Norton.

Stone, Lawrence. 1965. *The Crisis of the Aristocracy, 1558–1641*. Oxford: Clarendon.

Stürmer, Michael. 1967. *Koalition und Opposition in der Weimarer Republik, 1924–1928*. Düsseldorf: Droste.

———. 1974. *Regierung und Reichstag im Bismarckstaat 1871–1880: Cäsarismus oder Parlamentarismus*. Düsseldorf: Droste.

Sundquist, James L. 1983. *Dynamics of the Party System: Alignment and Realignment of Political Parties in the United States*. Rev. ed. Washington, D.C.: The Brookings Institution.

Sunkel, Osvaldo, with Pedro Paz. 1973. *El subdesarrollo latinoamericano y la teoría del desarrollo*. 4th ed. Madrid: Siglo veintiuno de España.

Terrill, Tom E. 1973. *The Tariff, Politics, and American Foreign Policy, 1874–1901*. Contributions in American History, No. 31. Westport, Conn.: Greenwood Press.

Thomas, S. Bernard. 1983. *Labor and the Chinese Revolution: Class Strategies and Contradictions of Chinese Communism, 1928–48*. Ann Arbor: Center for Chinese Studies, University of Michigan.

Thompson, F.M.L. 1963. *English Landed Society in the Nineteenth Century*. London: Routledge and Kegan Paul; Toronto: University of Toronto Press.

Thomson, David. 1946. *Democracy in France: The Third Republic*. London: Oxford University Press.

———. 1962. *Europe since Napoleon*. 2d ed. New York: Alfred A. Knopf.

———. 1978. *England in the Nineteenth Century (1815–1914)*. *The Pelican History of England*, vol. 8. Revised by Derek Beales. Harmondsworth, Middlesex: Penguin Books.

Thorburn, Hugh G., ed. 1979. *Party Politics in Canada*. 4th ed. Scarbourough, Ont.: Prentice-Hall.

Tidy, Michael. 1980. *A History of Africa, 1840–1914*. Vol. 1: *1840–1880*. With Donald Leeming. London: Hodder and Stoughton.

Tsokhas, Kosmas. 1984. *A Class Apart? Businessmen and Australian Politics, 1960–1980*. Melbourne: Oxford University Press.

Turner, Henry Ashby, Jr. 1985. *German Big Business and the Rise of Hitler*. New York: Oxford University Press.

Turner, Henry Ashby, Jr., ed. 1972. *Nazism and the Third Reich*. New York: Quadrangle Books.

Ullman, Joan Connelly. 1968. *The Tragic Week: A Study of Anticlericalism in Spain, 1875–1912*. Cambridge: Harvard University Press.

Ullmann, Peter. 1976. *Der Bund der Industriellen: Organisation, Einfluss und Politik klein- und mittelbetrieblicher Industrieller im Deutschen Kaiserreich 1895–1914*. Göttingen: Vandenhoeck und Ruprecht.

United Nations. 1958. *Yearbook of Food and Agricultural Statistics, 1957*. Rome: United Nations Food and Agricultural Organization.

———. 1961. *Statistical Yearbook*. 13th issue. New York: UN Department of Economic and Social Affairs.

———. 1984. *Yearbook of International Trade Statistics, 1982*. Vol. 1: *Trade by Country*. New York: UN Department of International Economic and Social Affairs.

———. 1986. *Yearbook of International Trade Statistics, 1984*. Vol. 1: *Trade by Country*. New York: UN Department of International Economic and Social Affairs.

Vinogradov, Juri. 1981. *Olbia: Geschichte einer altgriechischen Stadt am Schwarzen Meer*. Konstanz: Universitaetsverlag.

Vogt, Joseph. 1967. *The Decline of Rome: The Metamorphosis of Ancient Civilization*. Translated by Janet Sondheimer. London: Weidenfeld and Nicolson.

Walker, E. Ronald. 1933. *Australia in the World Depression*. London: P. S. King and Sons.

Wallerstein, Immanuel. 1974. *The Modern World-System: Capitalist Agriculture and the Origins of the European World-Economy in the Sixteenth Century*. New York: Academic Press.

———. 1980. *The Modern World-System II: Mercantilism and the Consolidation of the European World-Economy, 1600–1750*. New York: Academic Press.

Ward, Russel. 1977. *The History of Australia: The Twentieth Century*. New York: Harper and Row.

Wei, William. 1985. *Counterrevolution in China: The Nationalists in Jiangxi during the Soviet Period*. Ann Arbor: University of Michigan Press.

Weiner, Myron. 1967. *Party Building in a New Nation: The Indian National Congress.* Chicago: University of Chicago Press.

Westlake, Henry Dickinson. 1935. *Thessaly in the Fourth Century B.C.* London: Methuen.

Williams, Harry T., Richard N. Current, and Frank Friedel. 1969. *A History of the United States Since 1865.* 3d ed. New York: Alfred A. Knopf.

Williams, Philip M. 1966. *Crisis and Compromise: Politics in the Fourth Republic.* Originally published 1954. Garden City, N.Y.: Doubleday, Anchor Books.

Williams, Philip M., and Martin Harrison. 1973. *Politics and Society in de Gaulle's Republic.* Originally published 1971. Garden City, N.Y.: Doubleday, Anchor Books.

Wilson, Charles. 1976. *The Transformation of Europe, 1558–1648.* Berkeley and Los Angeles: University of California Press.

Wittfogel, Karl August. 1957. *Oriental Despotism: A Comparative Study of Total Power.* New Haven, Conn.: Yale University Press.

Woodside, Alexander B. 1976. *Community and Revolution in Modern Vietnam.* Boston: Houghton Mifflin.

Woodward, Dennis, Andrew Parkin, and John Summers, eds. 1985. *Government, Politics and Power in Australia: An Introductory Reader.* 3d. ed. Melbourne: Longman Cheshire.

World Bank. 1983. *World Tables.* 2 vols. Baltimore: Johns Hopkins University Press.

Woytinsky, W. S., and E. S. Woytinsky. 1953. *World Population and Production: Trends and Outlook.* New York: Twentieth Century Fund.

———. 1955. *World Commerce and Governments: Trends and Outlook.* New York: Twentieth Century Fund.

Zaionchkovsky, Peter A. 1978. *The Abolition of Serfdom in Russia.* 3d. ed. Edited and translated by Susan Wobst. Gulf Breeze, Fla.: Academic International Press.

Zeldin, Theodore. 1979. *France 1848–1945: Politics and Anger.* Oxford: Oxford University Press.

Zysman, John. 1983. *Governments, Markets and Growth: Financial Systems and the Politics of Industrial Change.* Ithaca, N.Y.: Cornell University Press.

Index